This book is dedicated to:

My friends and loved ones who have supported my staying at the office too long. Most especially thanks to my daughter, Alison, and her lovely family; Peggy Ascherman; Rich Hagle and especially Susan K. Jones --Steve Kelly

My grandchildren – Sheridan, Ronan, Daphne, Marlowe, and Bowden; and with special thanks to my long-time collaborators and friends, Rich Hagle and Steve Kelly.
--Susan K. Jones

ACKNOWLEDGMENTS

This book would not be possible without the visionary leadership of Ron Jacobs, sponsor of the annual Jacobs & Clevenger Case Writers' Workshop. Thank you, Ron, for your decades of support to direct and interactive marketing education as a teacher, author and philanthropist.

The editors would like to acknowledge the exceptional contributions of the authors of this book's cases and readings. Their names and affiliations are listed at the beginning of each piece. Their willingness to share their research, experience and knowledge with professors and students is very impressive, and much appreciated. Their generosity is exceptional as well; all contributors to this book have agreed that 100% of royalties will go to DePaul University's Interactive Marketing Institute.

The editors would also like to thank the past and present trustees and staff members of the Chicago Association of Direct Marketing Educational Foundation (now the Midwest Marketing Education Foundation) for conceiving and guiding the creation of the original DePaul Case Writers' Workshop, and for continued strong support of the Jacobs & Clevenger Case Writers' Workshop.

Thanks are due as well to Marketing EDGE and its trustees and staff for years of generous support and guidance to the Workshop. We especially appreciate the tireless efforts of Jeff Nesler, our close collaborator from Marketing EDGE.

We would like to acknowledge the great effort and support given to this and many other projects by Kathleen (Kate) Stevenson, Executive Director of the Midwest Marketing Education Foundation. Finally, we acknowledge and thank our long-time collaborator, Richard Hagle of RACOM Communications, for his belief in us, and for his unflagging dedication to excellence in marketing education.

The IMC Sourcebook

Readings and Cases in Integrated Marketing Communications

EDITORS

SUSAN K. JONES
Ferris State University

J. STEVEN KELLY
DePaul University

@2018 by Midwest Marketing Education
Foundation http://www.mefgroup.org/
Executive Director: Kathleen Stevenson (see web site above for access to Teaching Notes)

Catalog-in-Publication information available from the Library of Congress. Printed in the United States of America

ISBN-13: 978-1980324546 (Custom)
ISBN-10: 1980324546

THE JACOBS & CLEVENGER CASE WRITERS' WORKSHOP AND THE DEVELOPMENT OF THIS BOOK

Since its origins in the mid-1990s, the DePaul University Case Writers' Workshop (now the Jacobs & Clevenger Case Writers' Workshop) has nurtured the development of more than 60 original cases in Integrated Marketing Communications. The authors of these cases include professors, adjunct instructors and professional writers from all over the world. Case subjects include companies and agencies focused on financial services, product marketing, services marketing, online marketing, the non-profit world, and much more.

Dr. J. Steven Kelly is the Director of DePaul's Interactive Marketing Institute and an Associate Professor of Marketing at DePaul. He spearheaded the development of the Workshop with funding and direction from the Chicago Association of Direct Marketing Educational Foundation (now the Midwest Marketing Education Foundation), the Direct Marketing Educational Foundation (now Marketing EDGE, and Jacobs & Clevenger. These organizations have supported the Workshop because of the strong and demonstrated need among professors and students for timely, authoritative and meaty cases focused on direct marketing, interactive marketing, advertising, sales promotion and public relations.

As a former educator/trustee of the Direct Marketing Educational Foundation (now Marketing EDGE), former chair of the Chicago Association of Direct Marketing Educational Foundation, and current Midwest Marketing Education Foundation trustee, Marketing Professor Susan K. Jones of Ferris State University joined forces with Dr. Kelly in 2002 to help nurture case creation and prepare the cases for publication.

TABLE OF CONTENTS

The Future of Advertising or Whatever We're Going to Call It

By

Don Schultz, Northwestern University

In this opinion piece, the author speculates on the future of advertising. Arguing that the challenge of predicting the future lies mainly in the lack of an acceptable definition of the field, the author solves that problem by developing a set of postulates to create boundaries for the theory and practice of the discipline. The postulates of the present discipline are used as the base from which the future might evolve. Three scenarios are proposed for the future of advertising: (1) creeping incrementalism, (2) reversal of buyer/seller roles, and (3) reinvention of the field. The author suggests that those scenarios will develop and play out based on the developmental speed and acceptance of the various technologies identified.

SOME BACKGROUND AND POSITIONING ON THIS ARTICLE

Over the past few years, numerous conferences, seminars, colloquia, and the like have tried to address and resolve the definition and future of what has traditionally been called modern "advertising," generally with little success. What began a hundred or so years ago as a fairly simple process of sellers trying to attract the attention of prospective purchasers through various media forms and encouraging/convincing them to buy has morphed into a mélange of programmatic buying, public relations, product placement, social media, talking characters, content marketing, direct selling, timed coupons, and a host of other activities, some of them old line and others allied with new-wave technologies. The simple term advertising has fractionalized into a host of seemingly more specific but commonly marketer-generated topics, issues, and activities, often with their own definitional challenges. At the same time, it seems that consumers/customers/buyers have aggregated all of these terms into one omnibus term that they call very simply advertising or promotion. Thus, it may well be that advertising, as we have long known it, is an almost useless term beset by mini-definitions internally and globalization externally.

All of this conflict and confusion has resulted in a variegated field, focused primarily on creating or implementing short-term tactical activities rather than on developing long-term theory and strategic communication that can stand the test of time. While that has enabled advertising as we know it today to be a quite fluid and adaptable field, able to accept and include changing technologies and other discipline-related approaches, it has failed to enable the creation of a single, widely accepted theory base and definition of its own. And without that, advertising practitioners and academics alike have resorted to borrowing a multitude of concepts, approaches, and methodologies to explain how advertising is developed, the impact that it is supposed to have, and the results that it is supposed to achieve. Without a formal definitional yardstick, advertising is almost impossible to define today; and without a definition it is even more challenging to suggest what its future might be. How can we hypothesize, extrapolate, or predict the future of advertising if we aren't starting with a clear and commonly accepted definition of what advertising is?

The Challenges of Defining Advertising

As an applied science, the practical need for a definition of advertising has never really been required. Advertisers did their work, created messages and incentives, pushed that work out into the marketplace and waited for results. If consumers liked the outputs, the concepts were repeated. If they didn't, advertisers and their agencies abandoned them for new, more innovative, attention-getting, and acceptable approaches. That is evidenced by 2016's Super Bowl 50 advertising extravaganza in the United States, supposedly the showcase for the "best advertising ever," or at least the most expensive. Using that as a base measure of "good" advertising, we can say that advertising can be identified as communication that includes horses and puppies and embryos. It doesn't, however, include human gastrointestinal discomfort or the fictional character of a "puppy-monkey-baby." That isn't much of a conceptual or theoretical base on which to build a trillion-dollar industry.

Part of the definitional challenge has been created by the educational system that has developed around advertising, in other words, how the subject is taught, how the young are trained, and how the field is practiced. In the academic community, many beholders define the term advertising very tightly. For example, there are theories and definitions of advertising, of public relations, of sales promotion, of direct marketing, and now of social media, content marketing, and even "native advertising," all of which attempt to carve out a specific niche for the area. All have their own theorists, practitioners, and yes, deniers, so what we seem to have is increasing confusion, not rational discussion and development.

Advertising is based on attempts to engage consumers, primarily buyers, and influence them in their purchase or acquisition decisions. Yet how that is accomplished is still up for grabs, and that element of influence seems to be where most scholarly research and writing are focused. The end goal of such research often is to parse out the short-term effects of various marketing and communication tactics so that they can be copied or at least used as a base for moving the field forward. And while they might yield success in advertising, these tactical or strategic mechanisms would not constitute substantial enough fodder with which to build a definition or a theoretical base for the field and practice of advertising, and it's certainly not a format for defining the future.

Lacking a single, solid theoretical base, the preparation of new recruits for the practice of advertising has relied primarily on an apprentice system. That has been justified by the changing nature of the field.
Thus, advertising has emerged as an applied science, borrowing from many fields, such as psychology, economics, communication, sociology, and other social sciences. Today a number of new fields are being added, most of them "foreign" to traditional discussions of advertising, such as engineering, computer science, and neurology. Even the umbrella field of "marketing," under which advertising is traditionally subsumed, is an amalgamation of many other fields of study. Indeed, the term marketing, in spite of its increasing popularity, finds itself in the same position as advertising.

Definition Drives Theory Development and Explanatory Value

Advertising academics these days seem to have fallen into the Western linguist and social science trap of classification and categorization, taking a simple subject and trying to parse it down into what we believe might be the specific parts that make up its essence. In today's interactive, interlocking, multi•dimensional, holistic marketplace this approach seems totally unrealistic. Yes, scholars can parse the field down into its seemingly primary parts, but when separated those elements commonly simply re- aggregate themselves into another form and the process continues. Eastern philosophies of holism, inter•connectedness, interactions, and relationships seem so much more appropriate today to discuss what used to be "advertising" but is now primarily "marketing communications."

For the purposes of this article, I'm moving on from the definitional challenge that advertising presents and, instead, subsuming the term (and the practice of advertising itself) under the umbrella term marketing communications. From there, I'll build my perspective of what the future of marketing communications (including advertising) might be, leaning on my 50 years of academic research and observation—not to mention my even greater experience as a consumer.

TWO PRIMARY VIEWS

Being ever the intrepid adventurer, when the editor of this journal, Shintaro Okazaki, invited me to develop some opinions, reflections, and forecasts of what advertising might be in the future, I could hardly resist. I have been asking journal editors and conference session leaders around the globe to define the term. I have spent the majority of my life involved in teaching and researching the topic. The initial request that Shintaro made of me was quite simple. He instituted only minor constraints (one centering around word count). The charge seemed easy enough at the outset, but I hadn't considered the inherent complexities. For starters, there are two views of advertising that must be considered.

How Practitioners See Advertising/Marketing Communications

Advertising has generally been thought to encompass the creation and mass media distribution of persuasive messages by or on behalf of brand marketers from profit-seeking sellers. That notion has dramatically changed and evolved over the years. Advertising, as viewed from the practitioner's perch, now appears to be a moving set of interlocking pieces and parts involving multiple players/promoters who are constantly and continuously evolving, emerging, and adapting so that the field is being reinvented on almost a daily basis. That evolving cauldron of messaging, promoting, and incentivizing activities seems to come directly from the same evolution/revolution that is occurring among and within the key ingredients of the advertising process: people or, better said, customers and consumers. We can't hold them constant, so why should we believe that we should be able to hold constant the forms and functions being used to try to influence them? Therefore, whatever I write is or will face the same challenge: It may be accurate, relevant, and cogent today, but might well be totally worthless tomorrow. That's an accepted fact in today's marketplace.

The Academic View

The view is not the same from the academic or "ivory tower" theoretical perch. Academicians want stable models, consistent results, continuity of findings, and all of the other elements that create rigorous foundations of an actual science. We want to develop theoretical concepts that are repeatable or at least reliable. All of those wants are challenged because people, as our subject matter, are so unstable. They change and evolve and adapt and adjust to the continuously evolving environment in which they exist. It is, in my view, this instability in the marketplace that makes advertising and marketing communications such a challenging field of study, but one that is ever so much more interesting than many other topics. It is also this instability that creates the challenges of defining the topic and the field.

But in spite of these challenges, someone has to try and define the field if one is to speculate on the future. That task seems to have fallen to me. As a prelude to the future, one must make some assumptions. Thus, what follows assumes three critical ingredients, not just for the future of what we are defining as advertising but for the entire concept of market economies as relevant societal systems. We must assume that those will survive. If not, the issue of what is "advertising" or even marketing communications becomes truly irrelevant.

THREE KEY ASSUMPTIONS

I start by identifying three key factors that are the foundation on which this article is based. Although there may well be more factors than these, the three seem to capture the essence of today's situation.

There must be producers of goods and services who enter the marketplace with the intent of creating exchanges. Without exchange, there is no marketplace; and without markets, there is no reason for the producers to produce and certainly no reason for them to advertise or communicate. Thus, this concept of exchange seems to be central for the discussion of advertising/marketing communications. No markets, no advertising. End of story.

There are or will be actors or participants (i.e., people or organizations or others who will consume the outputs of the producers of the market economies). While this may seem an obvious and perhaps frivolous thought, there are those who today argue that the rapid movement to a machine-driven, robot-dominated, goods-producing system will destroy market economies. Their premise is that auto•mation and robots will drive workers from their jobs, resulting in the workers' loss of income and therefore consumption capacity. In other words, the development of automated systems will destroy the current consumption-oriented marketplace. Machines don't consume; therefore, producers will have no markets for their goods. And if there is no opportunity for consumption, there is no reason for advertising (Ford, 2015). (Note: There are those who argue for a marketplace of ideas and social justice fueled by advertising, but without manufacturing and consumption. The argument fails for lack of economic need or exchange activities).

Assuming the survival of marketplace economies and that automation does not totally destroy the system, those workers who are employed or otherwise engaged in commerce will create some type of value and thus be rewarded for their efforts through incomes, and their discretionary income is necessary to justify advertising investments by producers. Too often we ignore the fact that the majority of advertising activities are focused primarily in the areas of discretionary products and services. Those are reliant on consumers having discretionary resources. While foods are heavily advertised, as are liquors and automobiles and fast foods, all are really discretionary purchases by consumers. Absent income and discretionary resources—in other words, a subsistence marketplace—the demand and need for advertising are totally obviated. Brand choice becomes irrelevant when the buyer has no resources.

Without those three key ingredients and their ancillary and support areas, there is really no need for messages or incentives to differentiate one product from another, nor for attempting to shift consumer purchasing from one product category to another. If those three things do not continue to be available in the marketplace, we come to the end of advertising's future. We need go no further. But let's assume that market economies will continue for the present and press on with this discussion.

THE TRADITIONAL VIEW OF ADVERTISING

As mentioned, advertising today is an amalgamation and continuously evolving set of factors and processes. That makes it very difficult to identify the starting points of the disciplines and even more difficult to suggest when they might end. Thus, we can only identify a series of evolutions and activities that continuously morph and change. They are continuously being reinvented by academicians and practitioners as they are employed or evolve in the marketplace.

The crucible, of course, is the market and the consumer. If consumers respond or, better said, if advertising practitioners or academicians believe that consumers are responding in some form or fashion to advertisers' pleas and incentives, sellers will continue to invest their finite resources to try to influence consumers' purchasing decisions. Similarly, academicians will assume that their concepts and theories are correct, and they will create appropriate research agendas and teaching tools. They really have no other choice.

Advertising, given all of its forms and functions as we know them today, with the exception of direct response, is so imprecise that many advertisers spend because they have always spent or because their perceived competitors are spending. And academicians continue to develop reams of research because such research has always been done in the past. This lack of understanding regarding what causes the activation of advertising has resulted in the oft-repeated quote, "I know half of my advertising spending is wasted, but I don't know which half"—which is as accurate today as it was a half-century ago when it is said to have been coined (Advertising Age 1999). Surprisingly, it appears to be this lack of truly measurable results or accountability that seems to keep the advertising spending going. Advertisers continue to hope that, at some point, they will stumble on the magic key that will unlock an understanding of how "advertising really works."

That spending is, of course, totally dependent on the three factors mentioned earlier: exchange, consumers, and discretionary resources/income. Without all three of those the factors being present, advertising or whatever we call it would simply disappear. There would be no need for it, nor any resources to support it, and certainly no hope that it would ultimately reward the marketer who invested in it.

WHAT IS ADVERTISING TODAY?

Given the difficulty of defining advertising, as discussed, I will not try to define current-day advertising or marketing communications in a few words. Instead, I will try to identify a number of postulates, all of which are interrelated and inter•connected, and all of which provide a context for defining the field. If those boundaries can be confirmed, then it would seem much simpler to compare what advertising is with what it might be. For this approach to work, however, there must be some level of agreement between the writer's views and those of the reader and evaluator. Further, all of the following concepts must be viewed in context, and all must be judged based on their interactions with one another and the marketplace in general.

The concepts that I will use to define advertising or marketing communications today follow, and are listed in no order of priority:

Communication activities are developed by sellers, directed to consumers or users at any level, and commonly distributed by media organizations based on some type of fee payment.

The focus of the communication is on gaining attention and persuading audiences to consider or purchase the advertised or promoted product/service.

The messaging is based on some type of psychological model that is believed to represent the way that consumers or purchasing units take in, process, and react to persuasive messages and incentives.

The basic business model employed by advertisers, whether they recognize it or not, is that of a supply chain. (Note: This is not a part of a definition of advertising or marketing communications, but it is a necessary element, for it drives the entire management of the producing/selling organization.) This simply means that producers develop, make, and distribute products and/or services for which they have the capability and for which they perceive that there is some type of potential consumer demand.

As most of these firms are manufacturers and have been since the industrial revolution, the use-value of their products is built into them. Upon purchase, consumers can gain access to those uses and those values. Therefore, the basic business model of the firm is one of attempting to sell the inherent value of what has been made to people or consumption units whose value-in-use is generally unknown.

Measurable results of advertising have traditionally been tied to message preparation and distribution (i.e., the development of the advertising or marketing communication and incentives) rather than to the impact and results that those messages and incentives achieve when delivered. Thus, for the most part, advertising success historically has been and still is based on efficient message creation and distribution, rather than on message effectiveness.

When advertising is measured, it is usually done in one of two ways: (1) a calculation of returns on the costs of the tactics used or (2) some change in psychological or communication effect. The most widely used measures have focused on the impact of the message on end users through some type of communication impact (e.g., recall, recognition, or the like) or through some type of psychological measure, such as brand preference or intent to purchase on the next occasion, and so on. All have and continue to be used throughout the communication distribution chain. The most widely used measures, the attitudinal or human memory calculations, have been the most difficult to connect to financial returns, yet they are the favored ones. Given the multidimensional impact of advertising messaging, it has been difficult to parse out the impact of various media forms in the marketplace, creating even more difficulty in determining "how advertising works."

Branding elements—symbols, sounds, graphic elements, and the like—are integral parts of the advertising and marketing communications process. Those branding elements have intangible corporate value and may or may not be linked to the manufacturers or producers of the products or services being vended. Nevertheless, brands are considered the "public face" of the marketing organization and take on a "bigger than life" aura for many organizations.

Multiple theories and concepts have been developed over the years to try to support various marketer/seller suppositions of how advertising works. Most of those theories/concepts are based on limited marketplace results; thus, there is still tremendous speculation on the impact and effect of various advertising procedures and approaches by the spending parties. That's because most advertising spending is often based on rather spurious correlations of impact and effect. They are commonly based more on "hope" than true knowledge.

There is an almost incestuous relationship among advertisers, their agencies, media firms, and the research and measurement groups that estimate the size of media audiences. All have built models of how advertising "works," and all are interconnected and interrelated. Thus, there is little incentive for any of the participants to change or revise their historic methods or approaches, else the entire system would be challenged. As a result, advertising knowledge is severely restricted by a number of vested interests who seem unable or incapable of change. Further, each unit in the chain has limited incentive to change or redefine advertising as doing so might work to its own personal detriment.

Given these foundational postulates and their interrelationships, it becomes clear why forecasting the future of advertising is so difficult. If we accept the broad, general elements of what advertising (or marketing communications) is today, those accepted elements might provide a framework for what it will be tomorrow.

WHAT WILL ADVERTISING (OR WHATEVER WE'RE GOING TO CALL IT) BE LIKE TOMORROW?

For this discussion of what advertising or marketing communications might be in the future, I use the same approach as was developed for the present situation: a set of postulates that can be supported with today's knowledge. While these postulates are not provable today or may not even be supportable in the future, they at least provide a set of boundaries around which we can start to build a relevant view of what the future of what we now call "advertising" might be. Again, the postulates are listed in no particular order, but they do seem to move in a logical progression. As the reader will note, these postulates are much broader than the traditional terms used in the past to develop the concept of advertising. It is hoped that the rationale and support for that approach will become apparent as the elements are described.

Consumer knowledge and access to immediate sources of information and alternative products and resources will destroy the seller's traditional supply chain business model. That simply means that the traditional "inside-out planning" approaches, which have assumed marketer control of the entire sales, marketing, and communication system, are no longer viable. Therefore, the assumptions made in the traditional 4Ps approach (McCarthy 1960), which clearly was based on a sales model and supported by sellers' use of persuasive tactics leveraged against the buyer, will be sorely challenged—and already is.

That approach, which assumes the seller makes products with internal value and then aligns the other marketplace factors in a linear fashion to sell them to prospective buyers or consumers, is no longer relevant or even possible. Buyers simply have access to too much information and too many alternative product choices to make that model work. Thus, the traditional focus of advertising—activities designed to call attention to product differences and benefits—will substantially change if it survives at all.

The demise of the traditional supply-chain model will be replaced by a demand-chain approach. Sellers will have to focus more of their efforts on understanding buyer wants, needs, requirements, and the like, and less on generating production economies of scale to generate greater consumer interest and purchase. That will put much more emphasis on identifying and understanding buyer "pain points" and then creating products or service to fit those requirements. Thus, we will see a total reversal of the organizational structures of seller organizations and a growing emphasis on the use of reciprocity or shared value as a business relationship tool.

Prospective buyers will become the driving force in marketing communications going forward. That will necessitate changes in the internal structure of the marketing and communication departments within marketing firms. The marketing communicator of tomorrow will be more a knowledge worker than a creative manipulator, so communications professionals must be more focused on understanding and filling customer needs and wants rather than on trying to create those prospect needs/wants.
Research in all of its permutations will replace much of the traditional focus on communication creativity. We're seeing this transition occurring now with the emphasis on consumer data driving not just advertising but business decisions.

This shift to a holistic view of the buyer/customer will require more "generalists" in developing the marketer's planning process, as these generalists will understand how to apply actionable insights on the buyer/customer across marketing communications tactics and channels. Thus, the current focus on identifying and creating specialists and specializations will decline. Much of that activity will likely become automated based on big data and neural analysis. There will be increased emphasis on the internal effort to bring together communication, sales, distribution, and the like to create a complete, holistic package of solutions for buyers. This change will require managers who are more process focused instead of activity focused. Those managers will be the people who can gather all of the resources of the selling organization and present them as a seamless package to prospective and ongoing buyers. Whether these people will reside in the seller's organization or will be in some type of external agent group is not known at this time. It will likely be a combination of the two.

The entire philosophy of the selling organization will move from "selling what we have made" using persuasion approaches to meet organizational sales and volume goals to one of "helping customers find what and how they can solve their needs/requirements." Relationship selling will move to the fore in most marketing organizations, and much more personal attention will emerge than has been the case in the past. Connecting organizations with customers, rather than creating outbound messages and incentives, will become a key element of the advertising/marketing communications function in the future. That will likely mean major dislocations in existing marketing and advertising organizations.

Along with these more individually focused marketing communications approaches will come more emphasis on individual, one-to-one communication. This will be made possible by information technology, and it will be mandatory for marketers to build and maintain customer relationships. Most likely, this will mean the demise of traditional mass advertising and communication. Media will be much more focused on creating unique audiences that will appeal to sellers/advertisers rather than the broader, more general demographic groupings used by mass media today. Media planning and buying will become more of a customer-relationship-building approach rather than simply one of distributing the most messages at the lowest cost. Advertisers already are attempting to leverage data, analytics, and increased mobility to enable this sort of engagement and personalization, and the scope and scale of these efforts will continue to grow.

Thanks to this focus on specific individuals, there will be less emphasis on generating awareness and attention via advertising and marketing communications and more emphasis on generating customer and prospect response via programmatic buying. Because programmatic media buying will create a "closed-loop" system—that is, the seller will know who the prospective buyer is and will have some evidence of message delivery to that person—it should be possible to measure responses or sales results directly from their efforts, so programmatic buying will enable advertising and marketing communications to be more results oriented.

The foundations of research in advertising will shift dramatically with the increasing availability of large data sets, most of which will be based on behavioral data. Thus, the traditional academic use of small-sample, experimental research and then projections to the whole to develop communication concepts will give way to these large-scale, longitudinal data sets.

The same will be true for the professional community, where focus groups and research panels will be replaced by more detailed analyses of large-scale, longitudinal data sets. These changes will require new analytical skills by advertising/marketing communications researchers as they move away from regression and other limited-variable analyses to more robust methodologies.

The development of neural science and neural knowledge will have much to do with how and in what way advertising/marketing communications will be defined, as academicians and practitioners learn more about how the human brain acquires, internalizes, and is influenced by commercial communications. Because this is an emerging field it is too soon to identify what the impact will be, but it will probably result in major rethinking of the entire practice of advertising/marketing communications.

Many of the traditional concepts, borrowed in part or in whole from economic and psychological theory, will be replaced by behavioral economics and methodologies that actually explain the behaviors of consumers in the marketplace. They will likely negate some of the traditional assumptions and suppositions of how consumers might think or feel. Researchers will likely have to revise and replace many traditional concepts and beliefs as new information becomes available.

Integration of messages and promotions based on this new knowledge will become commonplace. Thus, a decline in the sellers needs for specific external agencies or specialists groups will likely decline as well. It is hoped that the specializations which have developed over time, such as public relations, sales promotion, direct marketing, product placement, content marketing, and the host of others, can be realigned, consolidated and included as parts of a holistic customer/prospect unit. That means the sellers will have to focus on individual customers and be able to provide ongoing help and assistance in customer's lives. In my view, that will make integration a key element in every seller's audience portfolio rather than something that is brought up at the end of the process. In short, more "advertising" or "marketing communication" generalists with broader and deeper customer focus will be needed rather than more specialists with detailed specific media and promotional tool capabilities.

Perhaps the greatest change to advertising/marketing communications in the future will be a new capability by marketers to actually measure the impact and effect of the marketing communication activities they employ. Attitudinal measures will be replaced by behavioral data, which means that, for the first time, advertisers/marketers will be able to actually calculate the returns from their advertising/marketing communications investments. As organizations learn what does and does not work, this will likely cause some dislocations in traditional advertising spending.

In line with this greatly improved ability to measure financial returns on advertising/marketing communications investments will come increased capabilities to determine the actual financial value of brands and branding. Today, brands are still too often a mysterious "black box" for marketers. It is generally assumed that brands generate some sort of financial returns on the investments made in them, but that value is often long term and indeterminate in modern corporations. Yet brands are commonly the foundation for most all advertising/marketing communications investments today. The ability to determine the actual financial value of brand equity among consumers and parse that out over time will be extremely helpful to the managers to either support or deny the true value of brands in the marketing organization's portfolio of assets.

One of the major changes in advertising/marketing communications will be the ability to develop more relevant forms of measurement, whether that be short-term tactical activities or longer-term branding and brand equity returns. Much of that will come from the development and managerial sophistication of data and data analytics. Thus, marketers and marketing organizations will be able to move from measuring historical returns to forecasting potential returns, which will enable managers to begin to treat short-term measurable returns as marginal returns on investments, turning traditional advertising and communication accounting on its head. That will likely mean switching from existing cost-accounting approaches to forms of actuarial science.

There undoubtedly will be other major factors that will influence and impact how advertising/marketing communications will be defined going forward, but these postulates at least set the stage for a more detailed discussion than is presently occurring in the field. It is hoped that this article will start that conversation.

POSTULATE REDUX: MITIGATING FACTORS THAT MIGHT REDEFINE THE SCENARIOS PRESENTED

The postulates just presented currently compose one view of how advertising/marketing communications can or might evolve. Readers will no doubt point out that they contain some challengeable speculations in addition to disputable facts and (understandably) do not account for unforeseen developments. The three factors identified at the beginning of this article— namely, the existence of an exchange, consumers, and discretionary income—may change more rapidly than I anticipate. That occurrence would have a have a major impact on all forms of free-market enterprise and would eventually encompass advertising/marketing communications as I outlined earlier in this article.

There may be other unforeseen factors, but for the present the discussion is limited to the three assumptions listed previously. Consider how they could be reframed to put them in a better perspective and in line with the postulates for the future: A substantial decline in consumer disposable income could occur. This could come from any of a number of sources, such as automation, radical environmental change, war, pestilence, crop failures, or other natural or man-made global disasters. If consumer incomes decline severely, there will likely be a short burst of promotional activity as marketing organizations seek to optimize the declining consumer demand coming from the curtailed resources.
Once past that optimization period, lack of consumer disposable incomes will precede the demise of advertising as we have known it. There will simply be no need for it.

Moreover, radical technological changes could impact advertising/marketing communications. Should a "master algorithm" suddenly be developed that would put an end to human disease or create instantaneous individual wealth, or provide systems that would solve all current energy needs effortlessly or other breakthrough developments, it could have major impacts and dislocations for all types of human endeavors.

For example, the sudden disappearance of all human disease—cancer, heart disease, diabetes, obesity, and so on— could have a severe impact on pharmaceutical firms, hospitals, insurance organizations, and a host of ancillary firms that have been developed to improve human welfare. Without disease, there would be no reason to call attention to alternative sources of health maintenance care or cure. The same could be true of energy sources, transportation, agriculture, or myriad other elements. Any large-scale technological improvements could severely undermine the need or corporate requirements for advertising/marketing communications and thus impact the demand for those activities.

Advertising/marketing communications is based on an imperfect understanding of how humans make decisions. Thus, there is currently incredible waste in trying to influence those consumer decisions through trial and error. If algorithms are developed that replicate human decision making, or other keys could be found as to how humans make commercial choices, demand for and investments in the discipline of advertising and, indeed, in all forms of marketing communications, would change dramatically. With knowledge of what will likely happen or what results might be obtained when marketing communications activities are employed, sellers would severely restrict or even make previous investments superfluous.

The rapid development and deployment of advertising/marketing communications decision making with automation and artificial intelligence would cut to the heart of market economies as they displace large numbers of workers, their livelihoods, and ultimately their disposable incomes. As automation takes over increasing amounts of formerly human work, and without alternative sources of income, traditional market economies will initially stall and eventually tumble into a chaotic morass from which they will find it difficult to recover.

While one could argue that these factors are ancillary to the future of advertising/marketing communications, I would argue that they are the sum and substance of the field. The fact that current practitioners and academics have, in essence, almost totally ignored them in thinking about or considering the future of the discipline simply reinforces the premise that advertising knowledge as we know and practice it seems to consist of a very shallow pool of tactical information and practice.

Unfortunately, the field appears to be continuing in this same pathway so that currently very little is being done to deepen or expand that reservoir. Too many advertising practitioners and academics are caught up in the thrill and excitement of the latest Hollywood celebrity's activities, with a primary focus seeming to be on the entertainment value of advertising while ignoring the more critical issues that face the field.

An example will illustrate the point: While a focus on improving racial diversity in advertising is clearly needed, it ignores the more substantial issues of income concentration/consolidation and the lack of consideration being given as to how the plight of low-income and unemployed families are dragging down various societies. Having more creative advertising to promote products that are beyond the reach of large portions of the population provides little value to anyone except the product maker and the marketing communications developer. More attention should be given to how advertising/marketing communications might have more impact on long- term societal issues that plague all societies. In other words, while we have our eyes turned toward the bright lights and big-screen stars, we're missing opportunities to help the field innovate and expand its impact, and prepare for the not-too-distant but very different future.
Clearly, the future of advertising/marketing communications is and must be based on consumers and their consumption capabilities. Ignore that and we ignore the very basis of what the field can, will, or should be about.

THREE POSSIBLE SCENARIOS FOR THE FUTURE OF ADVERTISING

It would seem there are three possible alternative tracks for the future of advertising/marketing communications. Each has its own values and importance, and each presents alternatives that must be considered. Thus, as a final argument, the three alternative routes that advertising/ marketing communications can or might take are presented as individual solutions for the future of the field.

Adaptation of the Current Practices Through Creeping Incrementalism

One possible future of advertising/marketing communications is that everyone involved will simply adapt and adjust to change over time—that is, they will slowly but surely evolve solutions to fit the changing nature of the marketplace. That would mean an acceptance of the change by the major leaders in the field and the development of tools and techniques to deal with and mitigate those changes. While this seems the most logical approach simply because it is the one that is seemingly already being attempted by both practitioners and the academic community, it is fraught with peril. Technology, consumers, and the entire marketplace are racing forward, and marketers, advertisers, and educators are struggling today just to keep up with those changes.

And the future will only become more intense. It is becoming increasingly clear that our present systems simply are not adaptable to or capable of moving at the speed of knowledge development and/or techno•logical change. In too many instances, while technology and other factors have increasingly changed everything around us, too many in the field continue to reject these radical changes, arguing instead for adaptation and evolution. Trying to force-fit traditional approaches and methodologies into radically different situations is not likely a rational solution to an increasingly and seemingly irrational marketplace.

The future (or, in some instances, the non-future) of advertising/marketing communications will likely follow this path unless major changes are developed immediately. An example of this short-term adjustment to major industry dislocations will illustrate this case. The rise of social media has caused major upheavals in the planning and implementation of advertising and marketing communications, yet many practitioners and academicians refuse to accept them. In trying to find ways to measure social media, industry gurus have suggested trying to convert all forms of media, including social, to one standardized measure: gross rating points (MarketingProfs, n.d.). Gross rating points grew out of traditional over-the-air and cable television planning.

It assumed one could estimate the total size of an audience and then deconstruct that total audience to determine what one percentage point of that audience might be. That's a gross rating point, or GRP. So the thinking goes that we'll simply convert all audiences into GRPs and suddenly have a common planning and measurement tool. That sounds really good, but the problem is the assumption that the audience size for all media vehicles is known or could be calculated. They aren't and can't be. In addition, the GRP measure was never anything more than a very questionable estimate of audience size—with error margins large enough to drive a truck through.

Assuming one could measure the audience size of social media or sales promotion, or any other form of advertising or marketing communication, the use of GRPs might be worthwhile. But when one tries to transfer that to other, interactive forms of media, the challenges become more than appalling; they become ridiculous. Trying to determine why the GRP methodology was recommended, the response given by advocates is that it was the only measure on which a committee could agree. That is not much of a reason and even less of a rationale.

Given this type of industry and academic approach to problem solving, it becomes clear that it is unlikely the adaptation of current practices can be the true future of advertising/marketing communications. The lack of a base is simply too great to overcome, no matter how creative the solution might be.

Reversal of the Buyer/Seller Roles

This is a truly innovative concept, but it comes with a large number of unproven concepts and supporting points. What is really being suggested is a total retrofit of existing advertising/ marketing communications thinking and practice. It is based on a realization by sellers that the increasing development of consumer knowledge and interactions with the various forms of communication will impact them significantly. That raises the potential solution of role reversal for advertising/marketing communications organizations. In other words, in this scenario, current buyers or consumers become inquirers, posting notices of their needs, wants, and desires. Then product suppliers and/or manufacturers bid to fill those needs. In other words, the marketplace becomes one giant eBay, with buyers and sellers interacting on a continuous basis. In this scenario, advertisers could be consumers who are signaling their needs. Current marketers could/would become responders, scanning the marketplace and making available products and services to fill those needs. The marketplace would thus become truly interactive, with buyers and sellers interacting on a continuing basis. The key ingredient here would be negotiation. There would be no set prices, nor would there be consistent demand. It would be a continuous, rolling exchange system between suppliers and consumers.

Is this type of interactive/negotiated marketplace practical or possible in a world of 7 to 8 billion humans and still growing? We already have seen glimpses of the potential in China. The electronic marketplace created by Alibaba, the Chinese online marketing giant, is providing the platform. Taking the form of Singles Day (the 11th day of the 11th month), this media-created marketplace celebrating the "singleness" of Chinese youth has grown enormously in a very short period of time. Starting with modest sales and revenues in 2009, the 2015 event generated 91.2 billion Yuan (USD$14.3 billion) and is predicted to grow substantially in the years ahead (BBC News 2015). In 2015, 40,000 marketers, representing 30,000 brands from 25 countries participated with almost all purchases been made through AliPay, the Alibaba financial site. It is a combination of technology, consumer demand, and marketer promotional capabilities combined into one giant interactive, electronic marketplace for one single day.

What is the role of advertising/marketing communications in this type of electronic event? It's quite limited, in the traditional sense of the word. Singles Day succeeds because sellers know that there will be available buyers. Buyers know, based on their marketing communications experience, that they can identify legitimate sellers based on their brands and other requirements built into the system.
Transactions are completed electronically. Distribution occurs based on agreed-upon requirements and availabilities. In short, the system works. And given technological developments, it will likely continue to grow.

What does Singles Day or any other electronic or technologically driven activity/event mean for advertising/marketing communications? That is still evolving, but it clearly changes the value and impact of what we have come to call advertising, since little media messaging is involved. Promotion occurs, but that is "on the spot" and primarily motivation to get the purchaser to buy now. Will this be the future of advertising/marketing communications? It will certainly have an impact, but how much is still to be seen.

Reinvention of the Field

A third alternative to the future of advertising/marketing communications is a total reinvention of the field and how it is practiced. That likely would come from the development of technologies that are now only starting to appear.

There is some evidence of what might happen to the field of advertising/marketing communications in the form of today's crude but growing field of programmatic media planning/buying. Even though it's in the very nascent stage of development, the machine-driven preselection of audience groups are matched with media availabilities and the negotiation is all handled automatically and electronically. Given that capability today, there is no reason not to believe this type of automated advertising/marketing communications development and implementation system, where machines talk to and negotiate with other machines without human intervention, will become the norm sooner rather than later. Other areas, such as consumer/prospect identification and the development of robots that can evaluate various types of audiences and even generate creative content, and then distribute that content, are on the horizon.

That could be quickly followed by the estimation or measurement of results of the advertising/marketing communications programs. That will be possible because most responses will be immediate and the measures will be financial returns, not attitudinal change. None of these speculations are really that far off in the future.

The big question this alternative proposes is this: Who will create and implement these types of changes? Will they be traditional advertising/marketing communications people who will become more skilled and capable of change? Or will they be "foreign" players, such as technologists trained in automation, artificial intelligence, probability models, and the like? This is truly the major question facing advertising/marketing communications today: Who will be your successors?

A FINAL THOUGHT

There is little question that advertising, or whatever we're going to call the field in the future, will change. The signs are too clear to ignore. Will that change be based on proactive research that works to understand all we can about the future, or will we continue to simply fill the gaps in what is perceived to be present knowledge? Will we continue to follow the same pathways and trace the same footprints of those who have gone before us, or will we set off on a new path, embracing change and acknowledging that new approaches are needed? That, to me, is the question of the future of advertising. Those decisions are being made today, and what concerns me most is that our sights are still set too low.

Academicians and practitioners alike must reach for the clouds, lest we be buried in the graveyard of the past.

REFERENCES

Advertising Age (1999), Special Report: "The Advertising Century," March 29, http://adage.com/article/special- report-the-advertising-century/ ad-age-advertising-century-timeline/143661/.

BBC News (2015), "China's Alibaba Breaks Singles Day Record As Sales Surge," November 11, http://www.bbc.com/news/business-34773940.

Ford, Martin R. (2015), The Rise of the Robots: Technology and the Threat of a Jobless Future, Philadelphia: Basic Books.

MarketingProfs (n.d.), "Marketing FAQs," http://www.marketingprofs.com/ FAQS/showfaq.asp?1. McCarthy, E.J. (1960), Basic Marketing, Homewood, IL: Irwin.

This reading is reprinted with permission from *Journal of Advertising*.

Don Schultz (2016) The Future of Advertising or Whatever We're Going to Call It, Journal of Advertising, 45:3, 276-285, DOI: 10.1080/00913367.2016.1185061

E-Commerce Shopper Marketing

By

Sara Master, Digital Marketing and Ecommerce Account Lead, Mosaic North America

Marketing to shoppers used to be a game of eyeballs. The more people who saw your message—the more product you sold. Today the game has changed.

But before we get into that change, let's quickly define what shopper marketing is:
The process of understanding shoppers and using that understanding to develop marketing that influences shopper behavior to positively impact consumption of the brand; usually at a specific retailer.

For instance, when I was on the Huggies account I was responsible for increasing consumption of baby wipes beyond diapering occasions (think of sticky fingers and runny noses). I specifically wanted the shopper to buy more wipes on Amazon through subscription. My target was the shopper (moms and dads) not the consumer (babies) and my channel was ecommerce.

In the old days of shopper marketing I would have put up a shelf sign in-store that specially told moms that Huggies wipes were "great for all baby messes, from nose to toes". That would have done it. Sales would have increased.

But in the new days of shopper marketing the brand is not in control. **The Shopper is in Control** (See Figure 1: Evolution of Shopper Marketing).

What does that mean? The shopper has more purchase choices than ever before, from brands to retailers to channel. They can shop online, or in store. They can subscribe, they can buy once. They have so many choices that control of the sale has gone past the brand or retailer and extended to the shopper. Therefore… The Shopper is in Control.

Figure 1: *Evolution of Shopper Marketing*

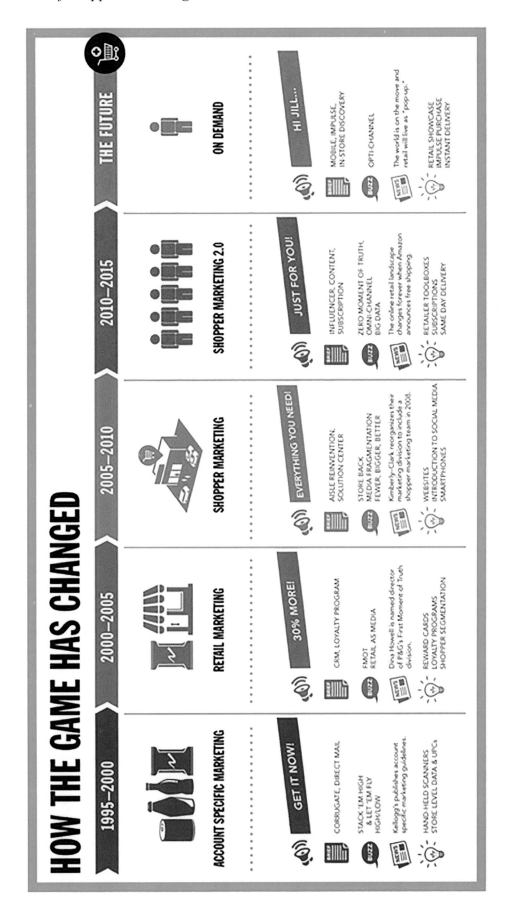

Because of this, in order for my wipes message to resonate, I needed to personalize it for my shopper (among other things: moms AND dads with babies in household who have an Amazon Prime account and are either buying Huggies wipes already or another premium brand). I also needed to ensure that, when shoppers actually clicked on my message (assuming it is some type of online ad unit), they landed at a place where they found the right product information to convince them to purchase.

Essentially what I needed to do was recreate the experience of picking up a box of wipes in the store, in the online world where the box is just a very small picture on a screen. That's a tall order, to take something life size that shoppers are trained to touch, and translate it to a digital environment—a retailer's Product Detail Page (PDP).
But it's also exciting because it offers opportunities to share new kinds of information like videos and reviews that a shopper can't normally consume in-store.

Today, we're going to walk through the ecommerce shopper marketing process. From creating Product Detail Pages (PDPs) to promoting products online to partnering with retailers on ecommerce innovations (things like Alexa or virtual gifts)—we'll learn in more detail how a shopper is in control, when it comes to online shopping.

Let's start at the beginning. Who's shopping online and for what?

You might be conjuring up images of harried moms buying diapers on Amazon, a lone Alaskan shopping for a Canada Goose coat on a cold winter's night, or a young urbanite finally finding that elusive vinyl record.

In each case, you'd be right. Online shopping crosses all demographics – age, gender, location, and socioeconomic statuses. In fact, 96% of Americans have made an online purchase in their life, 80% in the past month alone, according to a 2017 point-of-sale solutions survey by Square and Mercury Analytics.

Despite the examples above – diapers, coats, records – electronic goods, specifically computers and related items, were the most popular items sold online for decades. However, that shifted in 2015 when spending on apparel and accessories surpassed electronics. (Comscore, 2016).

In fact, Nordstrom has a new store concept that stocks no clothes, no cosmetics, no anything. Instead it offers shoppers a place to pick up and return online purchases as well as enjoy help from a personal stylist, tailoring services, beverages and manicures. The first of these Nordstrom concept stores is already open in Hollywood, California with more slated for later in 2018.

As ecommerce growth continues in non-perishable items of all types (from electronics to cosmetics) retailers are now considering the next big frontier: fresh food delivery.

Whether this comes in the form of grocery delivery, meal kit delivery, or something else entirely (like the Amazon Treasure Truck) is still anyone's guess. But moves like Amazon's purchase of Whole Foods; Albertsons (American's second largest grocery store chain) purchase of Plated; and Walmart's teasing of a home delivery service that asks employees to make deliveries on their way home from work; (Washington Post, 2017) all signal big changes in fresh food delivery in the immediate future.

While buying fresh food online is still trending, buying other items online has become a part of American culture. In the years to come projections are that online shopping will eventually outstrip in store shopping. According to eMarketer, between 2014-2016, online shopping was up 16%, while in store shopping was up 2.4%. Between 2017-18, eMarketer projected online shopping to go up 16% *again* but in-store shopping to only increase by 1.8%. This means that retailers and brands are looking to ecommerce as the key to driving future revenue growth.

What is driving all this online shopping growth?

The top three factors that are very or extremely influential in determining online shopping are: price (87%), shipping cost and speed (80%) and discounts (71%), per a 2017 point-of-sale solutions survey by Square and Mercury Analytics. Yet, when we remember that a shopper is in control, we should also consider that many shoppers go online to do research—read reviews and check for merchandise availability—before buying in store. (This is called "webrooming"). This online activity can lead to big business in-store. In fact, according to Forrester, "webrooming consumers will bring in $1.8 Trillion in sales in 2017."

Yet, despite activities like webrooming, online shopping continues to grow due to ease of purchase and faster delivery.

When shopping is happening online, how is it being done?

The short answer is: Mobile. About 60% of visits to ecommerce sites happen through mobile devices. However, ecommerce *purchasing* tends to happen on desktop with only 38% of ecommerce revenue coming from mobile (Wolfgang Digital, 2016).

Why are so many shoppers looking at items on mobile but purchasing on desktop? Most experts believe this goes back to screen size. Shoppers want to be able to really vet items visually before purchasing and the smaller mobile screen does not aid this (think of our PDP discussion at the start of this chapter).

Additionally, many shoppers dislike the task of entering in their shipping and credit card information through the mobile interface vs typing it in on their computer. These are areas of growth for ecommerce to overcome in the future. Remember that, because the shopper is in control, it is the retailer's job (in partnership with companies and shopper marketers) to make sure the online experience meets their expectations.

How can companies sell products online?

There are three ways companies sell their products online: direct to consumer, through multichannel retailers, and through pure play retailers.

When companies sell direct to consumer, they own the site they are selling through and usually it is the manufacturer selling directly without a retail store like Amazon or Walmart in-between. Examples of companies that sell direct to consumer include: Dollar Shave Club, Warby Parker, and Blue Apron.

Because it costs so much money to create and promote an ecommerce storefront, plus more time and money to manage the logistics of storing and shipping products, most companies sell their products through retailers.

These retailers may be multichannel or pure play. Multichannel retailers have both an online and a brick and mortar store presence. Examples of multichannel retailers include Walmart, Apple, and Nordstrom. Pure play retailers have a presence in just one channel, usually ecommerce. Examples of pure play retailers include Amazon (although that is changing with their purchase of Whole Foods and experiments with brick-and-mortar stores) and Chewy.com.

What are the steps to selling online?

The first step to selling online is to choose a selling method, either direct or through a retailer. Because this is a shopper-marketing focused document, we will assume that products are sold through a retailer. Therefor the first step is to select retailer partners at which to sell. This decision is called "Stage 0", and for the purposes of this discussion, we will assume that retailers selected include Amazon, Walmart and Target.

Innovation. **See Figure 2** for an outline of Stages 1-3 before you continue reading.

The Foundation phase, Stage 1, consists of two key activities. First is negotiation with the retailer. This is the time when the retailer will agree to accept and sell the products on their site. They will order the amount of product they wish to keep in their warehouse(s) to send to

Figure 2: Ecommerce Strategy

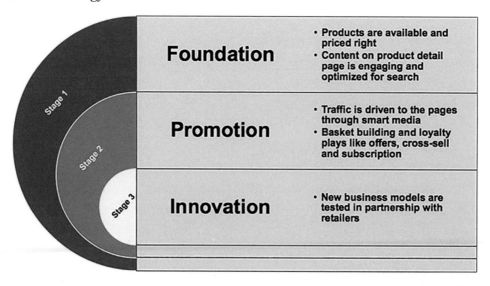

Following Stage 0, a company finalizes its go to market strategy through three stages: Foundation, Promotion and consumers when the product is ordered. The company will also negotiate the pricing and other terms of the agreement.

Following this, the second phase of Foundation is to **set the shelf.** The company will create "about" copy and images to upload to the Product Detail Page or PDP (the page where the shopper can add the item to their cart). See Figure 3 and Figure 4 for example about copy and example images. We'll explore best practices for creating copy and images later in this reading.

Once the terms of sale are negotiated with the retailer and the shelf is set, companies can move on to Stage 2, Promotion. The Promotion stage is characterized by two key activities. First, traffic is driven to the product detail pages through media placements like search ads and banner ads. And second, basket building and loyalty plays such as offers and subscription are employed. Again, we'll explore best practices for Promotion later in this reading.

Finally, companies enter Stage 3, Innovation. In this stage, companies partner with a retailer to test new business models and ecommerce ideas. For instance, when Target started testing their subscription model, they looked for a partner to test offer frequency and discount amount to determine the best combination of the two to drive purchase and loyalty.

Figure 3: "About" Copy for the Product Detail Page

	About this item	Customer Reviews	Item Recommendations

- Strong, shopper facing copy that is on brand

- Inform shopper; show product value and share reasons to believe

- Keyword rich without being keyword stuffed

- Asset Kit created with copy tweaked for key retailers (i.e. keyword list for Amazon; additional search headline for Walmart)

About this item

Disclaimer: While we aim to provide accurate product information, it is provided by manufacturers, suppliers and others, and has not been verified by us. See our disclaimer.

Cheap toilet paper doesn't hold up to the value of **White Cloud Mega Roll 2-Ply Ultra Strong & Soft** toilet paper. With Cloud Cushion technology for extra strength and softness, this Walmart toilet paper is our very best 2-ply bath tissue. And, because it's hypoallergenic and dermatologist approved, you'll find it perfect for all members of your family.

- Mega Rolls with 308 sheets is like having 4 rolls in 1!
- 12 Mega Rolls equal 48 regular rolls
- Ultra strong, soft 2-ply bath tissue
- Septic and sewer safe to help avoid clogs
- Lint-free with no residue left behind
- Available in 6 Mega Roll and 12 Mega Roll packs

Read less ▲

Figure 4: Example Images for the Product Detail Page

- Mobile first design

- Greater impact and context when images paired with copy

- Lifestyle images show usage, create aspiration, ecommerce video quickly shares reasons to believe

- Opportunity to cross sell, build basket, and share benefits of buying in ecommerce channel

Stage 0: Selecting Retailer Partners

In the second section, we discussed the factors shoppers take into account when selecting an online retailer. They are (in the shoppers' priority order):
- Price
- Shipping cost and speed
- Discount offers

As a shopper marketer, it is imperative to counsel clients (the company) to take this value equation into consideration when determining where to place big bets in ecommerce. Some retailers (Amazon, Walmart, Costco) offer free shipping in two days or less on most products. Others offer free ground shipping at a certain price point (Macy's, Nordstrom Rack, and many others) and still others require the shopper to pay for the full cost of shipping (HEB, most small specialty retailers).

Because shipping cost and speed are of a high priority to online shoppers, these factors heavily influence purchase and therefor the retailers that companies select to partner with.

Stage 1: Building the Shelf

Once a company has selected its preferred retailer partners, it is time to set the foundation for their ecommerce presence. Companies, with their shopper marketing team, will take action in the following areas: Retailer Negotiations, Product Detail Page Setup, Search, and Review Generation during Stage 1.

Before the products can be setup on the retailer's site, the selling company must negotiate the terms of sale with the retailer including pricing and participation in offerings like Prime, Free Shipping, Store pickup and Subscription. This is not usually considered a shopper marketing activity so we will skip ahead.

Following this, content can be created for the Product Detail Pages (PDP). There are two main types of content Basic—which is the minimum copy and images a retailer requires for a PDP, and Enhanced (Amazon calls it A+)—which is the "From the Manufacturer" content that appears further down the page (see Figure 5).

First, basic content is created. Companies start with "About" copy (see Figure 3) which includes product page title, "about" paragraph and "why buy" bullets and hidden keywords. All copy must be optimized to appear in the retailer's search results without being keyword stuffed. That means the copy must be useful to the shopper and include product details that help shoppers make buying decision. In the example in Figure 3, this includes details about the product size, strength and softness.

Following this, product images are created (see Figure 4). The first image on a product detail page is always a picture of the product (usually in packaging) on a white background. Retailers then allow for additional images and most companies opt to share the sides and back of their product packaging on a white background.

However, those companies are missing a strategic opportunity to visually share additional product features and benefits with their shoppers. To do so, more advanced companies may choose to share: lifestyle images showing the product in use, consumer reviews, cross-sell to other products and even video (Zappos.com is a leader in ecommerce video).

Once the basic content is created, companies create Enhanced (A+) content (see Figure 5). While many retailers like companies to have this content, its use by shoppers is limited. This is because most shoppers glean all the product information they want from the basic content at the top of the page. When shoppers scroll further down the page they are usually looking for product reviews or other "recommended" products. They are not looking for more information from the brand.

Which brings us to the final part of the ecommerce Foundation stage: Reviews. Many companies think that shoppers will organically review their products. And they do. However, having 50-100 reviews on a PDP is important for establishing shopper trust. In fact, **64%** purchases in the technology section is based upon the reviews and ratings posted about that particular product (Amzinsights.com, 2017).

Aside from establishing trust, reviews are used by Amazon and other retailers in their search algorithm, so products with more and better reviews appear further up in search results. Finally, as discussed in the second section, shoppers read reviews when "webrooming".

Reviews are so important that some companies have resorted to unscrupulous measures to obtain them. This includes paying others to write reviews or even creating fake accounts and writing reviews themselves. Now, many retailers have rules about how non-organic reviews are generated. Most retailers allow companies to share their product with shoppers in exchange for reviewing it—and that exchange must be called out in the review generally by saying "I received this product for free in exchange for a fair and honest review". Companies that go outside of these rules risk having their products removed from the retailer's website (Techcrunch.com 2016).

Figure 5: Enhanced (A+) Content

View larger

A Gentle and Reliable Clean - Anytime, Anywhere

View larger

View larger

View larger

For Hands, Faces and Surfaces

Use HUGGIES Simply Clean Wipes on hands, faces and bottoms, as well as everyday surfaces to gently and effectively cleanse.

For Your Family's Sensitive Skin

Hypoallergenic and alcohol-free, these versatile wipes are dermatologically tested to be gentle on your child's sensitive skin.

For Home and On-the-Go

At the kitchen table or at the playground, HUGGIES Simply Clean Wipes provide your family with a reliable clean wherever you are.

View larger

A shopper marketer's job is to help guide their client away from unscrupulous review generation to practices that are accepted by retailers and shoppers alike.

During the Foundation stage, companies work with the retailer to create a sales agreement for products online and then create the content that appears on the product detail page. This content must be search-optimized and include reviews.

Stage 2: Promoting the Product

Once a company has a strong foundation, it's time to promote the product. Generally, promotion can be divided into two portions: On the retailer's site off the retailer's site. Promotion on the retailer's site is negotiated and purchased through the retailer and can have added incentives like pricing and product placement on the site.

However, it is usually more expensive than off-site promotion, and there are limitations to the customization of the ad.

Promotions off of the retailer's site can appear anywhere the company chooses; they do not even have to be digital. Companies choose this type of promotion when they want to have more control over how and when the promotions occur, when they want to reach a larger audience beyond the retailers or when they want a more specialized message than they would be allowed to share on the retailer's site.

On the retailer's site promotion

For promotion on the retailer's site, it is usually best to start with sponsored search placements or "recommended" products. Sponsored search placements appear in shopper search results with the word "sponsored", see Figure 6. Recommended products can appear in many areas throughout the site but will almost always be a scrollable row of products with a headline such as "More to Consider", see Figure 7. Companies start with these types of placements because they appear when shoppers have raised their hand to signal an interest (either through searching a keyword related to a product or by browsing similar product PDPs). They are considered the fastest way to get your products into a shopper's basket.

The downside to the promotion methods above is that the shoppers don't learn anything about your product before clicking through to the product detail page. For new brands or new categories (teeth cleaning dog chews were new category several years ago) more explanation may be needed to generate a customer click. This is when other marketing methods on the retailer's site such as email, banner ads and homepage takeovers may be employed to share more product details to drive traffic to product detail pages or even product landing pages.

Off the retailer's site promotion

When companies want more control over the look, feel and placement of their media, they create promotions off of the retailer's site. The opportunities here are endless but can range from targeted banner ads to review generation to immersive brand experiences (think of liquor promotions like "The Johnny Walker Experience" or festival booths like the "Revlon Revelation" which invites shoppers into an air-conditioned trailer for a makeup consultation).

The key to strong promotions of this kind is to have a short brand message and a clear tie to buying in ecommerce NOW. Unsuccessful messaging will try to share all the reasons to buy a brand (or worse, multiple brands) on a banner ad without sharing any reasons to buy in the ecommerce channel.

One of the most successful ecommerce ads ever was done by Pampers for their value brand, Luvs. The ad features a front door with several boxes of Luvs stacked in front of it and invites shoppers to "Get Luvs delivered to your door". The ad was so successful that in ran in different formats for almost a year. Figure 8 shows an example ad unit which allows the shopper to click the icon of the online retailer they wish to purchase from.

In Stage 2, the most important promotion is search related placements on the retailer's site that drive to PDP. These paid search placements help drive sales on the retailer's site, which can increase organic search placement. Following search, a company should invest in on-retailer ad units and then off-retailer placements.

Stage 3: Innovation

In the Innovation stage, companies partner with a retailer to test new business models and ecommerce ideas. These new ideas are usually an output of a concept we discussed at the start of this reading: The Shopper is in Control.

With this mantra in mind, shopper marketers and their companies must consider what innovations they can make that will make shopping easier or better for the shopper. This may include subscription/auto-replacement, sampling, new pickup/delivery methods, voice ordering, and category reinvention. Innovation may be driven by the retailer who partners with a company and the companies' shopper marketing team to carry out testing and refinement of ideas, or it can be driven by the company that brings new thinking to the retailer.

Figure 6: *Sponsored Search Results*

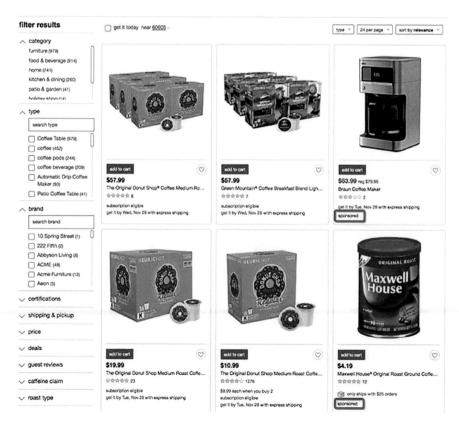

Figure 7: *"Recommended" Product Placements*

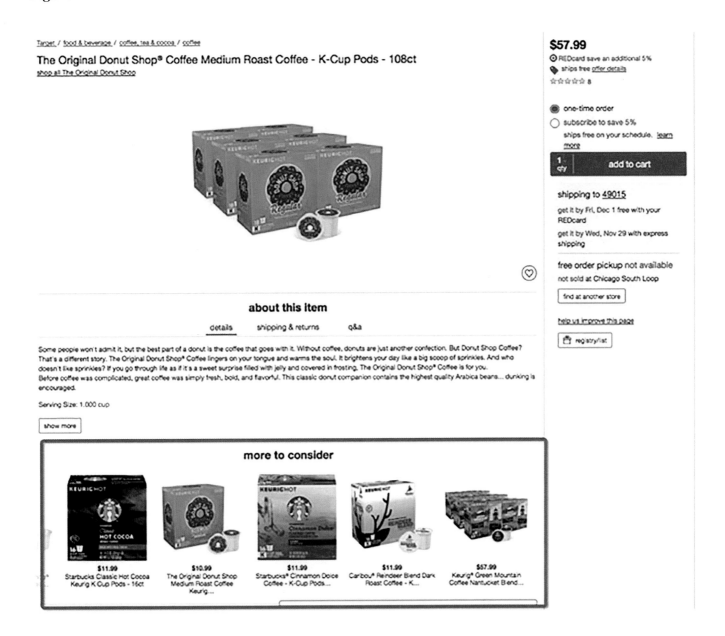

The important thing to remember is that a company should not engage in innovation until they have set their shelf and achieved healthy sales on the retailer's site. During this process, the company will start to forage for the connections at the retailer that are necessary for innovation.

Examples of smart innovation include:

- Partnering with a company launching delivery to sponsor free delivery. This appears to the consumer that the company is sponsoring delivery when $X of their product is purchased.
- Testing buy online pickup in-store discounts (i.e. 5% off when you buy online and pick up in-store). This kind of shopping is very valuable for the retailer and the company because they can avoid the cost of delivery which is almost always more than the cost to "pick" the item in store and have it available for pickup.

Figure 8: *Off Platform Ad Example*

- Joining forces to test offers to different audiences. For example, a retailer may wish to understand which audiences respond better to a $X off offer verses a %off offer. A company may partner with them to promote both offers to different audiences to determine which has the best redemption rate. The company would receive the offers promoted on the retailer's site for a discount to the selected audiences.
- A retailer may partner with a company to test various forms of category reinvention. For instance, a company may come to the retailer with a case for including coffee makers in searches for "coffee". That is, the company may say that including coffee makers in coffee search results will yield more sales for coffee makers without diluting sales of ground coffee. Testing this with select partners can help avoid losses associated with site- wide changes, and increase site sales in general.
- The new frontier of ecommerce sales is voice-activated search and sales (think Alexa, Google Home, Siri, etc.). With Google reporting that 20% of searches are now voice activated, both retailers and companies are scrambling for first-mover advantage in this space. (Marketing Land 2016)

Once the shelf is set and promotions are under control, shopper marketers can help their companies partner with retailers to innovate in the ecommerce space. This may include new forms of delivery, subscription or onsite categorization. The key here is that retailers and companies both bring innovative thinking to the table, and both learn from the partnership.

Personalization at Every Stage

No matter the ecommerce stage a company is in, personalization will always yield more sales—shopper marketers should have this in mind when developing content and marketing plans.

Depending on the retailer, personalization can range from recommended products based on past purchases to recommended products that compliment current items in cart (hamburger and French fries model) to custom offers only available to select shoppers. Generally, retailers will charge manufacturers for the opportunity to personalize their products to shoppers. But the data supports investing here:

- Personalized shopping cart recommendations influenced 92% of shoppers online. (Source: Kibo, 2017)
- 75% of consumers are more likely to buy from a retailer that recognizes them by name, recommends options based on past purchases, or knows their purchase history (Source: Accenture, 2016)
- Personalized home page promotions influenced 85% of consumers to buy online. (Source: Kibo, 2017)

As ecommerce continues to develop, there will be more opportunities to personalize product recommendations and offers to shoppers. Areas for shopper marketers to watch out for include: personalized ads using shopper name, customized product detail page content that adjusts to the shopper stage in the purchase funnel (first visit to that page or repeat) or emails reminding shoppers to buy products they may be running out of (e.g. you bought milk one week ago, it might be time to reorder your 2%).

Thinking about What's Next

While the roots of shopper marketing are in loud promotions that tell shoppers "Get it Now" and "Save" and "New and Improved" (Figure 1), the future is far more refined. Personalization will continue to allow messages to be more tailored to the shopper's needs and wants.

Therefore, as shopping, especially online shopping, becomes more personalized there will be more opportunities for shopper marketers to satisfy their client (the company) as well as provide value to the retailer *and* shopper. To do this shopper marketers must think mobile first, think commerce vs ecommerce (eventually the wall between shopping in store and shopping online will be totally gone just like in the Nordstrom showroom example) and remember that: The Shopper is in Control.

Social Media Marketing

By

Kelly Cutler, Founder and CEO, Kona Company

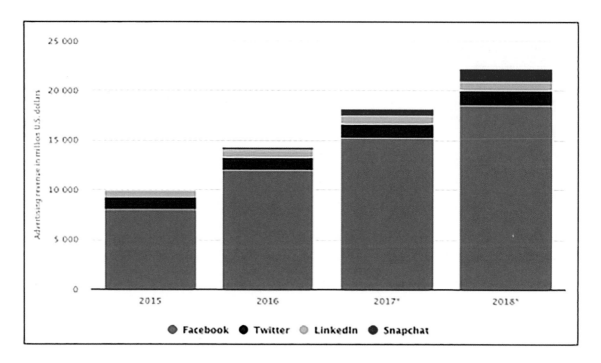

Social media marketing is a large and growing business. From 2015 to 2018 the social Media advertising business was expected to grow from $10 billion to nearly $23 billion in revenue.[1] Facebook leads the pack.

The growth of social media marketing is due to an increasing number of companies and brands utilizing social platforms like Facebook, Twitter and LinkedIn to reach their target audiences and drive more sales. For many companies, digital marketing has become the primary driver for acquiring new business. In fact, predictions indicate that digital will soon beat television in ad spend. As new entrants to the digital ad market (think Amazon and Pandora) continue to grow, there is still abundant innovation from digital's large players (think Google and Facebook).

This expansion is great news for marketers as it provides them with more creative opportunities to amplify their brand message in new and exciting ways. In this reading we will explore social media marketing at a deeper level and discuss how social channels can impact marketing programs for companies of all sizes.

Within social media marketing, there are many ways to connect with customers. Most companies engage in organic social media (think free), creating business profile pages within social networks and posting articles, content and updates to their news feed. Companies also frequently incorporate their organic social media strategy into an overall customer service strategy. Many marketers also use Facebook ads, sponsored tweets (Twitter), sponsored content (LinkedIn) and pre-roll video ads (YouTube.com) as part of an overall paid media strategy.

Figure 1: Social media ad examples on different platforms (clockwise from upper left) YouTube, Facebook, LinkedIn and Twitter.

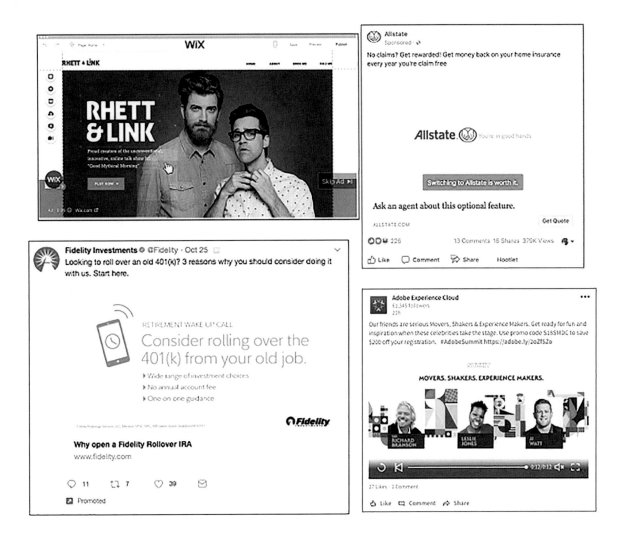

Content Marketing

As important as social media marketing has become, a foundational element for its success is content marketing. Companies must first develop a brand voice and establish their unique and valuable subject matter expertise. Then marketers can explore the best ways to provide valuable information to their customer base by engaging users with interesting content. In the Twitter ad example in Figure 1, Fidelity Investments is attempting to position itself as the expert in 401k investments. The eye-catching visual ad on Twitter drives users to a longer blog post that delivers worthwhile information, which ultimately results in Twitter users engaging more with the Fidelity brand.

Content Marketing can encompass many different formats and types. A single piece of content can be used in many ways to reach different people. This concept was named **COPE,** Create One Publish Everywhere[2], by the Content Marketing Institute. An example of COPE might be: if the same Fidelity tweet regarding 401k investments options also drive users to a short video that conveys the same information as the blog post.

Below are some interesting content formats for marketers to consider:

- Blog posts
- Articles
- eBooks
- White Papers
- Datagrams / visual posts
- Videos
- Photos
- Press Releases
- User Generated Content (UGC)
- Podcasts
- Slideshows
- How-to demonstrations
- Checklists
- Infographics

It is critical for marketers to understand the key role of content in a social media marketing strategy. In addition, they must also have a strong working knowledge of the products and offerings of the most important social networks.

Facebook

Facebook's monthly active user base grew to over 2 billion in 2017.[3] Over the last four years, this social behemoth has reported tremendous revenue growth leading to projections in global revenue for 2017 of approximately $30 billion.[4] More than 80% of all adult Internet users are active on Facebook.[5]

For marketers, Facebook offers many different organic and paid advertising opportunities to reach its loyal user base for large organizations, such as Amazon, Procter & Gamble and Walmart, and small and medium-sized businesses. Facebook ads can appear in many formats and locations: news feed on both desktop and mobile versions, right hand rail, within a Facebook page or the Messenger app.

Figure 1: Advertising opportunities on Facebook

Facebook's easy-to-use self-service ad manager gives business owners and marketers the flexibility to determine objectives and results. It also offers precise audience targeting based on a large number of demographic options, including location, age, interests, languages and relationships.

Figure 2: *Facebook's Ad Manager*

What's your marketing objective?

Awareness	Consideration	Conversion
Boost your posts	Send people to a destination on or off Facebook	Increase conversions on your website
Promote your Page	Get installs of your app	Increase engagement in your app
Reach people near your business	Raise attendance at your event	Get people to claim your offer
Increase Brand Awareness	Get video views	Promote a product catalogue
Increase your reach	Collect leads for your business	Get people to visit your shops

Figure 3: *Demographic Targeting on Facebook*

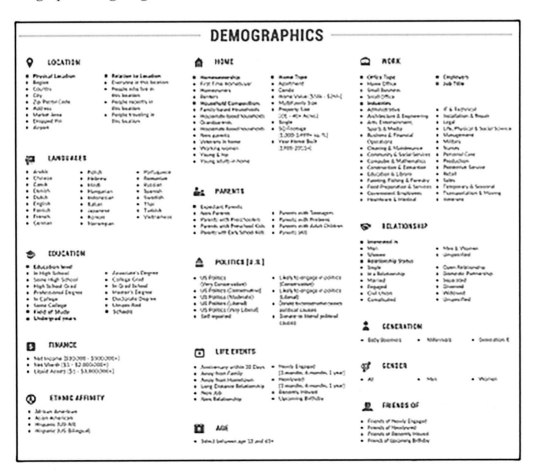

Facebook offers a variety of ad formats, including single or multi-image, video and carousel. The company recently announced several new formats including canvas, a full mobile screen experience; and collection, a catalogue display for retailers.

Advertisers can choose between a pay-per-click, CPC, or cost-per-thousand, CPM model when advertising on Facebook. CPC provides greater control for the way ad dollars are spent and typically delivers better results. With CPC, a user has to click an ad in order for the advertiser to be charged. Although CPM is a lower cost per user, advertisers are charged per 1,000 impressions, or eyeballs, so ad dollars can be spent quickly.

Marketers can use Facebook Insights to uncover a treasure trove of data about how their Facebook business profile, user base, and advertising are performing. These insights can be used to help marketers continually optimize campaigns and how they manage their Facebook presence.

Since Facebook offers so many benefits to advertisers large and small, many marketers regard Facebook as their most cost-effective and useful advertising platform.

LinkedIn

LinkedIn's monthly active user base in 2017 was 250 million[6] and revenue was $960 million.[7] More than 29% of all adult Internet users are active on LinkedIn.[8]

Figure 5: *Example of an ad on LinkedIn*

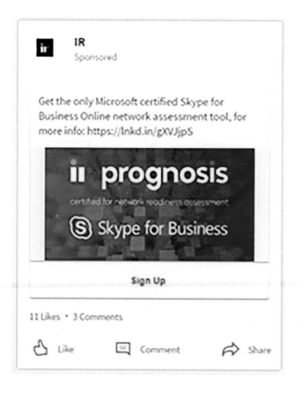

Since LinkedIn is a professional networking app, it offers specific business-related targeting. The platform provides advertisers with options to target individuals, based on seniority or job title, and specific companies and organizations. LinkedIn regards individuals with a large number of connections as thought leaders and influencers, and allows users to follow them; these individuals could also be targeted as part of an influencer marketing campaign. In terms of generating leads, creating brand awareness, or driving website traffic, options on LinkedIn include Sponsored Content, Dynamic Video Ads and Sponsored InMail ads.[9]

Twitter

Twitter's monthly active user base grew to 330 million in 2017[10] and quarterly revenue reached $589 million in the 3rd quarter of 2017.[11] More than 24% of all adult Internet users are active on Twitter.[12]

Twitter offers Promoted Tweets, Promoted Accounts and Promoted Trends as advertising options.

Figure 6: *Example of an ad on Twitter*

Since there is a limit to content length, Twitter is a great platform for marketers to introduce succinct content within a fast paced feed and engage in real-time conversations. Twitter best practices include posting regularly and establishing relationships with a community of loyal followers. Many users have come to expect customer service help on a company's Twitter feed, and this is another great way to engage with customers.

YouTube

In 2017, YouTube's monthly active user base was 1.5 billion,[13] with more than 30 million daily visitors[15], and global revenue of \$4 billion.[14] Every minute almost 300 hours of videos are uploaded to YouTube,[16] and nearly 5 billion videos are watched every day.[17] Many brands choose to host their own brand channel where they provide video content for users to view, comment and share.

Figure 7: Example of an ad on YouTube

YouTube also offers the following advertising options: TrueView Discovery Ads (appear in search results and on the homepage), TrueView In Stream Ads (a skip-able in-video ad) and Bumper Ads (6 second videos on mobile).

Pinterest

Pinterest monthly active user base was 200 million in 2017[18] and the company had a market valuation of \$12.3 billion.[19] More 26% of all adult Internet users are active on Pinterest.[20]

Pinterest is a creative and visual platform for sharing and exchanging ideas related to inspiration, products, design and short format how-tos. The popularity of Pinterest spans across generations.

Pinterest offers a variety of advertising options: Promoted Pins, Promoted Video Pins, One Tap Pins and Promoted App Pins. Compared to Twitter, the platform is 80% more viral and 3x more effective at generating leads.[21]

Figure 8: Example of an ad on Pinterest

Instagram

Instagram's monthly active user base grew to 800 million in 2017[22] and global revenue was $6.84 billion.[23] More than 28% of all adult Internet users are active on Instagram.[24] The platform is dedicated to providing users with the ability to post inspirational visual content and create a story using static and video imagery. Instagram content is easily shareable and appeals to all age groups. Because Instagram is owned by Facebook, the two networks share many ad formats and options for advertisers.

Snapchat

Snapchat's monthly active user base was more than 300 million in 2017[25] and global revenue was nearly
$1 billion.[26] 28% of Snapchat U.S. users are 18 to 24 years old.[2]

Figure 9: Example of an ad on Instagram

Figure 10: Example of ads on Snapchat

Snapchat is the most whimsical of the social platforms because it allows users to add pre-loaded creative to their own content. More than 10 billion videos are viewed daily on Snapchat.[28]

Snapchat offers Snap Ads, Filters and Lenses as advertising options.

Local

For many small businesses such as restaurants, hair salons, plumbers, travel agents and dry cleaners, online review sites are good for marketing. These sites include Yelp, Google+, Bing Places, Angie's List, OpenTable, FourSquare and many others. In 2017, 97% of consumers read online reviews for local businesses and 68% of consumers left a review for a business when asked.[29] As social media and mobile use evolves, most consumers will check review sites when looking for a local business.

Yelp is a top site for local business marketing. On average, 142 million users visit Yelp each month[30] to read and write online reviews of businesses. Yelp allows businesses to claim their business listing for free and offers a self-service ad platform, similar to Facebook's, and a full-service ad program.

There are many best practices[31] to follow to ensure online review sites are used strategically for local marketing

Figure 11: *Example of Local Advertising*

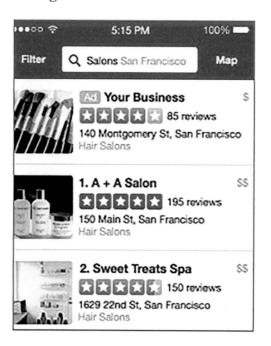

Influencers

Influencer marketing is defined by Wikipedia as a form of marketing in which focus is placed on influential people rather than the target market as a whole. It identifies the individuals that have influence over potential buyers, and orients marketing activities around these influencers. Influencers have the ability to change consumer behaviors, impact purchasing decisions and provide subject matter expertise for businesses and products. Influencer marketing harnesses the authority of these key individuals, using the social web. The most successful influencer marketing programs will clearly define the demographics of customers the company is trying to reach, and identify influencers with the largest and most targeted social following to reach them. Influencers can help drive more revenue for the brand as they provide high value content, or special information and access that consumers appreciate.

Tools and Resources

Social media marketing can be a complex and time-consuming endeavor for small businesses or teams. Fortunately, there are many tools and resources available to help marketers save time and be for efficient. Below are some important tools and resources for savvy marketers.

- Meltwater: monitoring and listening software
- Google Alerts: free updates based on keywords
- Hootsuite: management of multiple social media accounts in one system
- Crimson Hexagon: social analytics and analysis
- Sprout Social: social media management
- Kenshoo Social: management of social ad campaigns
- TapInfluence: influencer marketing
- Camtasia: video marketing
- Zmags: content creation
- Feedly: content aggregation
- Curata: content collaboration
- Canva: visual content creation
- PicMonkey: images and image editing
- Marketo: marketing automation

Conclusion

As the digital landscape grows, marketing continues to evolve. Social media marketing has become a complex and interesting place to develop relationships with prospects and customers. Through platforms like Facebook, advertisers can easily reach and begin a dialog with a highly targeted group of users.

As consumers insist on an increasingly personalized online experience, social media marketing platforms and tools will become an even more important part of an overall marketing strategy.

Endnotes

[1] © https://www.statista.com/statistics/426520/us-social-networks-ad-revenues/
[2] http://contentmarketinginstitute.com/2016/11/content-copeing-strategy/
[3] https://techcrunch.com/2017/06/27/facebook-2-billion-users/
[5] http://www.pewinternet.org/2016/11/11/social-media-update-2016/
[6] https://www.omnicoreagency.com/linkedin-statistics/
[7] https://www.omnicoreagency.com/linkedin-statistics/
[8] http://www.pewinternet.org/2016/11/11/social-media-update-2016/
[9] business.linkedin.com
[10] https://www.statista.com/statistics/282087/number-of-monthly-active-twitter-users/
[11] https://www.statista.com/statistics/274568/quarterly-revenue-of-twitter/
[12] http://www.pewinternet.org/2016/11/11/social-media-update-2016/

[13]https://techcrunch.com/2017/06/22/youtube-has-1-5-billion-logged-in-monthly-users-watching-a-ton- of-mobile-video/

[14] https://www.statista.com/statistics/289657/youtube-global-gross-advertising-revenues/

[15] https://fortunelords.com/youtube-statistics/

[16] https://fortunelords.com/youtube-statistics/

[17] https://fortunelords.com/youtube-statistics/

[18] https://www.socialmediatoday.com/social-business/pinterest-grows-200-million-monthly-active-users-infographic

[19] https://techcrunch.com/2017/06/06/pinterest-raises-150m-at-a-12-3b-valuation-as-it-makes-a-full-press-into-visual-search/

[20] http://www.pewinternet.org/fact-sheet/social-media/

[21] https://strongcoffeemarketing.com/quick-tips/6-reasons-you-should-be-using-pinterest-for-business/

[22] https://techcrunch.com/2017/09/25/instagram-now-has-800-million-monthly-and-500-million-daily-active-users/

[23] https://www.statista.com/statistics/448157/instagram-worldwide-mobile-internet-advertising-revenue/

[24] http://www.pewinternet.org/fact-sheet/social-media/

[25] https://www.omnicoreagency.com/snapchat-statistics/

[26] https://www.emarketer.com/Article/Snapchat-Ad-Revenues-Reach-Nearly-1-Billion-Next-Year/1014437

[27] https://www.statista.com/chart/8789/snapchat-users-by-age-group/

[28] https://www.theverge.com/2016/4/28/11526294/snapchat-10-billion-daily-video-views-users-stories

[29] https://www.brightlocal.com/learn/local-consumer-review-survey/#Q17

[30] https://www.yelp.com/factsheet

[31] https://fitsmallbusiness.com/yelp-for-business/

SNAP Inc.: Pushing the Limits of Social Media Communities and Advertising through Innovation

Excerpted from the work of :

Samer Sarofim, California State University-Fresno

It made big news in late 2013 when a young (almost 23 years old) entrepreneur, rejected a $3 billion dollar acquisition offer. Who rejects such an offer, particularly when it's tripled (the first offer was for $1 billion dollars)? More interestingly, who does so when the offering company is Facebook? According to Wall Street Journal (WSJ), Snapchat's (currently Snap Inc.) co-founder and CEO, Evan Spiegel turned down the $3 billion Facebook's acquisition offer.[1] Seemingly, what had been an arguable decision in 2013 became more justifiable four years later.

In February 2017, Snap Inc. made a successful Initial Public Offering (IPO). Operating less than six years, Snap Inc., according to some financial evaluations, was worth more than $40 billion dollars, shortly after the IPO. This gave Snap Inc. a market value that surpassed that of major corporations, such as e-Bay, Target, or Marriott. It's worth mentioning that the stock price of Snap Inc. increased by more than 40% after just one day of trading.[2]

A vital question is how such an upstart social media platform created an advertising avenue as well as an opportunity to build brand communities. The Snapchat app re-vitalized social media interactions by propagating the concept of short-lived posts and messages that lack a permanent footprint. Pictures, short videos, and messages survive for 24 hours before they are automatically deleted. With such short-term visibility of content, marketers seemed to be puzzled by how to create a community of brand fans and foster consumer-brand engagement. Yet, the popularity of the Snapchat app among consumers, particularly Millennials, encouraged marketers in major corporations to investigate creative techniques to increase brand engagement, despite the short-live nature of content posted on Snapchat.

Top Marketers Invest in Snapchat

For instance, highly regarded brands such as BMW, McDonalds, Under Armour, Gatorade, and Coca Cola stepped up to use Snapchat as a social media avenue to communicate with consumers.[3] Snapchat offers multiple ways to interact with brand followers. Brands can create user accounts that consumers can follow and receive notifications for brand posts. Further, brands can utilize paid media via partnering with Snapchat to create Sponsored Lenses and Sponsored Geofilters (Easter example shown here from Canbury Crème Eggs in the UK.)

Sponsored Lenses allow brands to create interactive filters that consumers can trigger and play with to edit and add action to their photos. Sponsored Geofilters allow marketers to associate a tiny stamp that represents their brand to events, retail chains, or even shared public space. When consumers take their pictures in the associated avenues, the pre-designed brand stamp will appear as an option to add to the picture. This way brands can spread across the social network.

In addition to interacting with consumers through free posts or paid Sponsored Lenses and Sponsored Geofilters on Snapchat, brands have the opportunity to create up to 10-second Snap Ads. Shooting vertical ads for the Snap Ads platform comes with logistical challenges since it changes the norms of the landscape dimension employed in creating video ads and hence requires additional resources.[4] However, brands seem to be willing to accommodate these logistical changes, especially since Snapchat encourages advertised by claiming that, when compared to horizontal ads, vertical ads achieve better viewing rates on mobile devices.[5]

Audi's Super Bowl Snapchat Experiments

With the opportunities and challenges that Snapchat brings to marketers and advertisers, many brands are taking serious steps to communicate with their fans via the several options available on this innovative social media platform. Audi, the high-end auto manufacturer, decided to early- adopt Snapchat in its integrated marketing communication strategy to create an engaging social media experience to the brand fans. Already an innovator, In 2011 Audi was the first brand to establish a hashtag in a Super Bowl commercial.[6]

With Audi's history of pioneering social media campaigns during the Super Bowl, they decided to go big by creating the first real-time campaign on Snapchat during the Super Bowl Sunday 2014. Building on marketing research with Huge (business consulting company), Audi examined the results of the second-screen viewing habits during the 2013 Super Bowl to find out that 59% of the Super Bowl TV viewers used mobile devices as they were watching the game.[7] In partnership with The Onion (digital media company),

Audi created a series of humorous snaps related to the game, and sent those snaps to brand followers. The Snapchat campaign was to promote Audi A3 model, which is an entry-price vehicle for the luxury brand. With their futuristic mindset, Millennial Snapchat users seemed to be a justifiable target market for the A3 model.

According to the Mobile Marketing Association video that was posted on Vimeo (see screen capture below and URL in footnote), Audi believes that the campaign exceeded their expectations.[8] Loren Angelo, director of marketing, at Audi of America said: "We realize the Super Bowl is no longer just a one-day event...It's a month-long conversation." [9]

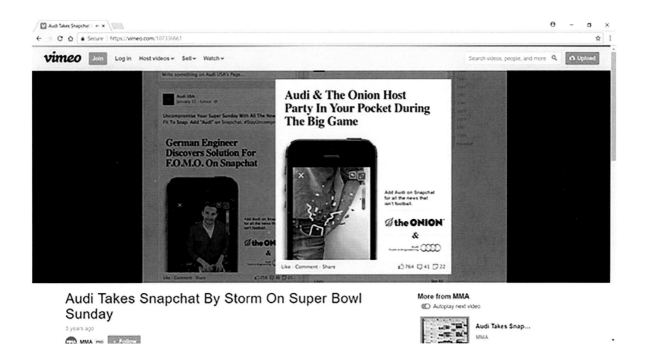

Audi Leads the Way with Snapchat Results

The results of the Audi Real-Time Marketing (RTM) Snapchat Super Bowl campaign were reported as follows:

An increase in Audi Snapchat followers by 5,500 on the game day
More than 100,000 Snapchat views
2,400 Twitter mentions for the campaign, with 2,500 new Twitter followers
9,000 new joins for the Audi Facebook page. According to *Advertising Age*, Audi outperformed the automakers in generating online mentions during the 2014 Super Bowl Sunday and 30% of those mentioned generated through Snapchat.

[1] Evelyn Rusli and Douglas MacMillan, "Snapchat Spurned $3 Billion Acquisition Offer from Facebook," *The Wall Street Journal*, November 13, 2013, accessed April 2, 2017, http://blogs.wsj.com/digits/2013/11/13/snapchat-spurned-3- billion-acquisition-offer-from-facebook/.

[2] Paul R. La Monica, "Snapchat is worth more than Delta, Target and CBS," *CNN Money*, March 3, 2017, accessed April 2, 2017, http://money.cnn.com/2017/03/03/investing/snapchat-market-value/

[3] Jamie O'Brien, "How 6 Big Brands are Advertising on Snapchat Discover," *Sprinklr*, October 12, 2012, accessed April 2, 2017, https://www.sprinklr.com/the-way/big-brands-advertising-on-snapchat-discover/[4] Alexandra Bruell, "Some Advertisers Struggle to Create Snapchat Ads," *The Wall Street Journal*, November 1, 2016, accessed April 2, 2017, https://www.wsj.com/articles/some-advertisers-struggle-to-create-snapchat- ads-1477994401.

[5] Garett Sloane, "Snapchat Persuades Brands to Go Vertical With Their Video," *Adweek*, April 26, 2015, accessed April 2, 2017, http://www.adweek.com/digital/snapchat-persuades-brands-go-vertical-their-video-164305/.

[6] Todd Wasserman, "Audi Super Bowl Ad Claims First Use of Twitter Hashtag," *Mashable*, February 2, 2011, accessed April 2, 2017, http://mashable.com/2011/02/02/audi-super-bowl-twitter-hashtag/#CGnelz70muqn.

[7] Jack Simpson, "Five seriously creative Snapchat campaigns and their results," *Econsultancy*, August 27, 2015, accessed April 2, 2017, https://econsultancy.com/blog/66867-five-seriously-creative-snapchat-campaigns-and-their-results/.

[8] "Audi Takes Snapchat By Storm On Super Bowl Sunday," *Mobile Marketing Association*, accessed April 2, 2017, https://vimeo.com/107336661.

[9] Christopher Heine, "Audi and The Onion's Snapchat Super Bowl Goes for Quick Laughs," *Adweek*, January 31, 2014, accessed April 2, 2017, http://www.adweek.com/digital/audi-and-onions-snapchat-super-bowl-goes-quick-laughs-155433/.

Conversational UX
How it will Change Search, Strategy, and Sales...Forever.

By Dan Golden, President and Chief Search Artist, Befoundonline

Since the advent of computers, humans have been fascinated by the prospect of talking with their machines. In Stanley Kubrick's *2001: A Space Odyssey*, Drs. David "Dave" Bowman and Frank Poole converse with the HAL 9000 on their trip to Jupiter. In the *Star Trek* series, characters regularly asked questions of and gave instructions to the ship's computer. The introduction of Apple's personal assistant, "Siri," in 2011, brought human interaction with machines to mainstream life, making real what had been only previously dreamed.

Since then, voice interaction with machines has grown at a furious rate. It began with voice searches on mobile devices. Internet connected speakers like Google Home and the Amazon Echo have expanded the capabilities of voice interaction and integrated machines into daily living. Voice interaction and the Internet of Things only promises to further develop the integration and relationship between human and machine.

This human-machine relationship will transform business. Increased consumer engagement through apps, social media, and email has established a comfort to engage with brands through technology. Improvements in voice search, especially greater machine accuracy in understanding user requests, have accelerated this change.

Voice search was only the first step. Digital marketers have scrambled to adapt search strategies to ensure they can engage with customers who prefer vocal interaction to gather information, make reservations, or place orders. A huge emphasis has been placed on a great user experience to accommodate these demands, capitalize on the opportunity and begin building a relationship with the consumer. The experience begins with voice, but often ends with a "traditional" visual user experience.

In this way, voice search is a unidirectional engagement. Technology, in the form of machine learning, and innate human behavior, will replace this visual step and transform the user experience. The next step in the evolution will be bidirectional engagement, aka conversation, or a conversational user experience.

In fact, it's happening now. And it promises to grow. Businesses, and especially marketers, need to understand how quickly this change is happening. They also need to understand how it will affect their strategy, what it means for search marketing and even their sales.

Many brands have already embraced this new user experience. Those that wish to thrive must it embrace it as well. This requires understanding the user, the technical elements needed for accurate results and the type of content that will be needed.

Conversational UX. What is it?

Conversational user experience (UX) refers to the interaction between a person and a machine. The way a person communicates with another person is very different from the way a person communicates with a machine. Human interaction involves more than words. It includes tone of voice, idiomatic phrases, non-verbal communication and personality.

Designers and programmers seek to make the experience between a person and a machine more natural. This has led to "conversational design," developing bots that use machine learning and AI to retain information, capture nuance of the user interaction and present a strong persona. While idioms and non- verbal clues may yet be far-off, machines programmed to understand and learn from nuance respond in a more conversational way.

Applications for Conversational UX

The question isn't where or how will conversational UX be used. The real question is where won't it be.

Mobile devices offer voice search. Google introduced voice search on desktop devices with a plugin for Chrome in 2013; since then, more apps have popped up with manufacturers building in more voice capabilities. Google Home and the Amazon Echo have brought voice activated machines into the home. Many new cars offer voice activation and integration with Google and other voice recognition apps like Dragon Drive. And the Internet of Things revolution is just getting started.

Basically, we're going to be talking to all of our electronic devices. Personal assistants like Siri may have started as basic voice search tools, but this will change. Daily interactions with machines like Amazon's Alexa will become a driving force for innovation. For voice-based user experience, this means more conversational experiences.

It's not unreasonable to believe a device's ability to "converse" won't be a major factor in its marketability. This might seem like a major concern for programmers and designers, but the reality is, it's a bigger challenge for marketers. Programmers only need to create programs and algorithms that encourage machine learning to better develop personas and conversational attributes. Marketers need to deliver:

- Content that answers user questions
- Proper technical set-up of web so content can be found
- Accurate keyword for SEO and SEM
- Local business information, i.e., up-to-date store hours
- Ecommerce options and voice-based simplified buying experiences
- Conversational apps
- Content for bots to deliver
- Automated customer service content

Programmers will deliver machines that will converse. Marketers will need to guarantee their businesses or clients offer the best experiences, via machine-based conversation.

How Soon Do Marketers Need to Start? How About Now!

It took years for voice search to gain mainstream acceptance since it debuted with Apple's Siri in 2011. One reason for slow adoption of voice interaction involved its new-ness. Another, and probably bigger, factor was accuracy. It took time for programmers to develop bots capable of "understanding" user requests. Use of this feature over time provided programmers with the information and feedback needed to develop the algorithms and machine learning tools to create more accurate responses.

Marketers should not expect conversational UX to develop as slowly. Voice interaction with devices is established. Machine learning, AI and algorithms and developed machine personas exist. Perhaps more importantly, as statistics show, people have come to rely on the voice-activated devices.

- "65 percent of Amazon Echo or Google Home users can't imagine ever returning to life without a smart speaker."[i]
- 42% of smart speaker owners say it's essential to their daily life.[ii]
- 40% of adults use voice search once per day.[iii]
- In 2014, 50% of people used voice search, according to a Google study. That number has only increased. [iv]
- 42% of people who use voice search say driving is a reason to use voice search.[v]
- 61% of smart speaker owners say having a smart speaker "is like having someone to talk to."

Reliance on voice search has far reaching impacts that marketers must take into account. A 2017 NPR – Edison Research report noted of smart speaker owners[vi]:

- 87% wanted the smart speaker to get answers without needing to type
- 13% use it to order food
- 10% use it to shop
- 35% use it for home lighting, thermostat and appliances
- 88% of smart speaker owners say their children (those who have children) like Alexa

Getting answers without typing equals research, or search queries. Ordering food and shopping are buying. Managing home lighting and other home appliances reflect an intersection of customer service and voice for brands. And children are getting accustomed to voice response from machines.

These statistics show the immediate need for marketers to embrace the conversational user experience.

Projections suggest the need is urgent. For example:

- Comscore says 50% of searches will be done by voice by 2020.
- By 2020, Gartner says 30% of searches will be done without screens.
- It's estimated there will be 21.4 million smart speakers in the US by 2020.
- 42% of smart speaker owners have two or more, while 45% plan to buy another one.

As noted, people communicate differently with machines. However, as programmers improve machine learning algorithms and AI becomes more advanced, conversational patterns will continue to evolve. Beyond the need to identify essential keyword phrases, marketers will need to adapt strategies for the upcoming changes in behavior, from search to sales.

Impact of Conversational UX on Business and Marketing

The success of smart speakers suggests that people will continue to become more comfortable speaking with machines. While sales conversion remains a small percentage of the user experience, research on products, services and brands is one of the primary reasons for talking with our machines. This promises to change the type of experience marketers must deliver, far beyond search results, although search is one of the most immediate elements marketers must address.

Several key areas marketers must address as conversational user experience evolves include:

- Search marketing
- Content marketing
- Voice actions
- Personal assistants
- Chatbots
- Brand Apps

Search Marketing

Even with increased use of voice search, the Search Engine Results Page (SERP) remains the primary means by which users see search results. The visual nature of the SERP with its paid ads, local listings, organic search results and shopping ads give marketers a margin of error. It's desirable to be the #1 result, but not essential. Conversational search will change that.

In conversation, rarely does a person give us multiple answers for a single question. The nature of conversation is that one question produces one answer. This won't change. When you ask Siri for the "nearest Chinese take-out", you don't want a list of nearby restaurants. The question demands one answer.

With conversational UX, marketers are no longer competing for a top 10 SERP result, or top three local result, or to grab one of four paid search slots. All of these – paid, organic, local – are competing for *one* spot. The answer to the user's question.

And that's only the first part of the challenge! Earning a top spot doesn't guarantee that a brand will remain there. With constantly evolving search algorithms, the best answer or result constantly changes. Users can always request for the next result, but the question remains, what will prompt them to do so.

Content Marketing

User queries of machines all have one factor in common. They all have intent, even if 61% of smart speaker owners say it's "like having someone to talk to." Machines can respond, but don't have opinions (yet!). As such they rely on content to supply the responses they give. With few exceptions, marketers supply that content.

Every question demands an answer. And answers today come in many different forms. They may come as a Quick Answer, provided by a Google Quick Answer Box. Featured snippets are another way to provide short, high-value content in response to questions. Rich cards offer another way to provide fast, concise information on academic courses, recipes, reviews, events and products. These content types along with website, ad and app content put the onus on content marketers to provide high-quality answers.

They also require trust. The search engine must "trust" the content is accurate and the best response to the user query. The user must also trust the response. The user must also trust the machine.

The first element of trust relies on standard elements of content marketing, user engagement, quality backlinks and SEO. The second aspect of this trust, the user trust, requires the source of the answer be trusted by the user. In marketing terms, this means the brand has credibility and likability. Failure on this point will make success in the top spot irrelevant. The third element falls to programmers and conversational design specialists.

Voice Actions

How people interact with machines is changing. The spread of voice-activation beyond the mobile device and into the home and car will alter expectations. This includes more personable machines, but also their ability to perform more actions.

Currently, there are three different types of voice requests: search, device command and home or appliance commands. Some examples of these include:

Voice Search

Check the weather: "Do I need a jacket today?" or "What's the weather like tomorrow?"
Answer trivia questions: "Where was Albert Einstein born?" or "How old is Beyonce?"
Check stock prices: "What's the Google stock price?"
Translate words or phrases: "How do you say cucumber in Spanish?"
Define a word: "What does gluttony mean?"
Convert between units: "What's 16 ounces in pounds?"

Solve a math problem: "What's the square root of 2209?"
Search within apps on your device: "Search for Thai food on Yelp"

Device Commands

Set an alarm: "Set an alarm for 7 AM"
Set a reminder: "Remind me to call John at 6 PM"
Create a Calendar Event: "Create a calendar event for dinner in Chicago at 7 PM this Saturday"
Check your schedule: "What does my day look like tomorrow?"

Home and Appliance Commands

WiFi: "Turn on Wi-Fi"
Radio: "Turn on Radio"
Security systems: "Turn off home security"
Lighting: "Turn on the light"

Marketers need to understand "the talk" of each conversation in order to stay connected to the way their customers speak and engage with their personal assistants, home speakers, cars and more.

Personal Assistants

Personal assistants may seem like the realm of programmers and developers, but marketers must understand each one's capability. Some like Apple's Siri, Samsung's Bixby, and Microsoft's Cortana come native with the OS of the device. Each one runs on different machine learning and Artificial Intelligence (AI) algorithms, meaning they don't all perform the same way.

For a marketer, this means that while the search request may be captured accurately by Alexa, Siri may not produce the same result, or vice versa. This makes keywords, tags and other technical elements vital to reach users on any platform. The variety of personal assistants adds to the diversity of language. Just as marketers have had to learn and understand the language(s) of their audience, now they must also account for the language capability of personal assistants.

Chatbots

A chatbot is a messenger service driven by machine learning algorithms and AI. Facebook messenger, WeChat and Amazon's Alexa are examples of chatbots (although Alexa is also referred to as a personal assistant). Chatbots, like personal assistants, will have a significant impact on marketers as they guide more and more people in the search to find answers, products to buy, or local restaurants, stores and entertainment.

Brand Apps

Many brands have built mini-apps specifically to enable their customers to interact via voice command. Others have integrated 'Ok, Google' into their app, although the degree of functionality varies. Examples of brand apps that feature conversational interfaces include:

Domino's Pizza. "I thought you'd never ask," reads the app. Dominos has made it simple to order pizzas, sandwiches, sides and desserts. Shortened ordering sequences improves the user experience while advanced integrations through "If This Then That" (IFTTT) with other mobile device apps like email or calendar enable Dominos to create a seamless user experience. Customers can buy pizza and then "Add a reminder to take your leftover Domino's for lunch," or "Let the team know in Slack when your order is out for delivery."

1-800-Flowers.com. Through the app's messenger platform, customers can use voice and/or manual swipe and typing (as may be necessary for some names!) to find flower arrangements, make a selection, give the recipient's name and speak the message for the note.

EWC. The European Wax Center app allows users to schedule reservations, check points, search FAQs and videos and more. Customers "ask my EWC" to perform actions. This simple phrase is an excellent example of how brands can use a standard phrase to begin the conversation.

Uber. With the Uber app, a customer can arrange a ride by saying "Ask Uber," another example of a trigger phrase to activate the voice feature of the app. Users can also change settings in the app such as the default pickup location.

Buying pizza or flowers, scheduling a wax and arranging a ride are only a few reasons to converse through an app. Whirlpool for example offers an app in the Apple AppStore and on Googleplay that users can download to speak with their "smart" washer and dryer. The iRobot Home app lets one speak with their Roomba cleaning robot.

The integration of "Ok Google" by some apps increases the conversational potential. Now, one can –

- "Scan my receipt on Walmart." (Walmart app)
- "Start my Lincoln MKZ." (Lincoln app)
- "Show rentals near me on Realtor." (Realtor.com app)

Conversation with machines is here. Now. It's no longer simply software platforms performing voice searches. Cars, appliances and robots now respond to voice. As more and more brands introduce voice into their apps, the conversation will evolve. For marketers, this has created an opportunity to connect on a deeper level with customers.

Recommendations to Capitalize on Conversational UX

Conversations are personal. While programmers have made significant advancements in AI and machine learning, personalizing the experience depends on marketers. The machines can only provide the content, information and answers available. Marketers must provide them to meet customer demand and capitalize on opportunity presented by conversational UX.

Five elements are needed to accomplish this. Before developing a plan, however, several questions should be asked to establish goals, set a direction and identify what departments or resources will be needed to execute the plan.

- What platforms are most important to your customers?
- What are the most used actions/features?
- What can we automate?
- What do loyal customers ask for?
- How can you promote repeat purchase behavior?

These represent only a few questions, but reflect the strategic approach needed to ensure any effort aligns with a brand's wider business goals. Once answered and a plan developed, it's time to get started.

Research

Research is the first and most important step of the entire process. It involves a thorough analysis of three essential parts: buyer demographic, buyer desire and buyer language.

Buyer demographic. This information lays the foundation for the buyer persona and helps to understand the deeper factors driving behavior and the language of the buyer. It includes metrics such as age, gender, income, and job type or title.

Buyer desire. A 2010 University of Texas marketing study reported that people buy based on emotion rather than logic or reason.[i] The research confirmed what marketers and sales professionals have known for years. How long? Well, in 1938, the *New Yorker* published an article on the legendary sales trainer Elmer Wheeler documenting his now famous "Wheelerpoint No. 1, 'Don't Sell the Steak; Sell the Sizzle.'"[ii]

The buyer desire represents the underlying emotional factors that prompt a choice. A marketer must know the client so well as to intimately understand the desire that makes the buyer want the product or service **and** make the decision that chooses the one offered by the marketer. Successful direct marketers have talked to this desire for decades by speaking to people of this desire in their own language. Conversational UX, however, elevates the importance of language so much it becomes a factor unto itself.

Buyer language. Advances in search engine algorithms and reporting have made it possible to know the buyer more intimately than ever before. Now, marketers understood the exact words used to search for a product. Prior to voice, marketers who leveraged this data could better position themselves. With voice, that remains true; however, voice introduces longer search phrases, making it essential to know the exact words and phrases used.

Conversational UX also doesn't end with a single search. Answers provided by Alexa, Google Home, Siri or any other personal assistant often prompt additional questions, commands or requests. This means content must be developed, *not only to answer the first question*, but also to provide content that addresses potential responses too.

How to Research Buyer Language

The age of voice doesn't jibe with lists of keywords. Word maps work better to understand buyer language and its relationship to specific keywords. To fully grasp the intent of the buyer, follow these three steps.

<u>Step 1.</u> Start with questions. People ask questions when doing search. So, in addition to Who, What, When, Where, Why and How questions, investigate "Which," "Are" and "Is" queries to.

<u>Step 2</u>. Look at prepositions. Words like "for," "with," "to," and "versus" are essential. Machine learning and AI may be able to develop some context, but realistically, the marketer who matches the buyer language will be the one the machines will see as providing the best answer.

<u>Step 3</u>. Listen. See what words your buyer's use most. Word clusters are great for this effort. The words used most are the ones around which to develop content, paid media and organic search strategy.

Own Local

Voice search is local search. Want to order a pizza? Alexa will look for nearby locations. People use voice search to find restaurants and to make reservations at home and on the road. Need to find a ride, schedule a wax, set an appointment or go shopping? It's local search.

Brands that want to survive with brick and mortar locations – either Small and Mid-Size Businesses (SMBs) or national brands – must own local search. Local success will require:

– Accurate and up-to-date Name-Address-Phone (NAP)
– Well managed Google My Business site
– Third-party and social business content regularly updated
– Managed review sites

Owning local search will require strategy. Social sites, indexes like superpages,com, yp.com and others, search engine local information, review sites and a myriad of other sites that capture local data will pose a challenge for brands. Both B2B and B2C businesses will need a clear strategy to engage with local search platforms and keep the data updated.

FAQ

The FAQ is back. A well-researched and structured FAQ answers the exact questions buyers ask. It also increases the chance to win a position as a Google Answer Box or Featured Snippet. Each of these delivers short, simple answers to a direct question that a reference site like a wiki cannot answer. A brand can leverage an FAQ to reach buyers by providing answers as though they were being asked in a conversation.

Schema

Research, local and FAQs apply to the user experience. Schema communicates the meaning of the data on your site to search engine AI. Structured mark-ups are available for:

- Articles
- Restaurants
- Local Businesses
- Software Applications
- Movies
- Products
- Events
- TV Episodes
- Recipes
- Reviews
- Music

Brands can take advantage of a variety of schema mark-up tools, including:

- Schema.org
- Google's Structured Data
- JSON LD
- Schema App

Connect Everywhere

Brands can elevate the conversational user experience they provide by connecting everywhere. Integrations are available for platforms like Actions on Google, Kik, Slack and many others. These integrations increase the amount of content available to search engines to provide in response to questions. The more connected a brand's content, the more questions it can answer.

Conversational UX: The Future of Brand Engagement

Conversational UX isn't about a friendly voice. While programmers continue to make advances in machine learning and AI to enhance the ability of a personal assistant to reply in a friendly voice, ultimately, conversation is about getting information. That's the responsibility of marketers.

As integrations continue to bring previously independent systems and data closer together, the efforts of marketing, sales and customer service will overlap, potentially becoming indistinguishable. This will happen:

As users get accustomed to conversing with brands through personal assistants drawing content from a brand's content infrastructure of web, app, and any other integrated systems;

As machines better understand user intent and can do more menial tasks like scheduling appointments and placing orders; and,

As marketers gain greater insight into the exact conversations and language taking place and craft content in reply to user demand and interest.

Voice search may be transforming the search landscape and relegating the practices of the past to history, but it is also increasing the proximity of the user to the brand. This shift promises to transform marketing from the traditional one-sided approach into a conversation between brand and user. This means conversational UX isn't the "next thing." Instead it is the future of brand-consumer engagement, a comprehensive brand strategy centered on a personalized conversation.

Like any conversation, it will require a lot of listening and work. The big difference? Marketers will have unilateral responsibility to do the listening and the work.

---

http://www.today.mccombs.utexas.edu/2010/04/do-you-make-buying-decisions-based-on-logic-or-emotion-a-tale-of-two- chickens/

https://www.newyorker.com/magazine/1938/04/16/the-sizzle

http://nationalpublicmedia.com/wp-content/uploads/2017/06/The-Smart-Audio-Report-from-NPR-and-Edison-Research- 2017.pdf

Ibid.

Comscore

https://googleblog.blogspot.com.au/2014/10/omg-mobile-voice-survey-reveals-teens.html

Katherine Watier

http://nationalpublicmedia.com/wp-content/uploads/2017/06/The-Smart-Audio-Report-from-NPR-and-Edison-Research- 2017.pdf

Marketing to Diverse Customer Groups

By

Jaime Noriega, DePaul University

According to the American Marketing Association:

"Marketing is the activity, set of institutions, and processes for creating, communicating, delivering, and exchanging offerings that have value for customers, clients, partners, and society at large."

There are situations where the diversity in a population requires, or can benefit from, the creation of specific market offerings for each diverse customer group; however, this reading will limit itself to a more common situation: a need for the creation of a specific selling message for at least some of the diverse groups.

Acknowledging Diversity in the Marketplace

There was a time when most countries' populations were by and large homogenous – at a minimum, this means most of the population is of the same race and ethnicity. In such markets devoid of diversity, advertising can be very straightforward and focus on showing the merits of the product being advertised. And if one or more protagonists *is* featured in the advertisement, their cultural identity is hardly noticed by viewers/ consumers. This is what happens in the absence of contrast. Sociologists have argued that any dimension of our self-identity is simply not salient (we are not directly aware of it) until we are in the presence of people who have a contrasting identity along that same dimension. For example, if an African-American female enters a room full of males, her gender identity will be the most salient (her identity as a female will be foremost in her mind); if this same individual enters a room where most of the people are Anglo, it is her race identity that will become most salient. For this same reason, when a TV commercial broadcast in Japan only features Japanese actors, Japanese consumers will hardly notice that the people in the commercial look just like them.

Even though the U.S. has always been a land of immigrants, the diversity of the population hasn't always been acknowledged by marketers. It wasn't until corporate America became aware of the growing purchasing power of minority groups that they began to produce advertising featuring minority actors and models. As early as the 1920s, advertising featuring African-Americans was targeted exclusively to these groups and was published/broadcast in media targeted to these individuals. Until the early 1960s, general market advertising in the U.S. featured mostly Anglo models and actors. It wasn't until U.S. marketers started to acknowledge minority groups as members of the general population that their advertising began featuring multi-racial/ethnic casts.

However, it is worth pointing out that just because diversity may be present in any population, this does not mean advertising should feature multi-cultural actors/models. Wherever there is animosity or distrust between people of different cultures, it may not be a good idea to feature a culturally representative group of actors/models in advertising.

A few decades later, corporate America began courting many other ethnic groups, either targeting them directly and singularly - especially if the group was assumed to require or prefer a language other than English – or by incorporating them into their general market advertising. More recently, marketers have begun to acknowledge the diversity presented by multi-racial consumers and those within the LGBT community.

Featuring an individual from a specific race or ethnicity in an advertisement is something marketers will do to culturally 'accommodate' viewers who share the actor/model's cultural identity, in an effort to have the viewer develop a positive response to the message. Studies have shown that when ethnic minorities receive a selling message, they prefer to see models/actors/ or spokespersons that look like them (Martin, Lee, & Yang, 2004); presumably, if consumers can relate to the faces they see, they are more likely to be persuaded to buy the advertised offering.

Research on confirmation bias suggests it may be possible to include different cultural elements in an advertisement in a very subtle way, so much so that consumers of a different culture may not notice these cultural elements.

Confirmation bias is the tendency to search for, interpret, favor, and recall information in a way that confirms one's preexisting beliefs or preferences. It is a type of cognitive bias and a systematic error of inductive reasoning. In theory, in a selling message scenario, it is possible for us to find the words or images which represent the ideas we respect, revere, or admire within the selling message and wind up feeling that the advertiser has accommodated our racial, ethnic, religious, or social identity. *Yet a person of a different cultural background may not necessarily 'see' these things in the advertisement*. This may be why the use of racially/ethnically ambiguous models in advertising seems to work so well. In fact, understanding how consumers (humans, really) process information may help an advertiser deliver a tailored message that for the most part, only the intended recipients will interpret in a culturally specific way. Confirmation bias may facilitate a favorably subjective interpretation of a selling message by consumers of various different cultures.

The Focus of this Reading

For the same reason that consumers in a racially/culturally homogenous society do not pay special attention to the actors/models they see in their advertising, previous research has suggested there is nothing special about featuring cultural elements in a medium where viewers fully expect to see nothing but these (Deshpande, Hoyer, and Donthu 1986). Because of this, I will emphasize more so how marketers attempt to reach diverse populations as part of their general market advertising, as opposed to how they attempt to reach them through targeted advertising.

Race and Ethnic Diversity

Marketers who wish to appeal to different ethnic or cultural markets within their general market advertising instead of, or in addition to, their targeted marketing efforts tend do so in one of two different ways:

Figure 1

Rainbow Coalition

Some advertisers feel the best way to appeal to a diverse cross section of the American consumer population is to be all-inclusive. These ads, which are hard to miss, usually feature one or more models/spokespersons of every conceivable race or ethnicity, presumably reflecting the actual population in the given marketplace (see Figure 1). These advertisements are noticeably different from other general market advertisements which will often include almost exclusively Anglo and sometimes African-American protagonists. In general, this all-inclusive approach may work just fine especially in major cities where people of different cultural backgrounds are more likely to coexist amicably enough. However, the potential danger of using this approach is best illustrated by putting it in an international perspective; this all-inclusive approach would be disastrous in some countries where although many different races and or ethnicities may coexist, they may not only not get along, they may even despise each other. The lesson is clear: whether or not all the relevant races and ethnicities are represented in one's advertisements is not as important as how those different individual groups feel about being depicted together. In some parts of the U.S. this may be a risky approach because market research is not likely to uncover these intergroup dynamics. Racial or ethnic intolerance is not a socially desirable trait; therefore, if asked, it is doubtful too many individuals would express intolerance for other races or ethnicities regardless of their actual feelings.

Everyone's Man/Woman

Many print and broadcast advertisers now feature models and/or spokespersons whose race or ethnicity is difficult to determine. Once the accepted standard, it is increasingly rare to see television or print advertisements in which the principal spokesperson is a blue eyed blonde. The assumption seems to be that almost any consumer will be able to relate to the spokesperson and feel the advertiser is somehow acknowledging their racial/ethnic/cultural identity. This recent and seemingly safer alternative which many advertisers now use is actually so common that it has now been ridiculed in a recent television advertisement for U by Kotex tampons. The TV ad cleverly parodies other commercials in its product class, calling them "obnoxious". In the commercial, an attractive young model dressed in white in an all- white background divulges the many advertising tactics used by marketers and at one point states: "…You can relate to me because I'm racially ambiguous…"

The growing popularity of this approach suggests it is working well. However, it is important to consider how this execution corresponds with empirical research. Studies have shown that when ethnic minorities receive a selling message, they prefer to see models/actors/ or spokespersons that look like them; presumably, if consumers can relate to the faces they see, they are more likely to be persuaded to buy the advertised offering. It should be pointed out then that featuring a racially ambiguous model or spokesperson in one's advertising is not quite the same thing as featuring a model of the same race/ethnicity as one's target market(s). Using a racially ambiguous model may *prevent negative feelings* a consumer may feel when receiving a persuasive message from someone outside of their racial/ethnic group; after all, the most accurate way to characterize a racially ambiguous spokesperson is to say they "could pass" for many races/ethnicities, whereas using a model or spokesperson who matches the target audience's race or ethnicity *promotes positive feelings* by delivering the same message via someone who is *clearly* a member of the racial/ethnic group being targeted.

Language Considerations

So far, this reading has looked at advertising to diverse consumer groups from the standpoint of using the 'right' people, images, and perhaps themes with which to make a lasting and meaningful connection with a prospective consumer from a diverse population. However, varying the language of a selling message in order to better connect with some diverse customer groups – whether they also understand English, or not – adds a new layer of complexity, challenges, and opportunities.

Backwards translation is a common tactic used in bilingual research which can be quite useful in advertising to ensure that a translated message gets across the intended meaning. When translating from English to Spanish, for example, one bilingual individual will translate the original English content into Spanish then a different bilingual individual will translate the Spanish translation back into English. The more similar the original content is to the English translation, the more accurate and proper the Spanish translation is considered. Still, the best advice for any marketer wishing to communicate in a language other than English is to translate the *idea* behind the selling message rather than the actual words in the message. Very few language combinations can rely on literal verbatim translations. Messages which rely on colloquialisms, humor, or a play on words are notoriously difficult to translate successfully.

Hispanics are the largest but by no means the only cultural group which may require a marketer to deliver his selling message in a language other than English. However, because there are so many different nationalities which comprise the group we refer to as Hispanics/Latinos it is sometimes challenging to find a word or phrase which has the exact same meaning across the many different versions of Spanish with which these distinct groups may be familiar. Depending on the demographics of the target area or the medium itself (there are many Hispanic newspapers throughout the U.S. which are specifically targeted to Mexicans, Salvadorians, Cubans, etc.); it may be worthwhile to deliver several Spanish language versions of the same selling message. A similar argument could be made for broadcast advertising which may require not only a slightly different version of the Spanish language script but possibly a slightly different pronunciation as well to reflect the most common accent and speech characteristics of the targeted group.

Another way in which a marketer can have a language gaffe in its advertising is through the inappropriate use of slang. In a 2005 McDonald's TV ad campaign for their double cheeseburger targeted at African-American consumers, a tagline referring to the sandwich states "I'd hit it." McDonald's marketers thought they were expressing the affirmation "I would eat that" in a very hip fashion, not realizing the expression they chose was more commonly used to convey a desire to have sex with the object to which the expression was directed!

There are many humorous examples of advertising translations gone wrong from the international marketing arena – a brief Internet search will yield a treasure trove of funny, embarrassing and even offensive examples. This is more likely to occur when a marketer uses a translator who may be multilingual but may not necessarily know much about the culture of the people for whom the translations are being made. U.S. marketers who decide they should translate their selling message when targeting us minority groups should go the extra mile to prevent such blunders.

The Special Case of Bicultural Bilinguals

There are other ways in which elements of language have been used to attract consumers from diverse populations. The most notable examples come from advertising targeted to U.S. Hispanics:

Ethnic Surnames

Within the past couple of years, U.S. audiences have also been exposed to numerous commercials where the protagonists are identified by their Hispanic family name either via a voice-over or by way of an inconspicuous small label at the base of the TV screen. These commercials are generally presented completely in English and as expected, the appearance of the people depicted in these commercials is probably best described as "ethnically ambiguous" more-so than "definitively Hispanic." The family members featured do not necessarily have any speaking roles but instead are shown interacting with one another in typical "slice of life" scenarios consuming the advertised product. The assumption is that Hispanic viewers will notice the Hispanic surname and feel the advertiser is somehow acknowledging their ancestry and perhaps even paying homage to their well-recognized strong sense of family. In following this approach, advertisers also implicitly assume that the average non-Hispanic viewer will either not notice the Hispanic surname or will not care; that is, will not feel excluded by the message.

A less common approach is to have the protagonist identified as Hispanic (again, by mentioning their surname) and at least one actor will utter a Spanish language word or phrase within an English language presentation. This is a bolder approach because even if the average American TV viewer has gotten used to seeing models whose ethnicity is very hard to determine, they may still perceive the non-English word or phrase as foreign, something which could diminish the relevance of the selling message and ultimately its ability to influence. This also assumes non-ethnic viewers either do not notice or mind the protagonists having a recognizable Hispanic surname. To the extent a bicultural individual notices and acknowledges the surname as an ethnic cue, it is possible that such an execution can make a special connection with the viewer.

Accents in Advertising

Aside from a few studies which have shown consumers generally prefer western European accents (Laiwani, Lwin, & Li, 2005; Morales, Scott, & Yorkston, 2012); there has been very little research in this area. Nevertheless, this has not kept some advertisers from using this tactic by featuring thick ethnic accents in their broadcast advertising. Two notable examples come to mind:

McDonald's broadcast an English-language television advertisement for one of their new McCafe line of products. The ad showed a young Hispanic woman whom the narrator identified as Julia, on her way home from work. The entire narration was done with an unmistakable Hispanic ethnic accent; and as if to make sure viewers understood the intent, during a very brief scene a man on the subway was shown reading a newspaper and for a split second, one could see the name of the publication: Acento – the Spanish language word for accent.

Another example came from Nescafe brands. This commercial featured two Hispanic protagonists, a traffic officer and a girl whose attention he captured with his matador-like antics while directing traffic. As in the McDonald's example, this commercial was also narrated by a male with a distinctive and unmistakable Hispanic accent.

These companies may have used a narrator with an identifiable ethnic accent in order to better connect with their presumed target market and this tactic could in theory resonate with Hispanic consumers. However, there is a serious risk in using this tactic to appeal to Hispanics living in the U.S.: Not all bicultural bilinguals speak the host language with a thick native accent; and those that do may not necessarily feel good about it. Unless there is reason to believe a majority of Hispanics in any given market are accepting of their ethnic accent when speaking the host/dominant language, this may be a particularly risky execution. It is also quite possible that individuals who either do not speak with an accent or are reluctant to admit that they do, would be offended if it were evident the selling message was targeted directly to them. Such a reaction would be akin to the cultural affirmation observed in previous studies of cultural frame switching. Instead of feeling accommodated by the advertiser, these individuals would very likely feel marginalized and manipulated and would not experience positive thoughts or feelings about the advertised brand.

There is perhaps one safer alternative for using accents in order to engage an individual's ethnic self-identity – using the proper accent when making reference to Spanish language brands. For example, when broadcasting advertising for a Mexican restaurant with a traditional Spanish name it may be helpful to make sure the name is pronounced correctly (as a Spanish word) even if the rest of the commercial is broadcast entirely in English. This small detail may be just enough to have the listener engage their ethnic self-identity. And because it can be easily argued that's how you pronounce the brand correctly, it is less likely the listener will question any ulterior motive by the advertiser. It is also possible such an execution may help the perception of the restaurant among English monolingual consumers since the 'correct' brand pronunciation may enhance perceptions of authenticity.

LGBT Consumers

In 1994, IKEA became the first national advertiser to feature a gay couple in one of their TV commercials. Following such a bold move, the retailer faced much criticism including angry calls, threats of a boycott, and even a bomb scare. When interviewed about their decision, IKEA's then head of marketing for the East Coast, Peter Connolly, gave a cautious response: "We're not trying to promote a certain lifestyle or make a statement, this is just part of our overall strategy to try to speak directly to all kinds of customers."

This rather non-comital stance seems to align well with how it appears the LGBT community would like to be regarded. Representatives of the LGBT advocacy group GLAAD – which until 2013 stood for Gay & Lesbian Alliance Against Defamation, but is now simply known as GLAAD – have addressed the issue of advertising in the past and made it clear they would like advertising targeted to them to feature an aspect of gay life that people rarely see: their daily lives. Instead of showing gays and lesbians marching at gay rights rallies, suffering from AIDS, or any number of other stereotyped settings or activities, advertisements targeting this consumer group should show them going about their daily life the way all other consumers do. The only thing that should set apart advertising targeted to this group should be the people in the ads and the relationships depicted in them.

Following such a seemingly 'safe' strategy may make marketers wonder if it will be clear they are targeting this group of consumers. After all, what could be worse than targeting a specific consumer segment and having members of that segment not recognize this? It is perhaps this reason that makes marketers feel they need to make their intent more obvious. Many existing ads targeted to the LGBT community will feature settings, images, or copy which makes it clear the protagonists in the ad are in fact members of the LGBT community (see Figure 2), even if such an approach opens the door to controversy.

Although it may be simple to portray gays and lesbians in a respectful non-stereotypical manner, it is worth pointing out that the acronym LGBT also includes individuals who identify as bisexual or transgender. Is it possible to portray an individual who is bisexual or transgender in one's advertising without running the risk of being offensive or insulting? Fortunately, this is not a choice advertisers must make to be all inclusive in their efforts to reach the LGBT community. Instead of featuring actors or models depicting any of these groups, many advertisers have chosen to feature the gay pride rainbow colors in their advertising and/or packaging (see Figure 3).

Figure 2

Figure 3

Unique Attempts at Marketing to Diverse Customer Groups

Is it possible to advertise in mainstream media but communicate with your audience entirely in a foreign language? As improbable as that may seem, one major U.S. corporation has successfully done exactly that. Jimmy Johns, a national sandwich chain which prides itself on lightning quick deliveries has produced and broadcast a series of three commercials: one in Spanish, one in Japanese, and one in Hungarian (see figure 4). These commercials stand out because they are placed in mainstream English- language media but broadcast entirely in their respective foreign languages, the only English phrase spoken during the entire commercial is the brand "Jimmy Johns" followed by a tag line at the end which is spoken entirely in English. It should be noted however that the average English-speaking viewer will completely understand all of these commercials even if they do not understand a single word spoken in them. They work simply because they are funny. The comedic scenarios do not require fluency in any of the three foreign languages. This is really key because this means the commercials are likely to work equally well for ethnic viewers who understand the dialogue and for English monolinguals who will still understand these scenarios where a clearly illustrated difficult situation is remedied by Jimmy John's ridiculously speedy delivery.

This represents a unique and bold approach no other advertiser has ever attempted, certainly not in a national campaign of this scope. These commercials really stand out because of the immediate contrast effect that is created when one is watching English-language television which is momentarily interrupted by a foreign language commercial. There is an immediate recognition by those who understand the foreign language and the extreme contrast effect of the shift in Language has a potential for engaging a bicultural individual's ethnic identity. Once that occurs, the advertiser may gain access to the consumer's distinct ethnic associative network.

The Special Case of Bicultural Bilinguals

There is some empirical evidence which suggests using a bicultural individual's native language in a selling message may be advantageous because the language itself and/or certain words have a deeper more emotional meaning for the individual (Puntoni, De Langhe, & Van Osselaer, 2009). This is a simple but impractical strategy since it assumes all targeted consumers will understand and prefer to read selling messages in their native language.

Figure 4

Nevertheless, such an execution could influence a consumer's affective reaction to a selling message; however, by specifically engaging one of the two distinctive cultures a bicultural individual embraces, it may be possible to also influence their cognitive reaction to a selling message.

Following the ethnic-language-only approach also fails to acknowledge what makes a true bicultural individual unique: he/she can fully embrace either cultural identity. If a marketer chooses to communicate with such individuals using only their native language, they will miss out on the consumer preferences which may be more easily and/or fully accessed when engaging the host culture identity – which presumably is more likely to be engaged via exposure to the host language.

Language is only one aspect of an individual's culture but it is a defining aspect for bicultural bilinguals. Recent studies suggest that in some cases it is possible that each of a bilingual's two languages can facilitate different types of thoughts and emotions. Recent studies in the field of marketing also suggest a marketer can exploit bicultural individuals' dual identities by strategically matching the language of execution to a given product category in order to make a selling message more relevant and more persuasive.

Noriega & Blair (2008) considered how the interaction of language and context could influence the thoughts Spanish-English bilinguals would report in response to a print advertisement. Subjects who saw a Spanish-language print ad for a fictitious restaurant reported more thoughts about friends, family, home or their homeland but only if the ad also mentioned dinner rather than lunch. This group also recorded more such thoughts than subjects who were exposed to identical ads in English.

Evidence that matching the language of a selling message to the cultural context associated with the advertised offering may also result in stronger perceptions of message relevance also comes from Noriega & Blair's (2008) alternative thought protocol coding of their second study (Study 2). Results indicated that subjects who viewed the Spanish language version of the Dinner ad were twice as likely to express thoughts about the product (restaurants) than subjects who viewed the English language version of the dinner ad (19.76% vs. 9.52%, p ≤ .001). This finding was not stressed in their original article because it was not the focus of their study.

Exposure to an advertisement for the product category of restaurants resulted in more thoughts about restaurants when that exposure was in the language in which the bilingual subject was more likely to think about dinner – the subject's native language. The U.S. Census shows there are more than 50 million American inhabitants who speak a language other than English at home; therefore, it stands to reason that because dinner is an event one is more likely to experience in one's home, for a bicultural- bilingual, it is likely that thoughts related to dinner (including the product category of restaurants) may be more easily, quickly, and/ or naturally accessed with a native language cue.

More recently, Carroll & Luna (2011) showed that Spanish-English bilinguals exhibited more positive responses to print advertisements when the language of the ad matched the language more likely to be associated with the usage context mentioned in the ad copy. Ads that described the use of the product with family and friends performed better when presented in Spanish whereas ads that described the use of the product at work performed better when presented in English. Both of these studies suggest a specific combination of language and context activated their subject's corresponding cultural identity; and as a consequence, elicited distinct responses from them. More to the point, these academic studies also stress the relevance of this alternative view of multiculturalism to the study and practice of marketing.

This research stream suggests that from a marketing standpoint, it may be possible to use the language of the selling message as a prime to engage either of a bicultural bilingual's cultural identities in order to differentially access distinct associations in consumers' minds, something which may ultimately aid in persuasion. And because priming is a general phenomenon, it may also be possible to use other aspects of an advertisement besides language to communicate at a deeper more meaningful level with one's target market.

Code Switching in Advertising Targeted to Hispanic Consumers

A linguistic tactic a few advertisers have used recently when targeting Hispanic bilinguals is that of code-switching. By definition, code switching involves the use of both the immigrant/native language and the dominant/host language. However, code-switching is recognized not as a linguistic tool but rather as a social tool meant to convey group membership. This would seem to indicate that code switching will either prime both cultures equally or prime the culture the individual believes is responsible for making him a bicultural individual. It could be argued then that if a bicultural individual is in the presence of members of the host culture, he will credit his immigrant/native culture for making him a bicultural; if such were the case, it seems code-switching is more likely to engage the immigrant/native culture. However, this is little more than conjecture; at this time there simply is insufficient empirical research to determine if or how exposure to code-switching can differentially engage one or more of a bicultural individual's cultural identities. Nevertheless, the use of code switching as an advertising tactic deserves a closer look for other reasons.

In keeping with the basic premise of speech accommodation theory (Giles & Coupland, 1991), it has been suggested that some advertisers are now using code switching in order to acknowledge and connect with the dual identity many bicultural bilinguals are presumed to hold (Bishop & Peterson, 2010). However, this premise may be based on a flawed understanding of how a bicultural individual manages his dual identity. There is no compelling evidence that a bilingual's bicultural identity is equally activated or even equally accessible at any given time; if anything, the cultural frame switching literature seems to suggest either of a bicultural's identities can be differentially activated - depending on the context in which the individual finds him/herself or by the strategic use of culturally relevant symbols (Hong et al, 2000) or language (Ross, Xun, & Wilson, 2002).

The assumption that a bicultural individual exists at all times in a dual-identity state of self-awareness is simply without empirical merit. Furthermore, although psychologists have long believed that developing and maintaining competence in both cultures may be instrumental in attaining psychological well-being (Lambert, 1977; Rashid, 1984; Martinez, 1988; Rogler, Cortes, & Malgady, 1991), the idea of an individual simultaneously displaying two separate identities (especially if they are potentially conflicting) smacks of a dissociative identity disorder; a significant departure from psychological well- being. A more accurate interpretation may be that each of a bicultural individual's cultural identities may be in a 'ready' state whereby a sufficiently strong cultural prime may activate either identity.

As an important side note, it is worthwhile pointing out that if a code-switched selling message does somehow activate both of a consumer's cultural identities simultaneously; then ideally, the offering being advertised should also have a distinct appeal for this dual identity. Yet judging by the product development literature, no such product orientation yet exists. Global marketers understand the need to create products that are culturally relevant to consumers living in the countries where these are sold by adapting the elements of the marketing mix as deemed necessary. Creating (or communication the virtues of) a product for a single individual who embraces, and is therefore motivated by, a bi-cultural identity is simply not even on the radar for U.S. marketers at this time.

Even if it were possible for code-switching to serve as a prime to engage a bicultural individual's ethnic identity (the identity we have argued is more likely to be primed), unlike other tactics marketers have used in the past, code-switching may require certain conditions be met before a bicultural individual 'accepts' it as a legitimate means of communication. Consider the following quote:
"Contact forms such as (code switching) are context bound, practiced by bilinguals for bilinguals..." (Anderson & Toribio, 2007:235).

A recurring theme found in much of the literature on code switching is that of identity. Just as language has long been recognized as a marker of identity (Bourhis, Giles, & Tajfel, 1973; Gumperz, 1982; Miller, 1999; Toribio, 2000), it has also been suggested that the use of intentional code-switching during conversation is also an explicit strategy bilinguals sometime use to express their bilingual/bicultural identity, group membership, and a sense of solidarity (Gal, 1978, 1979; Beebe, 1981; Gumperz, 1982; LePage & Tabouret-Keller, 1985; Milroy, 1987; Fernandez, 1990; Zentella, 1997; Bailey, 2000; Toribio, 2002). Lipski (1985) has gone as far as to argue that the successful use of code-switching may require membership in the community where it is practiced. This implies, at least, that the very act of code switching is or should be reserved for an entity that is genuinely multicultural or, perceived and accepted as such - yet it is difficult to conceive of a brand possessing a bilingual and/or bicultural identity, so how is code-switching by such an entity interpreted by bilingual consumers? One could argue that in most such cases use of language mixing in advertising does not fit any existing definition of code switching. In fact, what a marketer is doing when it chooses to mix different languages within a single selling message is better defined as 'language crossing'. Rampton defines language crossing as follows:

"…language crossing…refers to the use of a language which isn't generally thought to 'belong' to the speaker. … (it) involves a sense of movement across quite sharply felt social or ethnic boundaries, and it raises issues of legitimacy…" (Rampton, 1998:291).

Given the various examples and definitions of code switching and the theories that inform these, about the only natural and 'unforced' expression of code switching in a marketing context seems to be the verbal exchange—the dialogue—between a bilingual salesperson and a socially comparable bilingual consumer. This straightforward description helps to emphasize how unnatural it may seem for a bilingual to receive a unidirectional code-switched appeal from an anonymous entity which is not immediately or easily accepted as having a similar socio-cultural or bilingual identity as the viewer/listener.

To get a radical sense of how manipulative and contrived the use of 'Spanglish' (Spanish-English code-switching) may seem when used in advertising targeted to Hispanic bilinguals, just imagine the late Dave Thomas (Wendy's) or the late Orville Redenbacher of (Redenbacher popcorn) addressing T.V. commercial viewers in this manner. Admittedly, these examples may represent extremely un-ethnic brand identities; nevertheless, it is quite possible that some brands, by virtue of their country of origin, name, logos, slogans or spokespersons, can simply not pass themselves off as having a "bilingual" or "bicultural" identity that would give them the socio-cultural license to legitimately use code-switching in their advertising targeted to bicultural consumers.

Most bilingual consumer studies have been done with Hispanic bilinguals because this is the largest minority group in the US known to speak their native language (primarily at home). This does not present a limitation because the cognitive processes involved in first and/or second language learning and usage is identical for all human beings. In other words, the same results should be expected for any other language combinations, not just Spanish & English.

New Challenges

Advertising to diverse consumer populations has become a riskier proposition in the current socio- political environment; following the 2016 presidential election. Until now, any company that wanted to reach out to a formerly disenfranchised minority group may have faced minor backlash in the way of a story or editorial here and there; but in general, these progressive - albeit perhaps opportunistic - advertisers had no reason to fear their bottom line would be significantly impacted. However, the level of intolerance, prejudice, and narrow-mindedness that has suddenly become okay to voice and even act on since then, has given these advertisers a reason to question just how much they should reach out to any consumer group outside of the traditional general population. Ironically, now more than ever, communications technology allows advertisers to micro-target their consumers – preventing members of the general (non-minority) population from seeing a message they may find offensive or intolerable – however, the same level of technology makes it nearly impossible to hide any selling message from individuals who are steadfast in their desire to promote an oppressive, ultra-conservative, nationalistic agenda by criticizing any selling message that acknowledges any group(s) outside the conservative mainstream. This opens the door to having any broadminded commercial appeal scrutinized and condemned at the national level.

As recently as 2013, this issue came to the forefront of American culture and dialogue when Cheerios decide to produce and air a TV commercial featuring an interracial family (Figure 5).

Figure 5

The vitriolic backlash the company received through social media was a strong indication that although rarely vocal, there are still a number of consumers who do not want to see this social reality on television. A more common approach many companies have taken is to 'hint' at the racial, ethnic, or sexual identity of the consumers represented in their selling messages – rather than overtly display or acknowledge them. One such example is a TV commercial for Consumer Cellular in which an elderly couple is seen interacting with a biracial young girl – presumably, their granddaughter (Figure 6).

However, her relationship to the couple is never mentioned and she doesn't utter a single word throughout the entire commercial. The only apparent acknowledgment revealing the uncommon arrangement is given by the older female protagonist's first lines: "Our generation really has gotten used to a whole new world." She looks at the young girl and her husband looking at a tablet computer as she delivers her last few words. To this the husband adds: "It's been hard sometimes, but switching to Consumer Cellular, easy."

Figure 6

How a viewer may interpret such a commercial is difficult to say. What is the "whole new world" to which the woman refers? What part of this "whole new world" has been "hard sometimes"? Is it accepting that one's son or daughter has decided to marry outside of their own race, or are these innocent references to the seemingly daunting technology represented by the tablet computer? Such ambiguity allows advertisers like Consumer Cellular to cautiously reach out to a growing consumer population in a way that does not come across as obvious pandering, and without necessarily drawing the ire of those who would oppose this growing social reality.

Conclusion

As long as there is diversity in the consumer marketplace, marketers will have an incentive to make a special connection with consumers whom they believe will not or cannot relate to their general market advertising. Marketers must make an effort to understand the diversity in the marketplace beyond the superficiality that so often results in failed campaigns, damaging PR, and the growing impact of social media reaction.

References

Anderson, T. K., & Toribio, A. J. (2007). Attitudes towards lexical borrowing and intra-sentential code-switching among Spanish-English bilinguals, *Spanish in Context*, 4(2), 217-240

Bailey, B. (2000). Language and Negotiation of Ethnic/Racial Identity among Dominican Americans, *Language in Society*, 29(4), 555-582

Beebe, L. (1981). Social and situational factors affecting the communicative strategy of dialect code-switching. *International Journal of the Sociology of Language* 32, 139-149

Bishop, M. M. and Peterson, M. (2010). The impact of medium context on bilingual consumers' responses to code-switched advertising, *Journal of Advertising*. 39(3), 55-67

Bourhis, R. V., Giles, H., Tajfel, H. (1973). Language as a determinant of Welsh identity, *European Journal of Social Psychology*, 3(4), 447-460

Carroll, R., & Luna, D. (2011). The other meaning of fluency. *Journal of Advertising, 40*(3), 73-84.

Deshpande, R., Hoyer,W. D., and Donthu, N. (1986). The Intensity of Ethnic Affiliation: A Study of the Sociology of Hispanic Consumption, *Journal of Consumer Research* 13(2): 214-220.

Fernández, R. M. (1990). Actitudes hacia los cambios de códigos en Nuevo México: Reacciones de un sujeto a ejemplos de su habla, (49-58), In: Bergen, John J. (ed.) *Spanish in the United States: Sociolinguistic Issues*. Washington, DC: Georgetown UP

Gal, S. (1978). Variation and change in patterns of speaking: Language shift in Austria. In D. Sankoff (Ed.), *Linguistics variation: Models and methods* (pp. 227–238). New York: Academic Press.

Giles, H., Coupland, N., & Coupland, J. (1991). Accommodation theory: communication, context, and consequence, (1-68), *Contexts of accommodation: Developments in applied sociolinguistics*, New York, N.Y.: Cambridge University Press

Gumperz, J. J. (1982). *Discourse strategies*. Cambridge: Cambridge University Press.

Hong, Y., Morris M. W., Chiu C., and Benet-Martinez V. (2000). Multicultural Minds: A Dynamic Constructivist Approach to Culture and Cognition, *American Psychologist*, 55(7), 709–720.

Laiwani, A. K., Lwin, M., & Li, K. L. (2005). Consumer Responses to English Accent Variations in Advertising, *Journal of Global Marketing*, 18(3/4), 143-165

Lambert, W. (1977). The effects of bilingualism on the individual: Cognitive and sociocultural consequences, (15–27), *Bilingualism* ed. P. A. Hornby, London: Academic Press

Le Page, R. B.; Tabouret-Keller, A. (1985). *Acts of Identity: Creole-based Approaches to Language and Ethnicity*, New York, N.Y.: Cambridge University Press

Lipski, J. M. (1985). Linguistic Aspects of Spanish-English Language Switching, *Center for Latin American Studies*, Arizona State University

Martin, B. A. S., Lee, KC. C., and Yang, F. (2004). The influence of ad model ethnicity and self- referencing on attitudes, *Journal of Advertising*, 33(4), 27-37

Martinez, A. R. (1988) The effects of acculturation and racial identity on self-esteem and psychological well-being among young Puerto Ricans. *Dissertation Abstracts International, US, ProQuest Information & Learning* 49, 916-916.

Miller, J. (1999). Becoming audible: Social *identity* and second *language* use. *Journal of Intercultural Studies* 20, 149-165

Milroy, L. (1987). Language and Social Networks (2nd edn). Oxford: BlackwellMorales, A. C., Scott, L., and Yorkston, E. A. (2012). The Role of Accent Standardness in Message Preference and Recall, *Journal of Advertising*, 41(1), 33-46.

Noriega, J., & Blair, E. (2008). Advertising to bilinguals: Does the language of advertising influence the nature of thoughts? *Journal of Marketing, 72*(5), 69-83.

Puntoni, S., De Langhe, B., & Van Osselaer, S. M. J. (2009). Bilingualism and the Emotional Intensity of Advertising Language, *Journal of Consumer Research*, 35(6), 1012-1025

Rampton, B. (1998). Language Crossing and the Redefinition of Reality, (290-317), In: Auer, Peter (ed. and introds.) *Code-Switching in Conversation: Language, Interaction and Identity*. London, England: Routledge

Rashid, H. M., (1984). Promoting Biculturalism in Young African-American Children, *Young Children* 39(2), 13-23

Rogler, L. H., Cortes, D. E., Malgady, R. G. (1991). Acculturation and mental health status among Hispanics: convergence and new directions for research, *American Psychologist*, 46, 585-597

Ross, M., Xun, W.Q. E., and Wilson A. E. (2002). Language and the Bicultural Self, *Personality and Social Psychology Bulletin*, 28(8), 1040–1050.

Toribio, A. J. (2000). Language variation and the linguistic enactment of identity among Dominicans, *Linguistics*. 38(6) 1133-1159

Toribio, A. J. (2002). Spanish-English code-switching among US Latinos, *International Journal of the Sociology of Language*, 2002(158), 89-119

Zentella, A. C. (1997). Latino youth at home, in their communities, and in school, Education & Urban Society, 30(1), 122-13

Multichannel, Omnichannel and Integrated Marketing – Same, or Different?

By

Susan K. Jones, Ferris State University

There are numerous buzz terms used frequently in the world of marketing. It's natural to wonder if they all mean the same thing – or something different. For example – is Integrated Marketing the same thing as Multichannel Marketing? How about Omnichannel Marketing? Are these terms interchangeable, or do they have distinct meanings? In this reading, we'll look at how multichannel marketing is actually a less sophisticated marketing method than omnichannel, and how Integrated Marketing Communications (IMC) fits into the picture as the ultimate marketing method.

Are Multichannel Marketing and Omnichannel Marketing the same? No.

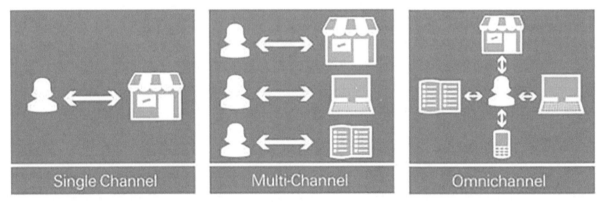

Graphic Source: http://mimeographs.wordpress.com/2013/07/28/multichannel-vs-omnichannel/

As you can see from the illustration above, multichannel marketing takes place in silos between customer and channel – via retail store, online, or catalog. At one time this was fairly revolutionary – just the concept of a firm doing its marketing via brick-and-mortar, online and print catalog instead of through a single channel – but it certainly wasn't as seamless as it could be. Omnichannel Marketing – a big step up – puts the customer at the heart of the multichannel strategy – with mobile as a key and central component. Now let's drill down into the marketing methods behind multichannel, omnichannel, and integrated marketing.

What is Multichannel Marketing?

Multichannel marketing uses multiple media – a print catalog, a web site, and brick-and-mortar stores – to effectively reach and serve a targeted customer group. A sophisticated database must integrate across all of these channels for customized communication between buyer and seller.

A fine example is Williams-Sonoma. The firm's catalogs and stores are so well integrated that visiting a Williams-Sonoma store is like stepping into the catalog—and vice-versa. Store visitors may be treated to cooking demonstrations, sampling, and advice on food preparation and presentation. The catalog offers how-to sidebars and recipes, while the Web site picks up on the same look and feel with beautiful "lifestyle" photography, recipes, and tips for creative cooks.

Here we see Williams-Sonoma's integration of "look and feel" across their catalog (top left), web site (top right) and store (below)

It's vital to measure your multichannel marketing efforts to make sure that the whole campaign has greater results than the sum of its parts. Melissa Duplantier, the public affairs officer for the American Red Cross South Louisiana Region and a master's level Integrated Marketing student of mine, did some research on this score and here is what she found:

"A recent study by global management consulting firm Kurt Salmon shows that print catalogs have served to help boost online sales. The study found that compared with customers who only shop online, those who use catalogs spend more money and return more often. The study also found that customers who utilize both channels who are the most valuable of all finding that:

'The average order size made by customers online is approximately 6% lower than orders placed directly through call centers using catalogs. For example, during one calendar-year period, we observed that Internet-only customers of one specialty retailer placed orders of $80 on average, whereas call center/catalog customers' average orders totaled approximately $90. Customers who utilized both channels saw their average orders climb even further, to more than $92.'"

As the digital marketing firm Atipso relates, accurate measurement of your multichannel efforts makes scaling – or rolling out your campaign – easy and secure. In other words, you have a good idea of what will happen when you expand to more customers. Accurate measurement also ensures you have control of your data and that you won't waste time and money on false starts. Finally, measurement can help you determine which channels produce the best results and which may need to be scaled back or modified.

Another way to look at multichannel marketing measurement is to look at appropriate KPIs or Key Performance Indicators, per Robyn Bragg writing for Nonlinear Creations. Across all the relevant media – mobile, mail, web, e-mail and face-to-face, Robyn suggests that marketers use the following measures:
- Reach – how many people are exposed to your message
- Acquisition – how many leads are you getting, and how high is their quality
- Conversion – how many leads are you turning into sales
- Retention – what is the long-term value of customers obtained through various channels

To ensure that you are maximizing your chances for success with multichannel marketing, there are several elements of crucial importance.

First, make sure that your marketing efforts have an **integrated "look and feel"** across all of your communications with prospects and customers.

Second, **integrate your online marketing efforts** and use strategic methods to draw prospects and customers to your web site. When they arrive, make sure that you provide them with a clear path to the information you have promised.

Third, **integrate your Customer Relationship Management process** across all of your channels so that the same updated and personalized information is actionable at every touchpoint.

Fourth, **adopt a "channel agnostic" viewpoint**. A sale is a sale, whether it is registered online, in the store, or via phone.

Fifth, **continue your strategic use of offline media** to ensure an integrated communication plan that optimizes the benefits of each medium in communicating with customers

The Next Step Up: Omnichannel Marketing

As mobile marketing continues to grow in the favor of our "always on" consumers, Omnichannel Marketing takes the forefront. And Omnichannel Marketing is much more than a promotional plan as John Bowden of Time Warner Cable explains: "Multichannel is an operational view – how you allow the customer to complete transactions in each channel. Omnichannel, however, is viewing the experience through the eyes of your customer, orchestrating the customer experience across all channels so that it is seamless, integrated, and consistent. Omnichannel anticipates that customers may start in one channel and move to another as they progress to a resolution. Making these complex 'hand-offs' between channels must be fluid for the customer. *Simply put, omnichannel is multichannel done right!"*

http://blog.marketo.com/2014/04/the-definition-of-omni-channel-marketing-plus-7-tips.html

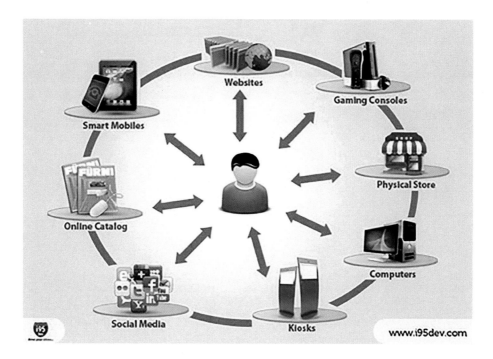

Omnichannel Marketing with the Customer at the Center

It may seem daunting to move from Multichannel Marketing to Omnichannel Marketing, but as we have noted before, it's all about putting the customer's needs first. James Green of marketingland.com suggests that we walk in our customer's shoes, first and foremost. That means following the path from suspect to prospect to buyer to repeat customer and making sure that every step of the way is smooth for the customer.

Green emphasizes the importance of measuring everything. It's vital to segment your audience, too – all the way down to 1-to-1 marketing whenever possible. That means you'll be developing content that addresses the specific behaviors of your customers – not providing them all things to all pieces.

A **use case** is a written description of how users will perform tasks on your website. It outlines, from a user's point of view, a system's behavior as it responds to a request. Each **use case** is represented as a sequence of simple steps, beginning with a user's goal and ending when that goal is fulfilled.

We want to make sure that all departments are involved in the development and perfection of use cases – not just marketing and sales. For example, customer service can be of great help here in identifying stumbling blocks for your web and mobile visitors.

Next, you'll want to make sure you are listening and responding on the customer's preferred channels and devices, whether that's phone, e-mail, live chat, mobile, or web form. Finally, START TODAY. As Ron Jacobs, President of Jacobs & Clevenger notes, "We are in the Omnichannel era and we need to heed our customers' growing sophistication".

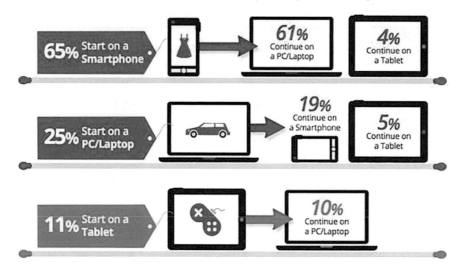

Chart from Telco 2.0 Research

As you can see from this exhibit and the one on the next page, today's consumer may take a rather circuitous path to a buying decision. Luckily, with today's CRM software, social listening and multiple dialogue methods, we can strive to be there with that next important piece of information no matter what step our customer has reached in the journey.

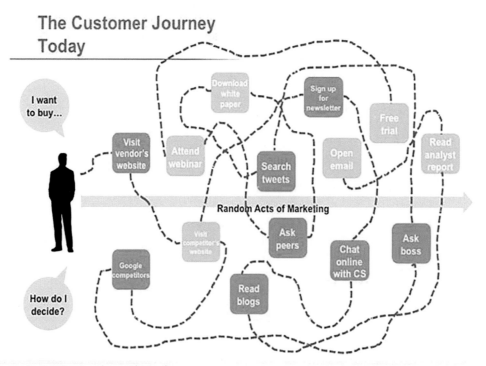

How does Integrated Marketing Fit In?

Is Integrated Marketing the same as Multichannel Marketing or Omnichannel Marketing? Integrated Marketing is "more than a marketing message strategy across channels" – it's "weaving together digital and physical channels to engage consumers' emotions, deliver brand experiences, and form ongoing relationships."

(Forrester Research)…this is the "holy grail" we seek as Integrated Marketing Communications (IMC) practitioners. We'll close with the visual below, which shows how IMC, done right, provides a beautifully integrated experience for consumers – the ultimate in seamless marketing.

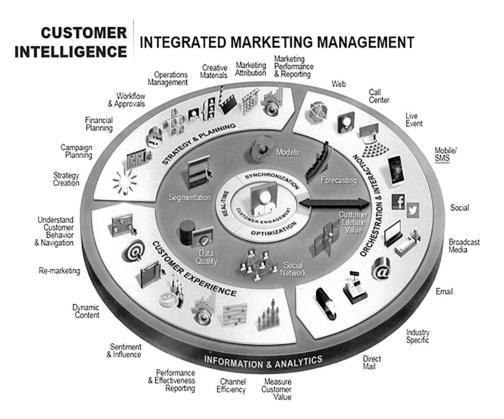

Graphic Source: SAS -- http://blogs.sas.com/content/customeranalytics/2013/07/08/integrated- marketing-management-the-big-picture-in-one-view/

A Creative Person's View of Direct and Digital Marketing Media

By

Susan K. Jones, Ferris State University

Direct and digital marketing media may include any channel of communication that invites a direct response. Even skywriting can be considered direct marketing if it includes a call to action and a telephone number or web address. Marketers have enthusiastically integrated the Internet, e-mail, and, more recently, mobile marketing and social networking sites into their media options. That said, smart marketers still make frequent use of the tried and true: various forms of direct mail, print advertising, telephone, broadcast, or digital media.

Every good direct and digital marketing plan calls for an outline of media objectives and strategy. Creative people can be of great help in determining appropriate media for a given marketing plan, based upon the creative advantages, disadvantages, and budgetary impact of various media alternatives. This reading discusses the basic pros, cons, and relative costs of entry for the most frequently used direct and digital marketing media.

DIRECT MAIL

Creative Advantages

- Almost unlimited format opportunities: size, looks, colors, paper, use of gimmicks, extent of copy, three-dimensional packages, pop-ups, etc.
- Extremely well targeted if market segmentation is done correctly.
- Allows for personalization and relatively private communications. As direct marketing expert Denny Hatch notes, "What makes direct mail different is that it goes to an individual person and has a letter. It's the only place in advertising where one person can make an emotional connection with a reader in his or her home."
- You may utilize all technological advances as they hit the market—you needn't wait for the medium to catch up, as you often do in dealing with space advertising vehicles and many Web sites.
- Ability to take advantage of database management and computer applications to reach highly defined markets with highly targeted messages—even individually targeted messages using variable data printing.
- Helps you learn in a controlled environment. You can develop test cells you want, not be at the mercy of a publication or broadcast medium, or limited by their ability to do A/B splits, geographic and lifestyle splits, etc.
- Highly responsive; only properly executed telephone marketing has higher response rates among direct marketing media.
- Allows you to use inexpensive formats like postcards, double postcards, or self-mailers to draw timely attention to an offer or opportunity on a Web site or landing page.

Creative Disadvantages

- Expense may bar entry. Space ads can be placed much more cheaply to test viability of a concept. Direct mail packages routinely cost $600 per thousand to $1,000 per thousand or more, even in large quantities.
- May be difficult to discover and reach a wide enough audience to meet volume goals, given limited universes and "list burn-out," a phenomenon in which good outside lists are barraged with so many offers that their value declines rapidly— especially if not replenished constantly with fresh names.
- Post office restrictions must be followed to the letter. Risks include paying extra postage and producing packages that cannot be mailed.
- The post office is less reliable on timing of delivery than broadcast and most print media. In addition, horror stories persist about non-delivery of significant amounts of standard mail.
- Direct mail is very complex and requires coordination of lists, creative production, and mailing. Other media are much easier to prepare for.
- Most direct mail does not come "invited into the home" the way ads do as part of a magazine, newspaper, Web site, or TV show selected and often paid for by the prospect.

MAGAZINES

Creative Advantages

- Ability to reach mass markets with magazines like *Better Homes and Gardens* and *National Geographic*, or very carefully segmented markets with magazines like *Golf Digest, Popular Mechanics, Prevention, Maxim, Working Mother*, etc.
- Rising costs of direct mail and dearth of good lists in many market segments make magazine advertising cost effective where it wasn't years ago.
- Mass magazines offer larger circulations than many lists, providing more exposure.
- Magazines come invited into the home, unlike much direct mail. This facilitates trust among readers, and a predisposition to feel positive about advertised products.
- No barrier to entry: 1/6- or 1/12-page black-and-white ads in mail-order sections of mass publications can be had for as little as a few thousand dollars; even less in highly targeted magazines with small circulation.
- Excellent color reproduction capability.
- More format options are available than in the past: pre-prints, bind-ins, tip-ons, promotional items enclosed with the publication in see-through mailers, personalization, scents, samples, etc.
- Generally much easier to produce and less difficult to coordinate than direct mail.
- A/B splits and regional editions are sometimes available. Testing can be done fairly inexpensively.

Creative Disadvantages

- Limited format possibilities due to page sizes and advertising configurations.
- Long lead time. Closing dates can be months ahead of cover dates.

- Lack of control over position. Some publications bunch ads together, creating ad "ghettos" without surrounding editorial. Response may vary a great deal between far- forward and far-back ad positions.
- Relatively slow response and a long shelf life make magazines hard to evaluate and react to for further testing.
- Relatively impersonal medium. Although personalization and customization are possible in some magazines, relatively few offer this option, or if available it may be limited to high-volume advertisers only.

NEWSPAPERS

Creative Advantages

- Immediate, authoritative, and newsy.
- A good medium for quick testing. Newspapers have late closing dates and yield quick response, so results are available fast.
- Fairly broad local coverage of a mature, literate audience.
- National newspapers like *The Wall Street Journal* and *U.S.A. Today* offer broad reach; excellent regional testing possibilities at affordable cost.
- Comes invited into the home by subscribers—and read in many households almost immediately upon receipt.
- Editorial-style ads let you trade on the publication's franchise as a respected source of news.
- Inexpensive to test. Many publications will even provide layout and typesetting so a concept can be tested in small papers for a few thousand dollars, then expanded as warranted.
- A/B split testing available in some local papers as well as zoned editions, splits by ZIP+four designation, etc., in some markets.
- Some segmentation can be achieved by advertising in specialized sections such as home and garden, lifestyle, sports, autos, entertainment, etc.

Creative Disadvantages

- Sharply declining readership among younger consumers make this medium problematic for many attractive target markets
- Poor color reproduction in many cases; poor photo fidelity.
- Impersonal medium.
- Position and format limitations abound.
- A mass medium with little selectivity except by city and suburban zones in many cities.
- Can be a complex media procedure to create a national campaign using local newspapers.
- Local events and conditions can affect ad response, jeopardizing projectability of results.

FREE-STANDING NEWSPAPER INSERTS AND WEEKEND MAGAZINES

Creative Advantages

- Many of the same advantages as direct mail: format flexibility, good color reproduction, control of production.
- A plus over direct mail: exact timing, since your ad or insert arrives in a specific day's paper rather than whenever the standard mail happens to be delivered.
- Huge and concentrated reach. For example, *Parade* magazine has a circulation of over 22 million and a readership of 54 million each Sunday, with most all of the reading done in a 48-hour time period.
- Co-op inserts like those of Valassis and News America (Smart Source) allow for cost- effective testing in a small number of markets, and roll-out potential in the tens of millions.
- Advertising in newspaper-circulated magazines such as *Parade* provides good testing possibilities and mass roll-out quantities.

Creative Disadvantages

- *Parade* Magazine readership and ad revenues are declining as the population of newspaper readers declines and ages.
- In some markets there is a great deal of clutter among free-standing inserts (FSIs). In addition, studies show that certain market segments almost never read FSIs.
- This is a mass medium with relatively little opportunity to target prospects. It may be effective only for relatively low-end, mass-appeal products and services. Individual FSIs can be nearly as costly as direct mail, yet response is considerably less than direct mail.
- Format opportunities for FSIs are constrained by what newspapers will accept and can insert.

BILLING INSERTS/PACKAGE INSERTS/CO-OPS/CARD DECKS

Creative Advantages

- Extends reach for direct marketing programs that have proved effective in mail and/or space.
- Affordable: may cost only a tenth to a fourth as much as direct mail (because the costs are shared with other advertisers), with results proportionately lower.
- Ability to control your own color quality and production within the confines of size and format restrictions.

Creative Disadvantages

- Format and size constraints, especially in card decks and co-ops.
- Usually not considered a stand-alone medium—most often used to extend the reach of successful, proven programs.

- Must be controlled to ensure your offer is being promoted in a compatible medium. Co-ops range from mass-market coupon envelopes to the exclusive ranks of executive card decks.

TELEPHONE

Creative Advantages

- Immediate, personal, selective, and very flexible. Allows for spur-of-the-moment up- selling and cross-selling to customers.
- Allows you to ask specific questions to gain market research information while selling or reinforcing sales.
- Highest response medium when done appropriately; also most costly per prospect contact.
- May be used as a primary selling medium or a follow-up for continuity sales.
- Works best with established customers, for following up qualified leads, for business- to-business pitches, for proactive customer service, or when you have specific questions to ask.

Creative Disadvantages

- More consumers consider outbound telemarketing an invasion of privacy than any other main direct marketing medium; indeed, about 80 percent of Americans signed up for the federal Do Not Call list in the first years it was available.
- Creatives must adhere to the specific and strict telemarketing regulations of the Federal Trade Commission regarding disclosures, prizes, misrepresentations, etc. The Data & Marketing Association provides information that outlines these rules in detail.
- Does not allow for visuals.
- Even a well-written script will not come across well unless the representative delivering it has been well trained, speaks clearly, and speaks with enthusiasm.
- Expensive on a per-call basis, although a small test may be designed at a reasonable rate to test viability.
- Many consumers are virtually unreachable by phone because of government Do Not Call lists, long work hours, unlisted numbers, and screening calls on caller I.D. systems.

E-MAIL

Creative Advantages

- Immediate: messages arrive in the recipient's mailbox seconds or minutes after they are sent, and usually are dealt with relatively promptly on receipt.
- Outstanding testing flexibility. Testing of lists, offers, sender names, subject lines, and creative approaches can be done very readily with very quick results.
- Attractive, digital, and colorful HTML e-mails have largely replaced less appealing text formats.
- Much lower cost than most any other medium, with the best return on investment of any medium ever invented (more than $25 for each dollar invested, per the Data &Marketing Association).

- Excellent for verification of orders, shipment alerts, and other customer service functions that normally are welcomed by buyers.
- High penetration among literate, affluent customers both at home and at work.
- Exceptional ability to customize e-mail delivery schedules and messages based on customer or prospect input and interests.

Creative Disadvantages

- The broad-brush connotation of "spam" has tarnished the image of e-mail as a promotional medium.
- Potential for deletion of promotional e-mails, even among opted-in customers, is very high.
- E-mail messages and delivery plans must be developed with great care since responsible e-mailers offer customers and prospects the opportunity to opt-out in response to any message. An annoying or poorly targeted message, or too-frequent communications, may have dire consequences for your e-mail list.
- Even an HTML e-mail is quite limited in appropriate format and length.
- Not as cost-effective as the phone for customer service purposes.

MOBILE MARKETING

Creative Advantages

- Immediate and timely—great for limited-time offers and opportunities that customers and prospects can take advantage of immediately, while out and about in the marketplace.
- A very personal and "always on" medium—many people are "joined at the fingertip" to their mobile devices.
- Pinpoint targeting of customer/prospect and exact location are possible.
- Very trackable with great database-building opportunities.
- Great for impulse purchases as consumers can pay with a few clicks on their mobile devices.
- Potential to create easily updatable apps that build brands, build relationships with customers, and/ or become profit centers.

Creative Disadvantages

- Perceived by many as intrusive, unwelcome, a possible privacy invasion and, in the case of immediate geographically targeted offers, even somewhat creepy.
- The challenge is to make an offer that is integrated with your larger campaign, and is more than simply a price appeal.
- Under scrutiny by the Federal Communications Commission with potential limitations coming on use and release of mobile customer data.
- Limited target market in the United States due to the need for consumer opt-in for respectful mobile marketing.
- Fragmentation due to a wide range of carriers and devices in use.

SOCIAL NETWORKING SITES (INCLUDING BLOGS)

Creative Advantages

- The ultimate mass media of the twenty-first century with top sites boasting hundreds of millions of participants (Facebook tops two billion users!)
- Incredible opportunities for pinpoint targeting based on what consumers reveal about themselves and what they talk about on social sites.
- Ability to reach younger consumers and others who spend little time with traditional media.
- "Natural relevance" for ads and offers—for example, ads that appear at the bottom of YouTube videos that offer more information about the brand or product featured in the video.
- Ability to establish a very human, accessible brand personality.
- Ability to build brand loyalty through fan pages, people who "like" your product or site, and bloggers who report positive experiences with your products or services.
- Site visitor analytics, consumer reviews, and comments provide inexpensive yet valuable market research information.
- Highly inexpensive from the point of view of media cost.

Creative Disadvantages

- Consumer control is paramount in social media: consumers and bloggers may say negative things about your product or service in the social space.
- It is very time-consuming to keep social media sites updated and monitored on a continuous basis.
- Results of ads on social media sites can be measured in terms of click-throughs, requests for information, purchases and time on site, but the ROI of social media sites and fan pages can be difficult to measure.
- High noise level and much competition for attention to your message.

TELEVISION

Creative Advantages

- Best medium for demonstration.
- Endless possibilities for formats and forms: drama, slice of life, pitch man, testimonial, celebrity spokesperson, or some combination—in studio or on location.
- More and more targeting is possible with digital cable and satellite options, as well as niche cable networks with shows catering to specific demographic groups.
- Versatile medium—may be used for sales, lead generation, integration with or support of other media.
- Digital editing allows for easier and much less costly customization or editing of TV spots.
- Quick responses: you can get an initial read on a commercial in minutes as customers call the toll-free number or log on to a landing page on the Internet.

- By their very length, many direct marketing commercials eliminate clutter. At 90 to 120 seconds, they may consume much of the time allotted to a commercial break period.
- Infomercials—entire 30-minute shows with an advertising message—offer the luxury of time to explain, demonstrate, and sell a product or service in an atmosphere that seems more like a show than a commercial.

Creative Disadvantages

- Very expensive: often takes $100,000 or more for production and media to per- form even a simple test. High costs make this the realm of large and sophisticated direct-marketing firms—or start-ups with deep pockets.
- Finite amount of television time available on desirable networks and cable channels. Time is especially scarce in the year's second and fourth quarters, when general advertisers beef up their broadcast buys.
- The woes of general advertisers on television hold true for direct marketers: more consumers are "zapping" commercials of all kinds, eliminating them from digital video recordings and using remote control devices to sample other shows while commercials are on the air.
- Cable cord cutting means that many younger consumers do not watch television at all; rather they subscribe to Netflix, Hulu and the like to avoid ads.
- A fleeting medium: unless you can move the consumer to action in 120 seconds or less (or 30 minutes in the case of an infomercial), you have lost your opportunity since nothing is written down.

RADIO

Creative Advantages

- Stations with specific formats allow for considerable targeting to businesspeople, country music fans, classical music buffs, sports fanatics, and so on.
- Inexpensive to test on a local basis; most rates are open for bargaining.
- Radio networks and satellite radio allow for considerable nationwide reach.
- Timely and newsy.
- A good medium for fantasy and humor.
- Ability to go on the air almost immediately—copy can be written one minute and read by an announcer the next. Even studio-produced spots take little time to prepare.
- Creative direct marketers have found that they may use the strength of radio personalities to help sell their products: Sean Hannity touts LifeLock as protection against identity theft; money expert Dave Ramsey gains leads for mortgage brokers and term life insurance sales agents.

Creative Disadvantages

- Much the same as television: a fleeting medium with nothing written down; listeners may switch stations during commercial breaks.

- Except for satellite radio, a few networks and syndicated programs, it is a difficult and complex job to obtain national reach via radio.
- No visuals; no response device.
- Radio is often used by listeners as background noise; thus getting their attention with an ad may be difficult.
- Reports of listening audience may be exaggerated since many use radio as background noise at home or at work.
- The number of people who do most of their listening in cars cuts down potential response, since they may not have access to phone or paper and pencil. Near-universal penetration of cell phones helps cut down this problem, especially for drive-time pitches to businesspeople.

INTERNET AND OTHER DIGITAL MEDIA

Creative Advantages

- A "hot" medium, especially with younger and more affluent audiences.
- Many site visitors are willing to provide database information in exchange for samples, insider information, and specially tailored responses from you. This information also allows you to customize your presentation to each visitor upon his or her return or even "on the fly"—making one-to-one marketing a reality.
- Your presentation can (and should) be changed often to attract prospects and customers back again and again.
- Ideal for the integration of sales promotion techniques like contests or online voting.
- Non-linear medium allows browsers to delve deeper into parts of your presentation that interest them most.
- You can tell what interests visitors and what stops them short by analyzing the data from their visits.
- Advancing technology and allows for excellent color, motion, sound, and videos.
- Excellent for building public relations and providing wanted services to customers at very low cost to the provider—such as FedEx online package tracking.
- Relatively low financial barriers to entry for a basic Web presence, although effective e-commerce requires a considerable investment. A small firm with a good Web designer can afford to appear much larger and more sophisticated than it can in other media.
- Nearly unlimited potential reach and frequency if you can attract visitors to your site and intrigue them to return.

Creative Disadvantages

- Because best practices for Web site design and copy are so different from those in print media, it requires acquisition of a whole new set of skills on the part of seasoned creatives.
- Site visitors expect constant updates. Done right, this is a high-maintenance medium.

- Leading sites like Amazon and eBay provide streamlined and highly customized experiences for their clients, and customers quickly come to expect similar state-of- the-art applications and customer service features from every site.
- While colors online are vibrant and varied, the ability to produce a picture of a product with fidelity and clarity is limited.
- The downside of a non-linear medium is that customers who "click onto" a hyperlink or banner ad on your site may never come back to see your selling message unfold.
- Actual purchasing online can be frustrating and time-consuming even on the most user- friendly sites.
- Concerns persist about security of credit card information and other personal information online.
- At least parts of your site will most likely be open to access by all: competitors, "enemies," etc., and your mistakes can be heralded throughout cyberspace by disgruntled customers—an opportunity not easily available to them in any other medium.

HOW TO CHOOSE THE MEDIA MIX

For best results, start testing a new marketing concept in the medium where you have had the most previous success. If your firm or client is new, track the media buys of competitors for clues as to where the most fertile customer base might be. In most cases, direct mail, space advertising, e-mail and the Web will be your best bets for initial testing. Indeed, testing offers, pricing, products, and creative elements via e-mail or on a Web site can be inexpensive and quick. In some cases, firms may choose to begin with telephone marketing since they can obtain direct feedback from customers—not only on whether they will buy, but also on why or why not. If tests prove successful, then consider expanding to additional media such as television, radio, social media, mobile marketing, co-ops, and package inserts.

In evaluating any media selection, be sure that results are tracked not only on initial responsiveness, but also on continued performance levels. In most cases, your ultimate goal is to obtain customers with maximum value over time—not just individuals who have a high front-end response rate.

The Elements of Sales Promotion

By

Susan K. Jones, Ferris State University

According to the Merriam-Webster Dictionary, Sales Promotion consists of *"Activities and devices designed to create goodwill and sell a product;* especially*: selling activities (as use of displays, sampling, demonstrations, fashion shows, contests, coupons, premiums, and special sales) that supplement advertising and personal selling, coordinate them, and make them effective".*

Sales Promotion is an essential element of Integrated Marketing Communications (IMC), which includes the following components:

Integrated Marketing Communications incorporates
- **General Advertising** – which builds awareness, image and brands
- **Public Relations** – in this case, non-paid publicity through media
- **Direct and Digital Marketing** – which targets individuals to forge and build relationships
- **Sales Promotion** – *Short-term incentives* for the trade or for consumers

The emphasis of *short-term* is important. If marketers offer the same sales promotion incentives on a regular or predictable basis, then consumers will come to expect those special benefits as an entitlement whenever they buy the product or service.

As with every Integrated Marketing Communications plan, the way we deploy these four main elements focuses on our target customers. What media do they trust? Where do they spend their media consumption time? What combination of online and offline elements will best inspire their attention/interest/desire/action? In this reading we will cover the two main types of sales promotion, the pros and cons of sales promotion, and the range of sales promotion tools available to marketers.

Two Main Types of Sales Promotion – Push and Pull

Trade Promotion (Push) – Push strategies are those that put the product in front of the consumer to make sure the customer is aware of your brand when they are at the point of purchase. This is done through cooperation with the trade.

Consumer Promotion (Pull) – Pull strategies are aimed at inspiring customers to seek out your brand actively, even if it's not readily visible to them on the retailer's shelf or web site.

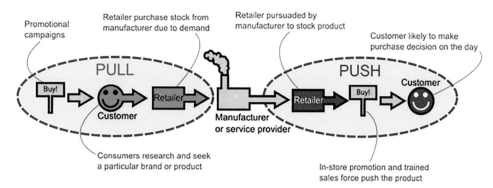

Illustration courtesy of http://marketing-made-simple.com

As you can see in the illustration above, manufacturers employ **push strategies** by incentivizing retailers to carry and promote their products in store. They may also incentivize sales staff to encourage consumer purchases of their brand. Manufacturers employ **pull strategies** through advertising and other mass media promotion, seeking word of mouth referrals (by social media and other means), and through various discounts and incentives.

Author Jon Gibson of http://marketing-made-simple.com (2017) does an excellent job of explaining these strategies further. He says:

> The term **'push strategy'** describes the work a manufacturer of a product needs to perform to get the product to the customer. This may involve setting up distribution channels and persuading middlemen and retailers to stock your product. The push technique can work particularly well for lower value items such as fast moving consumer goods (FMCGs), when customers are standing at the shelf ready to drop an item into their baskets and are ready to make their decision on the spot. This term now broadly encompasses most direct promotional techniques such as encouraging retailers to stock your product, designing point of sale materials or even selling face to face. New businesses often adopt a push strategy for their products in order to generate exposure and a retail channel. Once your brand has been established, this can be integrated with a pull strategy.
>
> **'Pull strategy'** refers to the customer actively seeking out your product and retailers placing orders for stock due to direct consumer demand. A pull strategy requires a highly visible brand which can be developed through mass media advertising or similar tactics. If customers want a product, the retailers will stock it – supply and demand in its purest form, and this is the basis of a pull strategy. Create the demand, and the supply channels will almost look after themselves.

Gibson also wisely explains that push and pull strategies are almost never mutually exclusive. They are used strategically in a combination that recognizes a brand's standing in the industry, its stage in the product life cycle, competitive pressures, and other concerns.

Two Types of Sales Promotion Incentives

Simply put, there are two types of sales promotion incentives. The first one is "Less" – providing a savings incentive to the customer. The second one is "More" – adding value through premiums, extra product, special opportunities, or other add-on incentives.

The Pros and Cons of Sales Promotion

While sales promotion should always be considered as part of an IMC campaign, it definitely has some pros and cons attached to it.

PROS

- **Attracts New Customers** – To gain the attention of new buyers, sales promotion strategies can offer them discounts, premiums and other incentives.
- **Good for Incentivizing Product Trial** – Whether distributed via sampling in-store, riding along with another product, or sent by mail, products trials can be helpful in convincing new customers to buy
- **Creates Urgency** – The short-term nature of sales promotions, with time and/or quantity limits, encourage customers to act quickly.
- **Easy to Measure on a Macro Basis** – It's fairly easy to count coupons redeemed and measure short-term sales increases inspired by sales promotion offerings.

CONS

- **Short-Term Strategy** – Sales promotion can gain attention and trial, but it's not cost-effective as an ongoing strategy to encourage brand loyalty
- **May Damage Brand Image** – Offering too many discounts and being highly promotional may lead to consumers thinking less of the brand in the long run
- **Easy for Competitors to Copy** – Most sales promotions can be copied very easily; finding a promotion that is unique can be difficult
- **Can Be Hard to Measure on a 1-to-1 Basis** – While it's easy to count coupons, a more involved process is necessary to tag buyers by name and gain information about them for the brand's database

Examples of Sales Promotion to the Trade

- Examples of Promotions to the Trade
- Contests and Incentives for Dealers and Salespeople
- Trade Allowances
  - Buying Allowances
  - Promotional Allowances
  - Slotting Allowances

- Point-of-Purchase Displays
- Sales Training Programs
- Cooperative Advertising

Examples of Sales Promotion to the Consumer

- Coupons – Paper and Online
- Contests
- Sweepstakes
- Games
- Gift with Purchase
- Samplings
- Tastings
- Social Media Offers

Fun Examples from Coke McDonalds
- What About Groupon and Living Social?
- Pros for Marketers
- Builds Short-Term Traffic
- Attracts New Customers
- Can Move Stale Inventory
- Increases Revenue on a Short-Term Basis
- Cons for Marketers
- Attracts Bargain Hunters Who May Never Buy Again
- Compromises Your Brand Image
- Unprofitable – Groupon or Living Social gets 50% of an already super-low price

Marketing with a Latin Twist: How Culture and Practices Morph as you Travel South

By

Mary Teahan, President & CEO at Qendar (Argentina)

This reading is targeted toward international marketing executives who want to be successful in Latin America (Latam). It provides some overall data on opportunities but concentrates on perceiving and adapting to cultural differences. The reading deals first with culture as it relates to business relationships with suppliers, partners and employees. Then it delves into some of the sales and marketing implications of cultural differences in the region.

Opportunities

Do you want to venture into data-driven marketing in Latin America? Certainly, there are opportunities. Latam GDP is close to one-third that of the US, according to the latest World Bank statistics.[3]

Country	2016 GDP (u$s B)
USA	18,570
Total Latam	5,459
Brazil	1,804
México	1,152
Argentina	585
Colombia	292
Chile	243
Peru	189

In entering the Latam market, as in most undertakings, there are opportunities and pitfalls. With respect to the latter, the old saying "the best way to make a small fortune in Brazil is to start with a large fortune" certainly comes to mind! Brazil is the largest economy in the region (perhaps the reason for being the brunt of the mentioned joke), followed by México and Argentina, as seen in the table above.

There are 33 countries in Latam, according to UN stats, which include the Caribbean. So a pretty classical Pareto relation exists: less than 20% of the countries – the six singled out above – represent almost 80% of the region's GDP.

---

[3] Source https://data.worldbank.org

Size, however is not the only determining factor in terms of market attractiveness: household income (hard to measure precisely in Latam) also varies widely by country. Below we see the statistics[4] for a proxy, GDP per capita, for the six largest Latam economies, as compared to the US:

Country	Population MM (est. 2016)	2015 per capita GDP (u$s)
USA	317	57,638
Total Latam	638	9,012
Brazil	208	10,080
México	128	9,830
Argentina	44	12,430
Colombia	49	7,130
Chile	32	14,340
Peru	18	6,150

Although far behind the US in per capita GDP, these countries are typified by unequal income distribution, so there are "the haves" and "the have-nots", with the latter bringing the overall country average down. The ones who pull it up are the large middle-class segments – led by Argentina and Chile, followed by Brazil and Mexico and, further back, Colombia and Peru – making these countries fertile ground for consumer marketing.

In terms of marketing media consumption, television continues to reign supreme, still representing over 50% of total media ad spend in Brazil, Mexico and Peru, and over 40% in the other three countries (as opposed to only 20% and falling in the US)[5]. But Internet ad spend is relatively high and growing, thanks to the availability of ever cheaper smart phones, meaning that most people are online.

In the age of data-driven marketing, Internet and social media access are key to effective marketing communications and sales. As of mid-2017, the six Latam countries stack up as follows on these variables[6]:

---

[4] Idem

[5] Various sources:
emarketer for Brazil and Mexico http://www.strathcom.com/wp- content/uploads/2016/11/eMarketer_Worldwide_Ad_ Spending- eMarketers_Updated_Estimates_and_Forecast_for_20152020.pdf AdLatina for Peru, Argentina, Chile and Colombia www.adlatina.com
Winterberry Group for US http://www.winterberrygroup.com/our-insights/outlook-data-2018-snapshot- evolving-role-audience-insight

[6] http://www.internetworldstats.com/stats2.htm Data as of June 30, 2017. Webpage last consulted on Feb. 17, 2018.

Country	Population MM	% Internet Use	% Facebook Use
USA	327	88%	74%
Argentina	44	79%	65%
Chile	18	77%	66%
Brazil	211	66%	66%
Mexico	130	65%	65%
Colombia	49	58%	53%
Peru	32	56%	56%
Total Latam	652	64%	57%
World	7635	52%	26%

So, while Internet usage is high in Latam with respect to the world average, the use of the dominant social network in the region, Facebook, – perhaps reflecting the gregarious relationship-oriented Latin personality – is more than **double** the world average and nearly 80% as prevalent (90% in some countries) as in the USA, making Latam a very attractive market for data-driven marketing.

We might be tempted to say that – with the high TV spend – these countries are still far behind the developed countries in marketing media use. However, other data show that those companies in these countries that have embraced data-driven marketing are not so far away from their colleagues in the more developed markets in terms of knowledge and capability. In Figure 1 below we see the results of a study of data-driven marketers in 17 countries[7], in which Latam (Argentina and Brazil) as well as the other developing nations surveyed (India and South Africa) stack up on a par with the developed areas in terms of the importance of data to their current marketing practice. It should be mentioned that the same survey shows that lack of agency/consultant expertise and lack of technology available in the market were not mentioned as barriers to the future growth of data-driven marketing in Latam.

The conclusion can only be that, while today Latin America lags behind the developed world in the sophistication of marketing practice, the knowledge and skills are there for state-of-the-art data-driven marketing to be done.

Figure 1: Comparison of the current importance of data to marketing in 17 countries

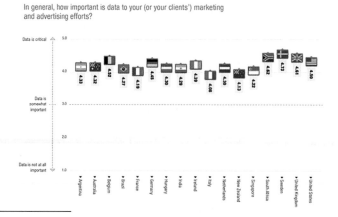

---

[7] http://www.winterberrygroup.com/our-insights/global-review-data-driven-marketing-and-advertising-2014

As also mentioned above, there are significant middle-class populations to be reached. So, some might suggest: just pick your country and dive into Latam! But is it so straightforward? … almost certainly not! Probably you will want to add up several countries to make for a larger market. However, succeeding in Latam is not that simple. In order to reach a larger market, you should choose more than one country (perhaps in stages), but you must be aware that success will depend on varying the tactics and maybe even to a certain extent the strategies in each.

There are major cultural dissimilarities among countries – which does not mean that you cannot have an overall "Latam strategy", but it does signify that you have to be very sensitive to the country differences.

Cultural Differences With and Within Latin America

There are language differences – Portuguese in Brazil and Spanish almost all the rest of Latam – but language is a minor consideration, compared to the cultural differences. And, although Latin American culture is largely Western (although with considerable influence from native peoples in many countries), such that the cultural variations are not as marked as in the case of Western versus Eastern societies, these differences can certainly make you or break you if you want to be successful at business in Latam.

Much has been written on some of the cultural shocks that occur in business interactions between North Americans and Latin American suppliers, partners, coworkers and subordinates. Some of them are sort of fun and/or funny! For instance, the initial handshake greeting is very rapidly replaced by cheek-to-cheek kissing. And you need to do this every time you meet business contacts as well as when you see your coworkers upon arrival at the office in the morning (but probably not when you just come back from lunch). Different countries have distinct protocols with respect to the kiss: you do it once on one cheek in Argentina but three times on alternating cheeks in Brazil for each greeting! Argentine males will exchange kisses, but Chilean men will not, etc.

Relationships are very important, so you would never want to meet or phone a colleague and get straight down to business matters. First, you need to ask after his or her family, or their recent vacation, or another personal subject to establish rapport… every time you call! And they will also ask about your personal matters. Only after these pleasantries will you move on to the object of the meeting or call.

Business lunches in Latin America are most often seen as social as well as work-related occasions. So if you invite somebody for lunch, you should definitely plan on spending at least two hours at the restaurant. Wine in Southern South America and hard liquor in Central and Northern South America will often be served, and sometimes plenty of it!

Whereas apparently superficial or anecdotic, these customs are actually quite important. Luckily, there is considerably more scientific measurement of cultural phenomena to discuss them in a more academic fashion. Let's start with regional differences with respect to the USA. The data for Figure 2 below come from a very recommendable website[8] that presents the results of the studies of Danish Professor Geert Hofstede on how values in the workplace are influenced by culture.

Power Distance

Here we see that the U.S. (and to a lesser degree Argentina) are much lower on the Power Distance variable, meaning that in these two countries, people strive to equalize the distribution of power and demand justification for inequalities of power. Meanwhile, the other countries in Latin America tend to accept that others have more power than they do and the people, supposedly, act accordingly. For instance, if you are a U.S. (or Argentinian) businessperson looking to do deals elsewhere in Latam, you need to realize that "what the boss says" holds much more weight in most Latin American countries than at home. By the way, this will be true in those cases in which you are the boss, as well as in instances when you are dealing with the subordinates of another boss.

Figure 2. Scores of some Latam countries vs the U.S. on cultural values (scales 0 to 100)

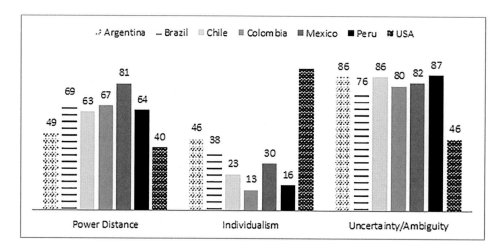

Individualism / Collectivism

The most notable difference displayed in Figure 2 is in the second set of columns, showing that Americans score extremely high in **Individualism**, as opposed to the Latin American countries (where the larger nations, Argentina, Brazil and to a lesser degree Mexico show a greater degree of individualism than the rest). According to Hofstede: *The high side of this dimension, called Individualism, can be defined as a preference for a loosely-knit social framework in which individuals are expected to take care of only themselves and their immediate families. Its opposite, Collectivism, represents a preference for a tightly-knit framework in society in which individuals can expect their relatives or members of a particular group to look after them in exchange for unquestioning loyalty.* Based on this, we could say that Latin American societies are more oriented towards the "we" than the "me". This gives rise to considerable paternalism within companies. Not only is what the boss or owner says "law" (see Power Distance, above) but, in turn, the boss is expected to

---

[8] https://www.hofstede-insights.com/models/national-culture/ Last consulted on February 17, 2018.

look out for his employees, long term. In the author's own experience, working in a local albeit very large family-owned business group in Argentina, an extremely qualified professional colleague whose opinions as a marketer demand much respect, once said, "Let's back off on this recommendation". When asked why, he said, "The boss does not agree. He is mistaken, but he is my *patrón*." *Patrón* means "boss" in Spanish, almost to the extent that *Don* or *Capo* means "boss" in Sicily... you know? This colleague had been working for the group for many years and has a very large family – many children – to support. Logically, he was caring for his family's long-term interest in bowing to the boss' point of view.

Also related to the collective society, we know that family values are high throughout the region and, as a consequence, geographic mobility is fairly low. An acquaintance says that American families get together for Thanksgiving and Christmas, but Latam families get together every Sunday! (And he is right!) So, if you are doing business in Latin America, these values will appear in daily work life. For instance, it is quite common for people to take the day off when it is their own or their child's birthday, because family comes first. People will be hesitant to move to another city (let alone another country) for a promotion – it's not that nobody moves, just that it's a really big deal and many people permanently accept less job advancement in exchange for staying close to their extended family.

Uncertainty Avoidance Indices

Returning to the third variable in the Hofstede graph, a huge cultural difference exists in the degree of tolerance for uncertainty and ambiguity, where the U.S. scores considerably higher than Latam.
According to the Danish scholar, countries exhibiting strong Uncertainly Avoidance Indices maintain rigid codes of belief and are intolerant of unorthodox behavior and ideas. Lower-score UAI countries have a more relaxed attitude in which practice counts more than principles.

Volatility

What does this mean for business? Perhaps because of the political and economic instability of Latin American countries, people fear the worst – since they know from experience that sh*t happens – and try to avoid taking chances as part of their own business decisions, because they know the volatility will reach them anyhow owing to the environment. A very savvy Latin American businessman friend once told me that he held most of his savings abroad in very low-yield but "safe" investments (like guaranteed bank deposits and US Treasury notes). This sounded strange, given that he is something of a wheeler-dealer at home. "I am accustomed to so much volatility in my own market – so much risk – that when it comes to my nest egg, I say 'enough" and act like the most risk-averse person in the world!"

A caveat: Don't be deceived over time by apparent reversals in instability, because they are temporal. Just when you think things are settling down, getting stable, that the country is turning around and is going into the future like a reliable "First World"[9] nation, ... kaboom! All Hades breaks loose. Argentina seemed to be on

---

[9] The term "First World" refers to so called developed, capitalist, industrial countries, roughly, a bloc of countries aligned with the United States after World War II, with more or less common political and economic interests: North America, Western Europe, Japan and Australia. http://www.nationsonline.org/oneworld/third_world_countries.htm

the right track from 1989 on, but in 2002 the economy took a nosedive and as a result a populist government gained control, taking the country back decades in economic development and aligning it temporarily with Cuba, Venezuela, Ecuador and Bolivia. As an international economist said, "Argentina doesn't even belong on that list!" Brazil appeared to be moving forward in great form in terms of economic growth, local technological development, and everything they had always wanted. They had reached number six in the world in national GDP, surpassing Great Britain. And then, in 2013 the economy down-cycled and… kaboom! Later from 2015 on, the political situation (impeachment, corruption, etc.) became chaotic… double kaboom! Even one of the more "stable" democracies like Chile has had its kaboom moments. Avoid being deceived by temporary cycles of apparent stability. Latin America is volatile.

So, don't be surprised, when doing business in these very unpredictable countries, if your local partners seem to be ultra-conservative in risk-taking! They know… Does that mean that you should not venture into Latin America? No, many international companies have very successful businesses in the region. They have learned to go with the flow.

Inter-Country Cultural Differences

It is important to note the variations in the first two Hofstede indicators in Figure 2, *among* the Latam countries themselves: between Argentina and Peru there are 32 points of difference regarding Power Difference and 30 points of difference with respect to Individualism (more when compared to Mexico). These are some of the intra-regional differences that you must take into account when venturing into Latam. Your partners and subordinates in Argentina will be more likely to engage you in debate regarding the best strategies and tactics to adopt, whereas you will need to encourage Peruvians to speak out.

In Brazil, where there is also considerable Power Difference, the author and several sources consulted[10] agree that normally your business contacts will never tell you "no", even when they are not in agreement; however, you will find it well nigh impossible to implement ideas to which they are actually opposed. You will need to develop a sort of sixth sense for when yes means yes and when it means maybe or even no!

Shorter Contracts

Hooker[11] relates many of the differences to the fact that in Latam, cultures tend to be high-context, signifying that they will be relationship-based and depend very much on personal communication. The US, Australia, Canada, and New Zealand, as well as much of Europe, have low-context cultures that are much more rules-based and depend on written communication. This contrast explains why contracts in the U.S. are so long and

---

[10] Alfonso Infante at https://streetsmartbrazil.com/doing-business-with-brazil-9-differences-from-brazil-to-us-and-other-countries/ last consulted on February 17, 2018. John N. Hooker, in "Cultural Differences in Business Communication" (Carnegie Mellon Research Showcase, Dec. 2008) says this behavior is common in many countries with high-context communications cultures and it has a lot to do with allowing your interlocutor to "save face".

[11] See footnote 6. Hooker states that probably the single most useful concept for understanding cultural differences in business communication is Edward T. Hall's distinction of low-context and high-context cultures, citing: Hall's *Beyond Culture*. Garden City, NY; Anchor Books, 1976.

detailed, as opposed to shorter more "flexible" contracts in Latam. In low-context cultures everything need to be specified in writing. In high-context cultures, things are more managed by the day-to-day relationship than by an agreement signed months before. Contracts in originated in Latam will tend to be much shorter, leaving much detail to the prevailing laws (like the Civil Code). Latin Americans actually find the length and detail of US business contracts to be overly complicated. They will sign them because they know that they are lengthy because of cultural differences, but they probably secretly look at their local colleagues and say "sheesh"!

Network or Perish

Networking is vital to doing business in relationship-centric Latin America[12] and reaching deals may depend much more on who you know than what you offer! When the author first arrived in Argentina from the U.S. for a job in banking several decades ago, she was impressed at how her colleagues instinctively picked up the phone and called old school buddies, family friends, neighbors and other personal contacts whenever a new business problem or opportunity presented itself. Her boss (a native) told her to develop a network or perish in business in Buenos Aires. For lack of local acquaintances, she resorted to becoming a "joiner" and being very active in professional associations to construct her own relationships as a necessary prerequisite for career success.

Bureaucracy

It is, according to Hooker, because of Hofstede's Uncertainty Avoidance Index, mentioned above (and somewhat in contrast to the lesser emphasis on rules in high-context societies), that bureaucracy – "red tape" – is so huge in the region. People like public officials who are in charge of controlling that certain things happen, or don't happen, try to get covered on multiple fronts and invent the most Kafkaesque requirements for getting permits to do almost anything. A typical skit on Argentine TV comedy shows a citizen trying to complete a government procedure who gets sent back time and time again by the public employee who needs to give approval, because there is always one more paper missing. It is to a great deal owing to bureaucracy that Latam countries rank so poorly in the World Bank's Ease of Doing Business Ranking shown below.[13] Argentina and Brazil are particularly outrageous! So, be prepared to do battle with red tape in order to do business in the region.

Country	World Bank Ease of Doing Business Ranking (out of 190 countries)
USA	6
Argentina	117
Brazil	125
Chile	55
Colombia	59
Mexico	49
Peru	58

[12] Hooker (2008).
[13] https://data.worldbank.org/indicator/IC.BUS.EASE.XQ

How Best to Navigate through Cultural Differences in Business Relationships

These differences can be frustrating. It is almost always best to have a trusted advisor who understands both your home culture and that of the nation where you want to do business, to help guide you around the pitfalls.

But don't make the error, however, of thinking that any Spanish-speaker from one of the Latam countries or from the US will naturally blend in culturally. Prejudices exist: Argentinians are said to be arrogant, Brazilians overly nationalist, Mexicans machistas (misogynous), etc. There are major cultural differences among Latam countries and whoever takes on a negotiating or managerial position in any one of them – even if he or she is a native speaker – must be aware of preexisting prejudices and act accordingly. This advice runs both ways: you must be aware of the differences between your culture and that of your colleagues and you must also be aware of how they react to your national idiosyncrasies.

As Thomas Becker[14] says in his enlightening book on doing business in Latam, you need to avoid the temptation toward cultural dominance (thinking your way is the best) and look for the cultural synergies, where adopting the local way will create value. But, his other recommendation is also very important: "never go native". Don't relax your performance standards or – above all – your ethical standards (and there will be temptations, given the rampant corruption in some Latin American business environments[15]).

...And, "So What?", you may say, in terms of marketing to consumers...

Alright, so Latin Americans are more respectful of authority and less individualist than some other nationalities. We have already established that these cultural differences are important in terms of how you can get business from your local reps if you are selling to Latam. And they are relevant to your success as a leader in the workplace if you are an executive posted to Latam. But how do they affect the actual marketing to consumers?

Luckily, according to Becker, and the author agrees, the numerous middle-class consumers are permeable to the shift from price perception to value perception. So, products and services aimed at the middle class can be marketed similarly.

The Bottom of the Pyramid

There is also a very large price-conscious segment in these countries and strategies for reaching the bottom of the pyramid should be considered when marketing to them. Varying the product (second brands, pared-back offerings, etc.) is a key strategy.

---

[14] Becker, Thomas. Doing Business in the New Latin America: Keys to Profiting in America's Next Door Markets. Praegler, second edition, 2010. pp. 177-180.

[15] According to Transparency International's 2016 Corruption Perceptions Index, other than Chile that ranked a commendable 24 out of 176 countries surveyed, the other five Latam countries singled out in this paper ranked between 79 and 123! https://www. transparency.org/news/feature/corruption_perceptions_index_2016#table last consulted on February 17, 2018.

Some cosmetic retail strategies could also be called for. For instance, in the 80s, a large Argentine chain of drugstores without drugs (*perfumerías*, as they are called locally; they sell toiletries and cosmetics but no medicines) had prime retail locations on city streets with large display windows. Their deliberate window dressing strategy was to clutter it up, because if they made attractive window displays, the clientele would interpret that they had upscale prices and not come in! The internal décor was also deliberately disorderly.

And the author will never forget visiting an appliance store client in the north of the country when she was commercial director for Whirlpool in Argentina. Part of the clientele were Kolla Indians from the Andes foothills (descendants of tribes subjugated by the Inca Empire). The storeowner told the author to observe the sales technique of the appliance salesperson as a married Kolla couple, dressed in their traditional garb, considered a refrigerator purchase. The salesman stood beside them and the fridge without saying a peep. The owner explained that culturally the Kolla are people of few words and if the seller tried to talk them up, they would immediately leave the store! Know your customer, right?

A more sophisticated example of marketing to the bottom of the pyramid comes from the satellite TV provider DirecTV in Argentina. Paid TV is a very mature product in middle-class Argentina, and the typical sales strategy is direct, telephone and digital marketing of monthly fees for distinct "plans" including access to different packs of channels. Just when everybody thought that there was nothing more to do in terms of marketing satellite TV, DirecTV detected a need in shantytown dwellers in and around the big cities. The shantytowns tend to flood and get very muddy when it rains. People often cannot even get out to get to work or school. So, some entertainment option for these downtimes is key. Satellite TV is great for that – since it brings not only cable channels but also network air signals, very popular in this socioeconomic segment that may not have good reception during stormy weather. Most cellphones in Argentina are prepaid (with only about 20% of accounts corresponding to monthly billing plans) and at the bottom of the pyramid they are all pay-as-you-go, because the people use the phone when they have money and not when they don't. Taking a cue from this, DirecTV developed a pay-as-you-go plan for satellite TV in Argentina (which has since been extended to other Latin American countries). To offer this service, a self-installation kit had to be created – both to keep costs down and maintain the visits of personnel to dangerous neighborhoods to a minimum – and a whole system of distribution had to be created through supermarkets, appliance stores, and other points of sale accessible to the target segment for obtaining the kit and periodically buying viewing time, since many of these people do not have credit cards enabling online payments: a whole new channel system, just for this service! They also created an SOS recharging plan that gives you two days' advance viewing time, chargeable against your next payment, in case you get "rained in" in your neighborhood with no balance on the account!

These are some examples of how Latam marketers adjust their products, pricing and distribution systems in response to local market needs and preferences.

Channel Strategy

Regarding the latter, big box commerce, hypermarkets, malls and outlets certainly did develop in Latin America from the late 1980s on. However, the Mom and Pop grocery store has persisted and even had a comeback, in which large chains like the French Carrefour (which is a major player in many Latam markets) have actually developed their own sub-brands of small neighborhood formats. Many people cannot afford cars, so the monthly trip to the hypermarket to stock up is not an option. Others that do drive may do their "big" shopping periodically in the large format stores, but will visit the local shops several times a week anyhow. Most upper-middle class households will have maids, so the lady of the house may not do the shopping at all, and expensive but laborsaving devices and products may not have the same appeal.

Kimberly Clark in Argentina developed a whole new channel for disposable diaper sales for their Huggies brand, initially aimed at low-end consumers, although they later realized that many upper-scale moms appreciated advice from a neighborhood diaper shop owner and preferred that channel over supermarkets.

Decades ago, when the author was in banking, McDonald's was planning their entry into the Argentine market. On a visit to the bank, the American expansion team asked her if she thought Argentinians would take to eating in their cars – obviously a big consideration related to real estate investment in the size of the locales. The answer was a resounding no. And to this day, McDonald's, which did make a successful entry into the market – with an upscale slant owing to costing and consequent pricing – has large seating areas in their restaurants and eating in cars continues to be an exceptional behavior!

Trust

Another big cultural difference in retail is the fact that it has traditionally been very hard to get your money back from a Latin American retailer once you made a purchase. You can exchange merchandise like apparel to get a different size or color, but if the retailer does not have what you need, you most often will have to take a credit voucher to buy something else someday in the future, as opposed to getting a refund. With rampant inflation having been the historical case in so many of the countries, your credit would devalue daily. So Latam consumers are very careful before purchasing. This is slowing changing, but the idea that once you pay "you're stuck" negatively impacts trust and is, beyond any doubt, a cultural challenge to distance selling.

Bargaining

One more cultural barrier for some channels is the long-standing habit of "bargaining" regarding price. Actually, Hooker[16] opines that haggling is a valid coping mechanism in high-context cultures as a means of reaching an agreed price with as little information exchange as possible. It is culturally firmly rooted in Latam; although in supermarkets and chain stores the fixed price as marked prevails, at their friendly neighborhood appliance dealer and other small retailers like clothiers, people will bargain. This often comes in the form of "If I pay cash or take two, how much will you knock off the price?" There is virtually no social stigma associated with price bargaining in these contexts. A certain preference for small formats for some categories of goods may spring from this. As a matter of fact, for big-ticket items, price shopping is a norm and people talk openly in social settings about how cheap they manage to purchase things. As such, the practice of *showrooming* (inspecting the merchandise in physical stores and then buying online) and

---

[16] Hooker (2008, p.6)

particularly *webrooming* (the opposite: checking prices online before going to the store to bargain) are very common.

ECommerce

Ecommerce is growing fast in Latam, but is far from the level reached in the U.S. In addition to trust and the opportunity to bargain, means of payment constitutes something of an obstacle. The percentage of unbanked consumers remains very high throughout the region (estimated at around 50% in Argentina), although there is a critical mass of credit cards in most countries that is sufficient for etailers to do their thing.

For ecommerce, logistics is a big obstacle. Direct and catalog marketing never really took off in Latin America (it reached higher proportions in Brazil, but still nowhere near the size of the U.S. or European DM industries) and consequently delivery mechanisms were developed mostly only for big merchandise like furniture, for instance, and even today tend to be citywide and not nationwide in reach. So, although some local versions of UPS and other delivery services do exist, they tend to be much slower and very much more costly than in the States. And this is the principal barrier to ecommerce development in the region.

Promotion

So, as marketers, we have talked about Product, Price and Place differences in Latam vis-à-vis the United States. What about the 4th P of Marketing, Promotion?

With the high degree of activity on social networks mentioned at the beginning of this reading, combined with the high-context relationship-oriented it should be no surprise that peer opinions weigh every more heavily in purchase decisions, as opposed to advertising. If you can get a commercial message to go viral (easier said than done, as most marketers know from experience), it can spread very widely!

In high-context Latin America, emotional appeals tend to be used more often in advertising than factual content. And with high risk-avoidance, the use of endorsers (entertainment or sports figures, famous physicians, etc.) is popular. Humor is employed, but less frequently than in the US, and more often when addressing younger consumers who tend to be have a more relaxed attitude toward audacity.

With cultural and, yes, racial differences among the countries in Latam, the models shown in advertising must vary. Using a supposedly "typical Latino" look for the same ad in Central and northern South America sometimes works, but it will not fly in Argentina or Uruguay, where the vast majority of people are descendants of European immigrants. Also, according to respective national census data, less than 0.4% of Argentines are Afro-Argentinians, whereas over 50% of Brazilians are blacks or "pardos" (as the national census bureau calls people of mixed-black stock), so a group or crowd scene in Argentina should not really include any blacks, whereas in Brazil it should!

Even when the visuals of a TV commercial can be successfully deployed over several countries, the language must be dubbed, because national accents vary tremendously. These are just some of the considerations to be taken into account in marketing communications in different countries in Latam.

Recommendations on Adapting Sales and Marketing to each Country Market

In summary, with respect to the actual sales and marketing differences, the author agrees with Nataly Kelly[17] when she recommends not only for Latin America, but also for the world in general:

1. Don't think of a "region" without recognizing the important country differences.

2. While you will probably want to maintain a degree of global branding consistency, you will need to adapt your sales and marketing channels to local realities.

3. Product should be adjusted to achieve "fit" one country at a time.

4. Pricing will also need to vary by country.

5. Let your local teams lead the way, not only regarding tactical matters, but also regarding strategy.

Final Considerations

There are ample opportunities to have the best of "luck" in developing your business in Latin America (and to avoid turning that large fortune into a small one!), do be very sensitive to cultural differences in the styles of doing business and leading human resources. And when you look at the sales and marketing aspects of the business, also consider culture and rely on the highly qualified and paid local executives that you have, hopefully, taken on!

Mary Teahan is President of Qendar Marketing for a Better Society, a marketing communications agency for non-profits in Argentina. She is also Academic Director of the Masters in Marketing and Communication degree program at San Andrés University in Buenos Aires. Past President of the Global Alliance of Data-Driven Marketing Associations. Former president of ALMADI, the Latin American Federation of DMAs. Former president of AMDIA, the Argentine DMA. President-elect of the Argentine Ad Council. Member of the Golden Brain Hall of Fame in recognition of contributions to advertising and communications in Argentina. An American, Mary has lived and worked in Latin America for many years.

---

17 Nataly Kelly, "The Most Common Mistakes Companies Make in Global Marketing", Harvard Business Review Online, September 2015.

BowTie Cause: Tied to Social Enterprise

By:

Stacy Neier Beran, Loyola University Chicago Mary Ann McGrath, Loyola University Chicago

How to Tie a Bow Tie

Step 1: Lift the collar.

Step 2: Place the bowtie around neck.

Step 3: Cross the longer end over the shorter end.

Step 4: Loop the long end under where the two ends cross.

Step 5: Fold the dangling end to make a loop.

Step 6: Drop the longer end over the skinny center of the bow.

Step 7: Pinch the bow together in front of the long end.

Step 8: Feed the middle of the dangling end back through the knot.

Step 9: Pull at the loops.

Step 10: ***Straighten*** the bowtie.[18]

Dhani Jones, Founder of BowTie Cause, elevated Step 10 to "***Rock*** the bowtie." Dhani's name was popularly recognized as a linebacker from 2007-2010 for the NFL Cincinnati Bengals. He was an expert with the pigskin, but his role in BowTie Cause demonstrated his expertise with social enterprise. As depicted in business press, contemporary company leaders wore hooded sweatshirts and laid-back sneakers: it appeared the secret to get market share and shareholder value up required entrepreneurs to dress down. Dhani's

---

[18] http://www.wikihow.com/Tie-a-Bow-Tie

signature bowtie, looped to perfection, instead symbolized the promise for enlightened community dialogue for the sake of common good.

Dhani recognized that bowties were a tricky accessory. He also recognized that the ten simple steps that resulted in one crisp bowtie could contain a message of support folded into its four corners. According to BowTie Aficionado, as few as 1% of men knew how to tie a bowtie.[19] Yet, through his daily practice, Dhani showed he knew what eluded most men. He not only knew how to tie a bowtie, but also how to rock a bowtie to support a cause.

Not only did the steps to properly tie a bowtie elude most men, but men additionally received mixed messages about when to wear bowties. When and why would a man wear a bowtie instead of a traditional necktie? The idea that a bowtie could generate attention, begin a conversation, and garner support for social injustice was the genesis for BowTie Cause. Through BowTie Cause, Dhani realized that a bowtie could transform a personal style choice into a symbol of social support.

Five years into its operations, BowTie Cause remained Dhani's signature contribution to society at large. As an organization, BowTie Cause had partnered with 109 causes, manufactured more than 5000 bowties, and donated $300,000 to a range of causes. Within a cluttered environment of fashion accessories and charitable causes, Dhani realized that BowTie Cause needed a clearly articulated Integrated Marketing Communications (IMC) Plan for gaining wider awareness and recognition as a signature solution to generate funds and awareness for various causes. What specific markets should be targeted? How could the bowtie be communicated as a symbolic icon related to specific causes? Not an expert in this area, he realized that there were far more than 10 steps involved in bow-tying to make this vision a reality.

The BowTie Cause Model

History of BowTie Cause

Dhani's path to create social change started with his time on the football field. During the sixth round of the 2000 NFL draft, the New York Giants selected Dhani as a linebacker after his record-setting career at the University of Michigan. Early in his NFL career, Dhani learned that Kunta Littlejohn, a childhood friend, had been diagnosed with lymphoma. For years prior to his diagnosis, Kunta had worn bowties. He vocally proclaimed that, "If you wanna be somebody, you gotta rock a BowTie." Dhani was at first skeptical about Kunta's statement but began to wear bowties in silent support of his ailing friend.

Dhani's initial uncertainty about Kunta's adoration of bowties soon turned into a signature for philanthropy. After retiring from the NFL in 2010, Dhani started BowTie Cause as a conduit to help others rock bowties in support of the causes that deeply impacted their lives. Dhani wanted the bowtie to be more than a fashion accessory and sought to associate the bowtie with social entrepreneurship. Dhani realized that donning a bowtie could support a cause, start a conversation, or be an advocate for change. As such, the BowTie Cause mission statement represented this vision:

---

[19] http://www.bowtieaficionado.com/2014/12/02/bow-tie-infographic/#.VZQCTWDvOS0

Our mission is to generate awareness – and funds – for organizations that make a difference. We accomplish this by telling the story of your organization through the design, creation and promotion of a signature BowTie.

As Dhani built relationships with organizations in Cincinnati (home of his final NFL team), Dhani recruited talent to lead BowTie Cause operations. Dhani served as Chairman of BowTie Cause, and his friend Kunta (now a cancer survivor) took the role as Chief Inspiration Officer. Amanda Williams joined

BowTie Cause as CEO nearly three years into operations; her finance and banking background brought strategic planning expertise. Amanda prioritized repositioning BowTie Cause as her first objective. She commissioned and guided a website relaunch that emphasized an improved user interface, updated logo, and a relevant tagline (*Get Tied to A Cause*). In conjunction with the website relaunch (www.bowtiecause.com), Amanda worked to streamline owned social media channels to reflect the improved style and to consistently communicate the mission. As the BowTie Cause Executive Team, Dhani, Kunta, and Amanda delivered the BowTie Cause model to highlight three key competencies. The team executed the BowTie Cause mission statement through consistent (1) organizational representation,
collaboration, and (3) process.

BowTie Cause is a social enterprise. Social enterprise—which is also called social venturing, social innovation, and social entrepreneurship—is a recent development in which organizations seek to meet urgent social needs while operating as a business. Social enterprises *are* businesses with the distinguishing feature of having a mission of providing social welfare services for people who are disadvantaged or otherwise excluded. Businesses which provide some significant benefit for the whole of society, in such areas as the arts, the environment, or community development, may also be considered social enterprises. They include for-profit and not-for-profit organizations, of which BowTie Cause is the former.[20]

To "generate funds," per the mission statement, BowTie Cause donates 25% of profit from online bowtie sales to the organizations represented by the customized bowties. Each uniquely designed bowtie captures the essence of its cause through color, pattern, texture, and other fabric embellishments. The suggested retail price for each bowtie was $57. The current price is $65. The added value for the cause organization results from the difference between the revenue from retail sales and the cost of bowtie production. Additionally, the initial $57 price point represented Dhani's Cincinnati Bengals number, so "57" was an extra nod to Dhani's leadership. The BowTie Cause model delivers economies of scale. For example, an order of 100 bowties costs $28.50 each to manufacture; for an order amount of 250 bowties, the cost is $27.50. See Appendix A for additional details about the cost structure and financial benefit to organizations.

The BowTie Cause model requires collaboration. The BowTie Cause team shares creative expertise with the cause organizations in the design of a bowtie that best portrays the mission of the cause. The cause partners know their historic roots and tactics as well as the needs of the populations they serve, but they generally

---

[20] John R. Boatright, "Social Enterprise," in The SAGE Encyclopedia of Business Ethics and Society, 2nd ed, ed. Robert W. Kolb (Thousand Oaks, CA: Sage Publications, 2017)

do not have social enterprise knowledge to design a wearable story. BowTie Cause guides partners through the manufacturing process and coordinates design, creation, and promotion. From the time of initiation, causes receive their bowtie orders in 12 to 14 weeks. Every bowtie prototype articulates the cause's story. The packaging of the bowtie also reflects the organization: each bowtie is packaged to promote the cause's story, logo, website, and social media channels. This balance between organizational representation and collaboration is anchored in the common mission to generate funds.

See Appendix A for an illustration of the process timeline.

Finally, the BowTie Cause mission explicitly aims to "generate awareness." BowTie Cause partners with organizations from an array of sectors. This flexibility allows BowTie Cause to work with groups that varied from sport teams' philanthropies, universities, and medical societies. Options for BowTie Cause to source prospective partners are endless. Increased diversification of partners enabled BowTie Cause to expand its reach and contribute to the fragmented cause marketing space. Appendix B lists BowTie Cause affiliates.

Cause Marketing and Social Enterprise

For BowTie Cause to grow through market expansion, it relies on an abundance of causes. Society's controversies, although largely unsought scenarios, create opportunity for BowTie Cause to be a contributor to causes that need both awareness and funds. Cause marketing, related to social enterprise, typically combines the cooperative efforts of a for-profit business and a non-profit organization for mutual benefit.[21] Dhani and the BowTie Cause team, as social entrepreneurs, regarded cause marketing as a means to benefit society. Consumers have an expectation that cause marketing will be part of any enterprise's operations. Per GfK[22], 63% of consumers reported only buying products that appealed to their beliefs, values, and ideals. Customers want to contribute to society through website clicks and in- store purchases, and cause marketing makes this convenient. "The number of consumers who say they would switch from one brand to another if the other brand were associated with a good cause has climbed to 87%."[23] This dramatic increase came at a time when charitable giving stagnated at 2% of the GDP.[24]

BowTie Cause incorporates both the spirit and the convenience of cause marketing. The uniquely designed physical bow tie itself serves as a beacon that exposes the larger public to a focal cause. The choice to exhibit the cause in the form of displaying the special bow tie is a touchstone to the inner values and priorities of its wearer.

BowTie Cause's Competitive Niche

Kunta pioneered the bowtie in the midst of a bowtie renaissance. Dhani articulated this "resurgence of the gentleman"[25] through his signature combination of dapper dressing and philanthropic efforts. As such, the

---

[21] http://www.entrepreneur.com/article/197820
[22] http://trendwatching.com/trends/enlightened-brands
[23] http://www.entrepreneur.com/article/197820
[24] http://www.ted.com/talks/dan_pallotta_the_way_we_think_about_charity_is_dead_wrong
[25] http://articles.latimes.com/2009/nov/29/image/la-ig-diary29-2009nov29

BowTie Cause team recognized favorable marketplace conditions to find success through a differentiated product strategy. The challenge for BowTie Cause was to signal consumers as to how and why "Rocking a Bowtie Cause bowtie" went beyond a fashion statement and morphed into a social statement.

The U.S. market for apparel and accessories surpassed $15 billion in a recent year, and sales of men's products have continued to outshine women's sales. An anticipated 3% increase in men's accessories indicated US consumers accepted product development in menswear and desired more options.[26] Yet, ties lost their place as a staple of corporate dress. With continued popularity of casual workplaces and stay-at-home employees, annual tie purchases steadily decreased as retailers responded to consumer preferences for "casual work wear."[27]

Despite slumping necktie sales, the marketplace for other men's accessories experienced resurgence. Decades of casual workplace dressing, including jeans and t-shirts, begged for an upgrade that allowed men to embody personal style through elevated products. Men desired comfortable, unfussy styles that also allowed them to "dress the part" for professional commitments. Unlike infinite consumer choices offered to women – scarves, jewelry, and handbags – men sought straightforward items to serve multiple purposes that merged "business casual and business comfortable."[10]

BowTie Cause saw this an as opportunity to merge this aesthetic with a premium product. Recent sales of men's denim signaled that men appreciated premium apparel to be used for multiple occasions. Sales of premium denim had first skyrocketed, then reached maturity and declined a near double-digit drop- off in sales.[7] Men appeared ready for low- to mid-priced garments to complement their premium-priced denim to keep their look fresh. In other words, there appeared to be an opportunity for appropriate accessories to supplement their casual dress. The durability of denim did not require constant replenishment, so while men wore-in their favorite jeans, their closets were void of other fashion- forward choices. BowTie Cause's masculine product assortment marked the brand's response to the expected industry uptick in men's accessories.

Men's fashion gravitated toward nostalgia, championed by society's fascination of popular culture influences ranging from Mad Men to Entourage. Products like pocket squares, cufflinks, eyewear, and bowties formed a mix-and-match wardrobe. Fashion-savvy men could simultaneously embody the well- groomed style of Mad Men's Don Draper and the laid-back look of Justin Timberlake. Nostalgic associations with bowties began to evolve. The historic image of bowties as "older" or "stiff" succumbed to modern interpretations of how men, representative of a range of lifestyles, "tied one on."

The playful, yet sophisticated, nature of bowties supported BowTie Cause positioning. As shown in Appendix C, survey participants expressed descriptions associated with the word "bowtie."

[26] Euromonitor International. Passport GMID.
[27] Mintel International Group Ltd. Mintel Reports.

Although consumers reported a range of perceptions about bowties, positive perceptions like "stylish" and "cultured" matched changing perceptions of luxury. Fifty-five percent of consumers reported that wearing a bowtie implied a sense of luxury.[28] With recent recession pressures lifted, luxury products satisfied a wider array of consumer desires. Product development freely combined form utility and fanciful appeal. In doing so, accessories responded to consumers' preferences for "masstige"[29] products, designed to blend mass pricing and distribution with prestige quality. Table 1 indicates how brands position luxury product offerings to fit three distinct preferences for luxury. This continuum ultimately points to opportunity for masstige products to include traits from each category.

Table 1 *Luxury Continuum*

Types of Luxury	
Accessible	Lowest, cheapest form of luxury that is accessible to most consumers in the marketplace
Aspirational	Middle tier form of luxury that most consumers aspire to attain
Absolute	Highest, most expensive form of luxury

Source: Euromonitor International.

Within the luxury spectrum, current positioning of BowTie Cause (see Fig. 1) held a unique position among menswear brands. Indirect competitors, like Coach and Ralph Lauren, earned market share through diversification across luxury categories. Attempts to penetrate each luxury category with a unique product line confused consumers about the true meaning of a luxury product. For example, Coach simultaneously offered $45 leather key rings and $598 duffel bags, leaving consumers skeptical about what the brand meant. Too many masstige product extensions threatened vulnerability and signaled loss of vision by the brand. Consumer confusion risked that brands could default on their core competencies.

Luxury Mixed with Cause

What differentiated BowTie Cause's positioning within a competitive luxury continuum was its focus on using the bowtie as signature of a cause. The rising popularity of bowties presented this opportunity.
While apparel brands with dominant market share boasted internal foundations as cause-related activity (like The Coach Foundation or the Ralph Lauren Pink Pony Fund), BowTie Cause products disrupted existing practice to invite both organizations and consumers to support *many* causes through *one* product. This contrasted with other brands' support of *one* cause through *many* products.

---

[28] Proprietary consumer data from BowTie Cause.
[29] https://hbr.org/2003/04/luxury-for-the-masses

Figure 1. BowTie Cause demonstrated positioning of a masstige product that represented multiple causes; this differentiated positioning created a niche amongst a fragmented industry of indirect competitors.

While BowTie Cause indirectly competed to gain market share from mainstream fashion brands, it remained a social enterprise brand. Similar brands like Livestrong and (Product)[Red] experienced admiration from global audiences who sparked dialogue about social causes through signature accessories. These brands combine consumers' dress and donation patterns. Like BowTie Cause, each brand achieved awareness through heavy endorsements by publicly-known figures. However, controversies arose from cause affiliations for both Livestrong and (Product)[Red] brands.[30] Consumers again became confused. Brands associated with causes needed to restore trust in fashionable products that made a societal contribution. BowTie Cause's positioning, therefore, was challenged to present a high standard of transparency about its organizational representation of multiple causes. Appendix D compares BowTie Cause to Livestrong and (Product)[Red].

The modern bowtie held appeal to philanthropic groups seeking original ways to tell their stories of support. Through philanthropy, consumers may contribute in three distinct ways. The "3 T's of Philanthropy" are donations of (1) time, (2) treasure, and/or (3) talent.[7] For many the modern frenetic consumer lifestyles suggest that time is a scarce luxury: finding adequate time to volunteer for favorite causes stressed commitments, to work and family. Consumers' tendencies to prioritize workplace commitments resulted in increased disposable income, so luxuries like bowties were attainable with earned disposable "treasure." The $65 retail price for a BowTie Cause bowtie enabled busy consumers to support causes consistent with their beliefs and interests, rather than expend precious time. Purchases from BowTie Cause satisfied the aspiration for luxury accessories while providing an accessible way to give treasure without depleting already scarce time to volunteer.

---

[30] http://www.conecomm.com/productred

Signature Segments

BowTie Cause has two distinct market targets – the ultimate consumers and the cause partners. The visual design of each bowtie required that the values of these two groups were consistent. Therefore, segmentation required BowTie Cause to satisfy needs both of wearers and philanthropies.

Ultimate Consumers

Through proprietary research, BowTie Cause had clearly defined consumer segmentation. The ultimate consumers of BowTie Cause prioritized clothing and philanthropy choices as special expressions of their identities. They were motivated to make purchases that brought them both esteem and confidence. Their choice to wear bowties was to garner both attention and respect from others. Straightforward demographics were inadequate to classify ultimate BowTie Cause consumers. This segment generated 30% of BowTie Cause sales, so up-to-date research was crucial. Three consumer segments emerged, designated as "Ringleader," "Happy-Go-Lucky," and "Old Guard."[31]

Ringleaders: The Primary B2C Psychographic

Among ultimate consumers, ringleaders formed the target market that combined altruism with action. Ringleaders not only shared their time and treasure through actively choosing causes to support, but they also rallied others to follow their lead. These consumers most closely resembled Dhani and Kunta's initial challenge to be somebody by rocking a bowtie. Ringleaders believed everyone can be someone, so as opinion leaders, they wore and worked for the brand. By wearing BowTie Cause, they mobilized others to build awareness and openly exchange conversations about causes, values, and visions for a better society. Ringleaders transcended gender expectations also associated with bowtie; they were made up of both men and women. Women in this category would also openly engage with BowTie Cause without regard for the masculinity of the bowtie. These women understood the cause; for them, the physical bowtie was secondary to their connection to the cause.

Happy-Go-Lucky: The Secondary B2C Psychographic

Given consumer perceptions of bowties as "quirky" (see Appendix C), the Happy-Go-Lucky segment promised to be central to BowTie Cause growth. Happy-Go-Lucky consumers primarily valued convenience in their purchase decisions. As such, BowTie Cause satisfied time utility through its "two for one" offering: Happy-Go-Lucky consumers simultaneously gave treasure to a cause while saving time during the e-commerce ordering process. However, to effectively persuade Happy-Go-Lucky consumers, BowTie Cause needed to appeal to the "feel good" factor involved with their investment of treasure. Happy-Go-Lucky consumers wanted to impact society but did so only after being pulled to the cause by the brand itself. Happy-Go-Lucky consumers did not seek social enterprises but instead depended on the brand to connect them to the cause

---

[31] http://www.conecomm.com/beyond-demographics-1

through tools like social media. Such behavior demonstrated the importance of BowTie Cause's openness to consistent dialogue with consumers about causes and values. Their need for convenience and reactive approach made BowTie Cause a head-vs- heart connection for them.

Old Guard: The Tertiary B2C Psychographic

Finally, a tertiary market included consumers who were traditional bowtie wearers. By combining luxury with cause, these Old Guard consumers stumbled into socially responsible purchases. They conventionally wore bowties – to special occasions rather than everyday – and routinely purchased based on price, quality, and convenience. Amongst old guard consumers, BowTie Cause posed an opportunity for brand switching: one-third of old guard consumers considered adjusting their brand preferences in favor of a brand associated with a cause. Old Guard consumers represented males over the age of 55, and BowTie Cause offered a relevant option for these professionals. Consequently, Old Guard consumers had more professional exposure that required attendance at high-profile events (like galas and auctions) hosted by the causes represented in the BowTie Cause portfolio. Old Guard consumers also had experience with traditional ways of donating and could be persuaded to adjust their donation preferences through an accessory already present in their wardrobes.

Cause Partners

Cause partners received explicit mention in the BowTie Cause mission statement. To effectively understand the stories within the diverse cause sector, BowTie Cause sought to articulate the organizations' missions in its design process. BowTie Cause generated 70% of its sales through organizational buying by cause partners.

To maintain existing wholesale relationships and cultivate new ones, the BowTie Cause team included a Cause Curator. As a business development professional, the Cause Curator reported to Amanda as the CEO and treated each cause organization as an account. The Cause Curator retained records and detailed notes of sales funnel cycles as well as to record all contacts with organizations. Collected data referenced information like email threads, dates of contact, and website pages. The Cause Curator communicated with causes through email, phone calls, Skype, and in-person meetings. Weekly workload allocation ensured the sales funnel matched sales goals projected from previous years' sales ledgers. The Cause Curator created a clear, standardized CRM implementation.

The Cause Curator role was to be the consistent contact with each cause organizations. Using proprietary CRM documentation, the Cause Curator organized relationships as "current" or "prospect." In both current and prospect relationships, the Cause Curator interacted with multiple stakeholders in organizations' buying centers and procurement groups. Users who directly benefited from the missions of the cause partners – cancer patients, veterans, or students – did not typically participate in the wholesale and design process. It was essential that the Cause Curator be knowledgeable and empathetic about the scope of services that could be represented in a bowtie. See Appendix E for excerpts from documentation generated by the Cause Curator.

For causes with existing relationships, the Cause Curator aimed to renew the relationships through production of existing designs or slightly modified and updated designs. For example, the Juvenile Diabetes Research Foundation (JDRF) exemplified the most established relationship within the BowTie Cause portfolio. The JDRF mission was "to find a cure for type 1 diabetes and its complications through the support of research."[32] To support its mission, JDRF collaborated with BowTie Cause to produce three distinct bowtie designs. Health-related organizations in general were the best sector for the BowTie Cause platform. For existing relationships, such as that with JDFR and other health-related organizations, the Cause Curator learned to coordinate buying opportunities with the budget cycle of the cause. Designing three JDFR bowties, for example, demonstrated a "modified rebuy." Such modified rebuys challenged the Cause Curator's abilities to penetrate the existing organizational structure, since new contacts were frequently involved. This selling goal, in turn, reinforced long-term relationships and avoided ad hoc transactions.

The Cause Curator also initiated new prospect leads. Although the Cause Curator sourced prospects from organizational websites and non-profit trade associations, personal referrals proved most effective. Internal referrals to new cause stakeholders working for the same mission but on different projects proved productive; referrals also came directly from Dhani. To support this "new buy" process, the Cause Curator shared the BowTie Cause materials (Appendix A) with prospects to describe the mission, process, values, and other specifications. In total, the branded collateral presented BowTie Cause capabilities as a long-term partner, rather than a transactional vendor.

In particular, local organizations showed the greatest potential as clients of BowTie Cause. Navigating these smaller, lesser-known organizational structures, however, proved a challenge and made an organized Request for Proposal (RFP) process essential. To identify the roles and responsibilities of stakeholders new to BowTie Cause, the Cause Curator was tasked to convert opening communication with prospects into pipeline opportunities. Therefore, understanding of the prospect cause's mission was necessary to demonstrate how BowTie Cause could generate awareness and funds, primary goals for these smaller organizations.

One Signature Communicated Through the Promotional Mix

Social Media

Clear segmentation addressed B2C and B2B opportunities, and therefore the promotional mix simultaneously required messages for ultimate consumers and cause partners. Social media content illustrated both the BowTie Cause mission and partners' missions. BowTie Cause tried to make its online voice relevant to its own brand and to the causes it represented. A content calendar recorded major events, such as National Hunger Awareness Day or World Environment Day, and queued relevant messages though online channels. Such content stimulated dialogue with Ringleaders and Happy-Go- Lucky consumers to view and create online messages. Metrics, including bounce rates, page views, etc., tracked month-to-month trends and set goals. Through a contract with Kooda Media, BowTie Cause measured impact in the digital environment

---

[32] jdrf.org

while keeping focus on generating funds and awareness. See Appendix F for excerpts from social media tracking, and see Appendix G for a sample timeline of social media content.

BowTie Cause took a risk by purposefully downplaying social media. Compared with BowTie Cause competitors, social media presence remained intentionally quiet. BowTie Cause maintained presence on Facebook (with approximately 7000 fans) and Twitter (with approximately 4000 followers). Google Plus, Pinterest, and Tumblr also directed clicks to content via Facebook and Twitter. All social and digital content was internally produced by BowTie Cause (in partnership with Kooda Media). For example, a promotional video about Dhani's involvement consistently appeared via YouTube and Facebook. More recently, Instagram emerged as a medium capable of visually highlighting the design of the bowties and wearers' experiences for nearly 500 followers. BowTie Cause understood it could not altogether avoid social media, rather it strategically attempted to use its own media to balance presence and sidestep noise. The goal was to control its presence in social channels and cohesively represent its brand with appropriate messaging in channels owned by its cause partners.

BowTie Cause strengthened its brand through the effective use of a hashtag: #TiedToACause. All social content - either about specific products or specific cause partners - mapped to this hashtag. Its simple text embodied its mission and encoded a message that stimulated meaningful online dialogue. This hashtag created a connective thread that openly invited new and existing consumers and causes to engage with their values. #TiedToACause became a digital signature and an extension of the signature bowtie.

User Experience (UX)

While the hashtag #TiedToACause was associated with social media interactions, e-commerce and wholesale purchases could not solely depend on social media posts. Social media use could contribute to the consumer experience, but could not be depended upon to initiate cause interest in the endeavor. The BowTie Cause website was the crucial touchpoint to unite the experiences of ultimate consumers and cause partners. After nearly four years of operations, BowTie Cause initiated a website redesign to enhance the user experience (UX). Such redesign was needed to unite aesthetics and function.[33] The redesign led to marketing research about consumer perceptions of the updated features. Per survey data, the most important visual cue within the upgraded website was the word "shop." This indicated that consumers visited bowtiecause.com with the intention to purchase. Additionally, users rated the design as visually pleasing (mean=4.16, on a 5 point Likert scale). Survey respondents reported the website design as "unique and innovative" (mean=3.93) and that website graphics were clear (mean=4.07). Consumers mostly agreed about ease of use (mean=3.91), ability to find pages within the site (mean=3.69), and customized orders (mean=4.0) See Appendix H for findings from survey data including heat maps and qualitative comments. Also, see Appendix I for integration of the website relaunch via social media.

---

[33] http://www.marketingprofs.com/articles/2015/27842/10-user-experience-testing-tools- marketers-need-to-know-about

Google Analytics

Although the proprietary marketing research commissioned by BowTie Cause implied consumers accepted the website's aesthetics and functionality, data from Google Analytics offered a different perspective. In 2015, consumers visited bowtiecause.com from desktop, mobile, and tablet devices equally. Each visit lasted approximately two minutes, so BowTie Cause had a short time frame to attract consumers' attention to its cause and products. Furthermore, the time users spent on the new website decreased by 30 seconds. The website perhaps became easier for consumers to navigate. Yet, consumers may have more quickly lost interest. After clicking through about 4.75 pages, 1 in 2 consumers "bounced" from the site. Additionally, the number of pages clicked slightly decreased since 2014, so returning consumers – knowledgeable of BowTie Cause's message and offering – may be navigating with greater efficiency.

Brand Ambassadors

Data about the user experience encouraged integration of social and digital interactions. The goal of the BowTie Cause promotional plan was to motivate purchase and the wearing of signature bowties. These objectives paralleled the mission to raise funds and generate awareness. With a sound online experience anchored, efforts began to involve personalities in the promotional mix. As a nationally known and popular athlete, Dhani served as the champion for endorsement. Dhani showed how to invest personal treasure with the purpose to "change the world."[34] He made the signature bowtie part of his personal mission. In doing so, he frequently referenced Kunta's story; thus, Kunta too served as a BowTie Cause Ambassador. Dhani's personal attachment to both philanthropy and style personified the ideal BowTie Cause Ambassador.

BowTie Ambassadors became a core medium to enhance BowTie Cause's promotional mix. Ambassadors represented BowTie Cause signature traits and embodied ringleader psychographics. Specifically,

A BowTie Cause Ambassador does not simply make a statement, they are a statement. Their actions, beliefs, and character speak to the things they stand for. A BowTie Ambassador rocks BowTies because of what they represent - not just because they are cool. A BowTie Ambassador is a leader, an influence, a catalyst for conversation and change.[35]

Ken Rosenthal, a Senior Major League Baseball commentator for Fox Sports, regularly showed how to rock a bowtie. Ken embedded the signature vision of BowTie Cause Ambassadors during each television appearance. Given the national popularity of major league baseball, Ken exposed BowTie Cause to fans who might have traditional expectations of how bowties are worn. Ken's primary reason to rock a bowtie remained simple: he wanted to "raise awareness for all the organizations with which BowTie Cause was partnered. Not only did Ken talk about various causes and his bowties during his Fox air time, but he also supported the BowTie Cause brand by driving fans to the site to shop online. Bowtiecause.com devoted a page linked to all bowties Ken wore on air. Ken was an energetic ringleader and an overall sales increase

---

[34] http://bowtiecause.com/the-cause/dhanis-words-mobile/
[35] www.bowtiecause.com

accompanied each of his Fox appearances. The sales boost was not only for the specific tie he wore, but also for additional bowties that consumers discovered on the site related to their signature style and donation preferences. See Appendix J for additional details about Brand Ambassadors.

However, like social media, BowTie Cause understood celebrity endorsements demanded cautious use. Consumer data collected[11] indicated that not all consumers considered celebrity endorsements as a purchase influence. Thirty percent of survey participants reported "likely" or "very likely" to respond to celebrity influence, and 21% reported they were "undecided" about likelihood to be influenced by celebrity endorsement. Further, 25% of survey participants expressed inclination to wear a bowtie when favorite athletes wore bowties. Dhani and Ken clearly activated the signature message as they rocked bowties in athletic settings. Given that nearly 50% of survey participants avoided celebrity endorsement influence, the Brand Ambassador tactic opened BowTie Cause branding to a wider variety of consumers who personified "celebrity" qualities, yet manifested ringleader traits.

Integrated Promotional Mix for Wearers and Causes

The core message of the promotional mix – to change the world by rocking a bowtie – integrated across social media, digital UX, and Brand Ambassadors. The message resonated through business development by the Cause Curator. Yet, due to its twofold segmentation, BowTie Cause diffused across the product life cycle at multiple rates. The purchase decision for ultimate consumers was a short journey to point, click, and rock the bowtie. The organizational buying process to reach the bottom of the funnel occurred far more slowly. The messaging potentially fostered the need for two campaigns to represent two BowTie Cause segments. Yet, a split in the cohesive promotional mix signaled a communication problem for this brand as it strived to establish a cohesive communication strategy for sharing stories, raising awareness and funds for myriad causes.

The Decision Problem

BowTie Cause lacked one cohesive IMC plan to enable cause-related organizations and philanthropic consumers to know and accept its signature bowtie as a visual symbol of support for worthy causes. They had many pieces in place, but as Dhani, Kunta, Amanda and the team met, they realized that they needed to question and reexamine every aspect of their efforts.
Several questions arose for review:

- Is there a clear statement of the position BowTie Cause has within the social entrepreneurship space?
- Is the current website responsive both to consumers and organizations?
- Can SEO be improved?
- Are there specific appeals that should be aimed at each consumer segment?
    - Should the BowTie Cause "Success Pack" be revised?
    - Should social media take a more prevalent role in the IMC mix? If so, in what form?
    - What other channels should be included in the communication plan?

- Should additional high-profile celebrities be sought as Brand Ambassadors? Who would do this and how should prospects be chosen?
- Should the product line be extended to include other accessories, notably those targeted toward women?

It promised to be an interesting meeting. One signature bowtie could be tied in ten steps, and yet they knew that their challenge was to produce a Marketing Plan that could "tie it all together."

Appendix A: BowTie Cause Success Pack

Thank you for your interest in collaborating with BowTie Cause. Our mission is to provide opportunities for socially-conscious organizations to spark conversation, raise awareness and ultimately generate funds. Today, we primarily accomplish this mission through the co-created design of signature BowTies and the engagement inspired by them.

Organizational Representation

Every BowTie comes specially packaged including bow tying instructions and a custom storycard, which incorporates your organization's narrative, logo, website and Twitter handle. the cost structure is outlined below:

Order Amount	100	250	500	1000 or more
Cost Per BowTie	$28.50	$27.50	$26.00	$23.00
Retail Value	$5,700	$14,250	$28,500	$57,000
Benefit to Organization	$2,850	$7,375	$15,500	$34,000

We suggest that each organization sells each BowTie at $57. The difference in the cost of the BowTie to the organization and revenue from retail sales directly benefits the partnering organization.

Collaboration

BowTie Cause will order additional BowTies to be sold on the BowTie Cause website and will take on the cost to fulfill this inventory. BowTie Cause will then donate 25% of the profit from the online sale of each BowTie to the respective organization.

Process

Added Value

- Each organization's story will be included on the BowTie Cause website with a link to the organization's website.
- Social media will be utilized to promote all partnering organizations.
- Each signature design will be entered into the annual BowTie Challenge. The winning BowTie will be worn by Ken Rosenthal at the World Series.

We look forward to collaborating with you!
Please contact info@bowtiecause.org with any questions.
Go to BowTieCause.com to learn more and see some of our incredible partnerships!

Appendix A: BowTie Cause Success Pack (continued)

BOWTIE CAUSE
SUCCESS PACK

BowTie Cause would like to thank you for your business! We are excited that you have selected the BowTie as an avenue for your organization to raise funds and awareness. Getting your powerful message across to as many individuals as possible is of the upmost importance. We are excited to begin the next phase of this collaboration to help your organization raise awareness for your cause by rockin' a BowTie.

This Organization Success Packet is a guide compiled of best practices from over ninety of our partnering organizations. As you work through the details of your event, we are always happy to answer questions you may have. If you have any suggestions as to how we can make this collaboration better, please feel free to share your feedback with your BowTie Cause contact.

BOWTIE CHAMPION

A BowTie Champion is a person (internal or volunteer) who is in charge of overseeing the project and communicating with BowTie Cause as your event approaches. Through past collaborations we have found that having a designated individual, a BowTie Champion, ensures your BowTie gets to customers and supporters in the most successful way. BowTie Cause will address all decision making with your designated decision makers, but the BowTie Champion will be the contact for BowTie Cause to make certain that your signature BowTie is successfully leveraged before, during, and after your event.

EVENT DETAILS

Event Date?...................☐
Emcee?.....................☐
Where is the event being held?
What is the atmosphere/vibe
of the event?..................☐
Pre event press event?
Ticket cost?..................☐
Who is attending?
(demographic)..................☐
Likelihood that attendee will
spend? (auction, table sales)........☐
What is the goal for the
BowTie Inventory? (pre-sale,
event sales)..................☐
Location for BowTie Cause at
the event?..................☐
How many volunteers
dedicated to supporting the
BowTie?....................☐

We would like to know as many details about the event as possible. The more information we have, the more help BowTie Cause can offer in order to make certain all aspects of the event are achieved.

BOWTIE MARKETING

Pre-event publicity material?........☐
How will the BowTie be
presented?..................☐
Mention during the event by
the emcee? (when, how often).......☐

Appendix A: BowTie Cause Success Pack (continued)

BOWTIE CAUSE COMMITMENT

Every collaboration creates its own unique experience; however, we hope to set a standard as to what you can expect from us throughout this process. BowTie Cause will use our available resources to assist in raising awareness for your event.

SOCIAL MEDIA

Two Tweets the week of your event . . . . ☐
One Facebook post the week of your event . . . . ☐
One Facebook post the week after your event (Only if images from the event are provided) . . . . ☐

If Dhani is scheduled to be at your event, we will need the following information.

INFORMATION FOR DHANI

Does Dhani have a speaking role at your event? If so, length of speaking time? . . . . ☐
Topic/talking points? . . . . ☐

BUT WAIT, THERE'S MORE...

After the event we would like to follow-up with your organization to make certain we have captured all pertinent information. This information not only helps us create better collaborations in the future, but it also allows us to fulfill our social engagement responsibilities to your organization.

1 - It is our goal to help your organization achieve it's sales goal for the BowTies; therefore, we are able to help with suggestions on how we can move any remaining inventory if needed.

2 - Please send BowTie Cause a few photos from the event. The photos will be used by BowTie Cause through our social media outlets in order to highlight your event.

3 - If you have any feedback on how we could improve the collaboration we would greatly appreciate it.

WHAT TO DO AFTER

Have we made BowTie Cause aware of the remaining inventory? . . . . ☐
Have we given the pictures of the event to BowTie Cause? . . . . ☐
Have we given our feedback to BowTie Cause about our experience? . . . . ☐

THANK YOU

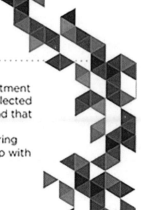

We would like to thank you for your commitment to your cause. We are so happy that you selected BowTie Cause to be a part of your event and that you chose the BowTie to help spread your powerful message. We look forward to hearing your successes and growing our partnership with you in the future.

Appendix B: BowTie Cause Partners

Organization Type	Organization Name	Organization Type	Organization Name	Organization Type	Organization Name	Organization Type	Organization Name
BowTie Cause Partners							
Armed Forces	USO		JDRF		Cancer Support Community		Hunger Network
	Armed Forces Foundation		Leukemia and Lymphoma Society		Autism Speaks		SPCA Cincinnati
Arts	Cincinnati Ballet		Livestrong		Pints for Prostates		Hibiscus Children's Center
	Cincinnati Pops Orchestra		Most Valuable Kids		Lighthouse Youth Services		International Swimming Hall of Fame
	SPIVA Center for the Arts		Cincinnati Zoo		Hope Starts Here	Foundations	Esophogeal Cancer Awareness Center
	Headlands Center for the Arts		Society of St. Vincent de Paul		Children's Tumor Foundation		American Brain Foundation
	Cincinnati Art Museum		Ronald McDonald House Charities		Chiquita Classic		Detroit Tigers Foundation
	Cora Jean's Old School Café		Alzheimer's Association		The Spirit of Construction Foundation		Envision Children
	May Festival		Boys Hope Girls Hope		James Beard Foundation		Lungevity
	Cincinnati Opera		91.7 WVXU		Cancer Family Care		The Jason Motte Foundation
Education	University of Michigan		Kenzie's Closet		Santonio Holmes III & Long Foundation		Life Center
	Cincinnati Country Day School		Maggie's Hope		Elizabeth Glaser Pediatric AIDS Foundation		Mito
	Breakthrough Cincinnati		Ferdinand's Ball		ALBA		Jewish Family Services
	University of Arkansas	Foundations	Pablove Foundation	Foundations	Mission Kids Child Advocacy		Lymphoma Research Foundation
	BTN Live Big		Stand Up To Cancer		Boy Scouts of America		Patrick Dempsey Center
	University of Toledo		Arkansas Commitment		Ulman Cancer Fund		Rock CF Foundation
	ICSJ		ALS Association		Ed Block Courage Award Foundation	Health Related	University of Michigan C.S. Mott Children's Hospital
	Morehouse		Cystic Fibrosis Foundation		Flying Pig Marathon		Arkansas Children's Hospital
	Page Education Foundation		Dress for Success		J. Kyle Braid Leadership Foundation		Scoliosis Research Society
	Syracuse University		Arkansas Prostate Cancer Foundation		National Kidney Foundation		University of Cincinnati Neuroscience Institute
	Nativity School		Village Life Outreach Project		Cooperative for Education		National MS Society
	Mullen		9/11 Memorial		Variety		This Star Won't Go Out
	The Space		Ovarian Cancer Research Fund		Mercantile Library	Specialty	BowTie Foundation
	University of Cincinnati		Easter Seals		The Spirit of Cincinnatus		
	Lupus Foundation of America		American Diabetes Association		SAGA		
	Carnivor		The Charlie Foundation		St. Elizabeth Foundation		
	Wine Down Wednesday		Heroes Foundation		The Salvation Army		
	Marvin Lewis Community Fund		Project Haiti		Transitions		

Appendix C: Survey participants word associations with the word "bowtie"

Appendix D: Comparison of BowTie Cause to Livestrong and (Product)ᴿᵉᵈ

	Livestrong	(Red)	BowTie Cause
Non Profit	Yes	Yes	No
Product Offerings	Multiple	Multiple	Few
# of companies partnered with	Multiple	Multiple	Multiple
Online/In Store	Both	Both	Online only
Celebrity Endorser	Formerly- Lance Armstrong	Bono & U2	Dhani Jones
Celebrity's Image	Negative	Positive	Positive
Cause(s) they support	Improving the lives of those with cancer	Funding HIV/AIDS programs in Africa	A wide variety of organizations from health to education to the armed forces

Appendix E: Excerpts from Cause Curator Documentation

Week of:

	Actual	Goal	
Emails	64	50	128%
Calls	5	20	25%
Meetings	6	5	120%
Follow-Ups	25	20	125%
Portfolio Contacts	5	2	250%
Networking Events	1	0.5	200%

Appendix F: Excerpts from Online Tracking Records

	Previous Week	Current Week Fans	Increase #	entions / RTS (T	Total Reach	#of Posts	gh Engagement Post(	Reach / Likes
Facebook	5713	5718	5		1.4K	7	6.17 Lupus BowTie announcement - Ken	10 Total Likes, Comments, Shares
							6.16 Quotes + picture of Ken wearing Pints for Prostate BowTie	16 Likes, comments, shares
Twitter	3357	3379	22	36 RTS | 45 Favs | 62	1.047 Impressions	29	6.17 Lupus BowTie for K Rosenthal	12 RTS | 473.4K impressions
Instagram	145	150	5			6	Picture of Mannequin w/ BTC BowTies covering it	22 Likes | 1 comme
Google+	9		-9		1589 views	2 n/a		n/a
Pinterest	4	4	0					
Blog	Transformations - Kunta Littlejohn							
Promotion?	Review BowTie purchase and receive 10% off	Doggie BowTies on Instagram						
Weekly Highlig	Twitter	Lupus BowTie announcement circulated well						

Appendix G: Example of a Social Media Content Calendar

Sunday	Monday	Tuesday	Wednesday	Thursday	Friday	Saturday
1 Galloping Pig Promo	2 Quote of the Day (Facebook/Google+)	3 Ken Rosenthal/Bowtie Promo (Facebook/Twitter) ADA	4 #BowTie Selfie Submission (Twitter/Instagram)	5 Blog Post	6 Ken Rosenthal/Bowtie Promo (Facebook/Twitter) ADA	7 Ken Rosenthal/Bowtie Promo (Facebook/Twitter) ADA
8 Galloping Pig Promo	9 Quote of the Day (Facebook/Google+)	10 Ken Rosenthal/Bowtie Promo (Facebook/Twitter) J Kyle Braid	11 #BowTie Selfie Submission (Twitter/Instagram)	12 Blog Post	13 Ken Rosenthal/Bowtie Promo (Facebook/Twitter) J Kyle Braid	14 Ken Rosenthal/Bowtie Promo (Facebook/Twitter) J Kyle Braid
15 Galloping Pig Promo	16 Quote of the Day (Facebook/Google+)	17 Ken Rosenthal/Bowtie Promo (Facebook/Twitter) Lupus	18 #BowTie Selfie Submission (Twitter/Instagram)	19 Blog Post	20 Ken Rosenthal/Bowtie Promo (Facebook/Twitter) Lupus	21 Ken Rosenthal/Bowtie Promo (Facebook/Twitter) Lupus
22 Galloping Pig Promo Father's Day	23 Quote of the Day (Facebook/Google+)	24 Ken Rosenthal/Bowtie Promo (Facebook/Twitter) Alzheimer's	25 #BowTie Selfie Submission (Twitter/Instagram)	26 Blog Post	27 Ken Rosenthal/Bowtie Promo (Facebook/Twitter) Alzheimer's	28 Ken Rosenthal/Bowtie Promo (Facebook/Twitter) Alzheimer's
29 Galloping Pig Promo National HIV Testing Day –EGPAF tie-in	30 Quote of the Day (Facebook/Google+)					

Appendix H: Survey Data about BowTie Cause UX Website Relaunch

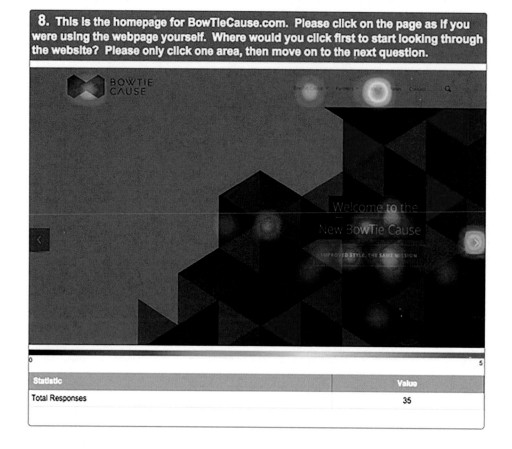

Statistic	Value
Total Responses	35

Appendix H: Survey Data about BowTie Cause UX Website Relaunch (continued)

Statistic	This retailer's advertised items are in stock.	This retailer provides information on how much an item costs with the shipping costs included.	This retailer provides accurate information about when orders will be received.	This retailer's website has a running total of purchases as you add more items to the cart.
Mean	3.96	4.09	3.91	4.07
Variance	0.63	0.45	0.54	0.43
Standard Deviation	0.80	0.67	0.73	0.65
Total Responses	45	45	45	45

Statistic	It is easy to get anywhere on this retailer's website.	I don't get lost on this retailer's website.	This website allows you to find a page previously viewed.	This website allows you to go back if you make a mistake or want to change your order.
Mean	3.91	3.84	3.69	4.00
Variance	0.54	0.73	0.63	0.68
Standard Deviation	0.73	0.85	0.79	0.83
Total Responses	45	45	45	45

Statistic	The website does not crash	The website pages load quickly	The retailer provides numerous payment options
Mean	4.20	4.18	4.14
Variance	0.68	0.76	0.49
Standard Deviation	0.82	0.87	0.70
Total Responses	44	44	44

Statistic	Overall, I am very happy with the service experience.	In general, I am very pleased with the quality of the service this retailer provided.	I feel pretty negative about this retailer.
Mean	4.14	4.30	2.34
Variance	0.59	0.49	2.00
Standard Deviation	0.77	0.70	1.41
Total Responses	44	44	44

Appendix H: Survey Data about BowTie Cause UX Website Relaunch (continued)

Statistic	The retail site is visually pleasing.	The website design is unique and innovative.	The graphics and pictures on the website are clear and crisp.	The text on the website is easy to read.	I do not have to scroll from side to side in order to see the whole page.
Mean	4.16	3.93	4.07	4.14	4.09
Variance	0.93	0.95	0.76	0.63	1.20
Standard Deviation	0.96	0.97	0.87	0.80	1.10
Total Responses	44	44	44	44	44

Qualitative data re: survey question, "What made you happy with your customer service experience?

Text Response
Professionalism, simplicity
Well, I purchased a stand up to cancer bow tie last year for my boss. I think that there were a few glitches in your system because I wasn't sure when it was getting shipped. I had to call a couple of times. I really wanted him to get the tie too...he wears a tie everyday but only owns two bow ties. We did have to "youtube" how to tie the bow tie...it was a bit confusing...but, we got it. If you have any coupons, I could use one for a future purchase. Thank you very much, Sincerely, Maureen L. Wright   gmail: littlemo78@gmail.com
How easy it was to navigate throughout the website!
The website is visually pleasing and easy to navigate
Easy to use website
The website navigation and the experience of buying clothing and supporting a cause.
EVERYTHING
Everything
Very easy and straightforward process. Easy to find what you want and easily purchase it.
The website looks clean cut and professional. The presentation is very luring!
I liked the fluidity
I enjoyed the layout of the website and how visually appealing it was. Since I've never owned a bow-tie, it made it easy to figure out which one I wanted, especially the search bar and items related to whatever else I was purchasing. I would recommend this website to my friends and would come back on it to shop for some fancy bow-ties! :)
Everything is quick and responsive. Love the color pallet chosen for the website.
Autism speaks bow ties!
The accessibility and organization of the site
Everything was made very easy, informative, and understandable to the consumer.
the colors on the website were really cool. It kept my attention and caught my interest.
I was tied to the cause of the bow tie i purchased. I just wish it wasnt as expensive or more money went to the cause.
I have purchsed several ties as gits. I have never had any problems and service & delivery are excellent. Also, my son will only wear Dhani's Bowties for a cause.
Well put together website, good products, and supports something worthwhile.
the website looks really colorful and appealing, and is also easy to navigate
The overall format of the page was something different and that something caught my attention
Love the many options of ties offered, and love that I can support so many different philanthropic organizations when purchasing these items.
The items are of high quality and are delivered promptly. Also, they support a cause that I believe to be important.

Appendix I: Social Media Presence Before and After Website Relaunch

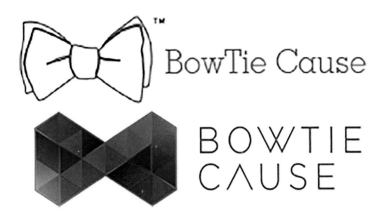

Logo

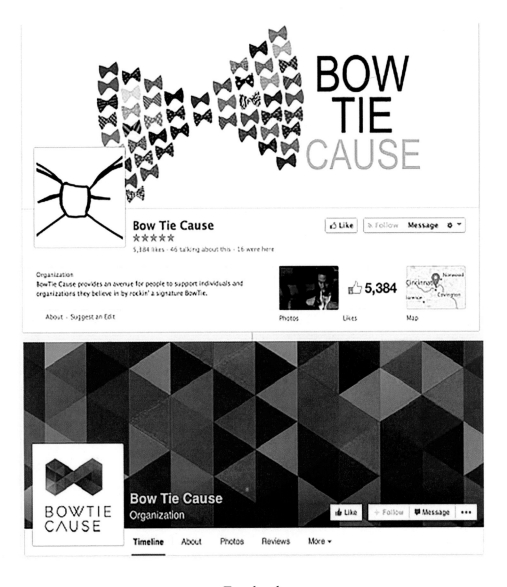

Facebook

Appendix I: Social Media Presence Before and After Website Relaunch (continued)

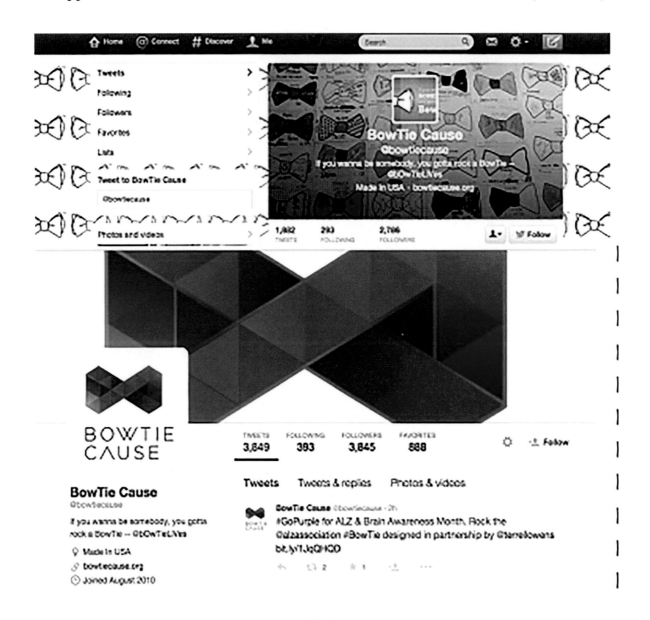

Twitter

Appendix J: BowTie Cause Ambassador Program

BowTies w/ Discount

Fit For:

- Local personalities / media
- Moderate social media following
- Example = News Anchors

BowTies Given @ cost. wholesale $44

Promotional Expectations

- Instagram #BowTieSelfie wearing BTC BowTie using Hashtag (#TiedToACause). Tag @BowTieCause.
- Twitter #BowTieSelfie wear BTC BowTie using Hashtag (#TiedToACause). Tag @BowTieCause.
- Twitter message about the reciept of BTC BowTies using Hashtag (#TiedToACause). Tag @BowTieCause.
- Facebook image post of BTC BowTie using Hashtag (#TiedToACause).

BowTies + Capital

Fit For:

- Highly visible personalities
- Social media following of 500,000+ (Twitter)
- Example = Justin Timberlake

BowTies Gratis + Capital

Promotional Expectations

- Instagram #BowTieSelfie wearing BTC BowTie using Hashtag (#TiedToACause). Tag @BowTieCause.
- Twitter #BowTieSelfie wear BTC BowTie using Hashtag (#TiedToACause). Tag @BowTieCause.
- Multiple Twitter messages about the reciept of BTC BowTies using Hashtag (#TiedToACause). Tag @BowTieCause.
- Facebook image post of BTC BowTie using Hashtag (#TiedToACause).
- Wear BTC BowTie to an event, appearance and provide image to BTC.

BowTies Gratis

Fit For:

- Well known, influential personalities
- High social media following
- Example = Ken Rosenthal

BowTies Gratis

Promotional Expectations

- Instagram #BowTieSelfie wearing BTC BowTie using Hashtag (#TiedToACause). Tag @BowTieCause.
- Twitter #BowTieSelfie wear BTC BowTie using Hashtag (#TiedToACause). Tag @BowTieCause.
- Multiple Twitter messages about the reciept of BTC BowTies using Hashtag (#TiedToACause). Tag @BowTieCause.
- Facebook image post of BTC BowTie using Hashtag (#TiedToACause).
- Wear BTC BowTie to an event, appearance and provide image to BTC.

How a Burger King Franchise Can Succeed in a Competitive Fast Food Industry

By

Bela Florenthal, William Paterson
University Manar Awad, M.Sc. Student, Birzeit University
Giuliana Campanelli Andreopoulos, William Paterson University
John Malindretos, William Paterson University

Abstract

In this study, we consider the owners of two Burger King franchise establishments that have been struggling financially over the past three years. The owners are looking to grow the revenue of their two struggling locations and remain competitive in the changing fast food landscape. They realize that their competitors are not only other fast food brands but also the growing number of fast casual chains, ethnic cuisine restaurants, and convenience store establishments. They notice that their target customers, Millennials, have become more health conscious and exhibit an increasing desire to diversify their palates. As a result, the franchisees struggle to meet Millennials' expectations in terms of their menu items. In addition, they do not keep up with innovative technology, such as mobile apps for ordering and delivering fast food items, that has been gradually adopted by competitors. Thus, the owners of the two Burger King locations are faced with two key challenges: (a) how to stay competitive and (b) how to be more attractive to Millennials.

The Fast Food Industry

Industry Trends

The fast food industry, including limited-service (order and pay before eating) and quick-service (minimal table service) restaurants, was a $570 billion industry worldwide in 2017, with $245 billion in the United States and showing an annual growth rate of 3.2% between 2012 and 2017 in the United States. The industry has long experienced rapid growth. The quick-service restaurant industry alone has seen an approximate 28% increase in revenue, from $159.2 billion in 2002 to $203.2 billion in 2015.

The fast food industry is dominated by three companies: McDonald's, Starbucks, and Yum! Brands, Inc. (including KFC, Pizza Hut, and Taco Bell), with the Top Five brands accounting for over 40% of the market share in the United States. McDonald's had the largest market share in 2015, at 17%, and Yum! Brands' 2015 market share was around 10.8%. McDonald's, Subway, KFC, and Pizza Hut were ranked among the Top Five most valuable brands worldwide in 2016. McDonald's brand value far exceeded that of its competitors, at about $88.65 billion in 2016 (Starbucks came in second, with a brand value of about $43.56 billion).

Fast food has long been the most favored choice of food for US consumers, mainly for its convenience, affordability, and speed. It appeals to those who are looking for a satisfying meal on a budget, including college students and families, with 34% of children eating fast food every day. These restaurant chains are desirable, as they provide a recognizable experience no matter what location a consumer visits. In 2016, 80% of consumers ate at a fast food restaurant at least once per month, and 44% at least once per week. Customer retention is fairly easy for fast food restaurants, and over 90% of fast food consumers indicate that they would likely sign up for a loyalty program if their favorite fast food restaurants provided one. The industry thrived even during harsh economic conditions, as fast food chains were able to capitalize on the 2008 recession by offering low-priced menu deals.

However, as consumer confidence and spending have increased over the past five years, the industry has struggled to keep up with changing preferences and the demand for healthier food options. Fast food chains compete with the food industry in general, whether with higher quality restaurants or lower end food establishments. Donut and bagel shops as well as coffee chains can become strong competitors if they offer fast food options.

The Burger Industry

Hamburger fast food restaurants largely dominate the market, accounting for 30% of US quick-service restaurant sales in 2016. Pizza parlors are the second largest segment, with 15% of the market share, followed by sandwich shops at 12%, chicken restaurants at 8%, and Mexican restaurants as the fifth major segment, with 7% of the market share. The hamburger is preferred mainly for its portability and customizability, with 57% of consumers eating hamburgers on a weekly basis. Nevertheless, hamburger sales growth has slowed in recent years, and industry watchers speculate that this growth has peaked, as U.S. consumers prefer more exotic cuisines. With the decline in sales and changing customer demands, large hamburger chains have refranchised. The most franchised chain is Burger King, which now owns only 1% of its US locations. By the end of 2018, McDonald's planned to have 90% of its locations worldwide owned by franchisees. The refranchising strategy benefits the parent companies' bottom line. With the burden of cost now transferred to franchisees, the parent companies have very low overhead costs and no direct costs, all while continuing to raise capital and pay off debt.

The top leaders in the burger industry are McDonald's, Wendy's, and Burger King. McDonald's has the leading position in the industry, having generated $35.8 billion in sales in 2015 as a result of operating 14,248 locations in the US (more than Burger King and Wendy's combined) and selling 75 hamburgers per second. It is no wonder that McDonald's is the largest fast food restaurant in the US and the largest restaurant company worldwide in terms of both generated revenue and customers served. Despite having the highest market share of the global fast food industry, however, the company has been losing market share to Wendy's and Burger King (down from 18.6% in 2014 to 12.8% in 2016). In 2011, Wendy's beat Burger King as the second largest burger giant in the United States, with annual sales of $8.5 billion, compared to Burger King's annual sales of $8.4 billion for that year. Wendy's is increasingly becoming a threat to McDonald's, as it has shifted its focus to improving its value menu, offering more low-priced options.

The main concern for the burger industry, and fast food in general, is that US consumers are becoming more health conscious. This would not be such a major threat if it were not for the ever-growing supply of cheaper healthy food. Because consumers have a wide variety of fast food options from which to choose, they also have more power to influence brands. Their preferences for healthier menu options force the fast food industry to undergo a transition by offering more healthy choices. Because many fast food chains have an unshakably bad reputation for being unhealthy they have decided to more aggressively emphasize low prices.

Competing Fast Food Options

Competing fast food industry products include pizza, pasta, sandwiches, and chicken as well as Mexican and Asian food. In 2017, the pizza industry had $45 billion in revenue in the United States, and had experienced an annual growth rate of 1.9% between 2011 and 2016. The key players in the pizza industry are Pizza Hut Inc., Domino's Pizza, Little Caesar's, and Papa John's International Inc. These top companies comprise 39.7% of the total industry revenue. The majority of the remaining pizza restaurants, 54.3%, are locally focused, independently owned stores. Industry growth had been rising slowly over the past five years since the recovery from the recession. However, as the economy improved, sustained growth was expected for the industry over the next five years.

A second major competitor to the burger industry is sandwich and sub store franchises, with $21 billion in industry revenue at the end of 2016. Jimmy John's and Subway dominated the market share. Despite the slow economic recovery, the industry had excelled in the past five years because sandwich shops could easily adapt to healthy food demands and offer highly desirable products at low prices. It's easy for consumers to switch from a heavy, unhealthy hamburger to a light, yet filling, turkey or chicken sandwich. The annual growth for 2011 to 2016 was a steady 2.8%. Strong revenue growth was expected to continue in the next three years.

Mexican and Asian foods have become increasingly popular in the fast food industry. Mexican restaurants were a $38 billion industry at the end of 2016; this segment rose quickly, with an annual growth rate of 3% between 2011 and 2016. Chipotle and Taco Bell, companies with the largest market share, have driven the rise in the Mexican restaurant industry. Industry revenue and the number of establishments were expected to continue growing in the next three years. This expansion and related demand can be attributed to increased immigration and increased acceptance of ethnic cuisine. For example, there has been an increase in demand for Tex-Mex, which is a fusion of American and Mexican cuisine. Statistics show that in 2016, three of the 20 leading food item trends on fast food menus included ethnic cuisine options.

In regard to such ethnic cuisines, Asian cuisine also has grown in popularity. Asian restaurants are the fastest growing fast food category worldwide. Global sales of Asian fast food restaurants increased nearly 500% between 1999 and 2015, with a 135% increase in the United States. A survey conducted by the National Restaurant Association (NRA) found that in 2015, 36% of U.S. consumers reported eating Chinese food at least once per month, and 42% were eating it a few times per year. This trend continued into 2017 as a Statista survey found that ethnic-inspired breakfast items were seen as the leading trend in breakfast/brunch restaurant menus by 68% of respondents, and 45% of respondents endorsed traditional ethnic breakfast items.

Consumers' increasing desire to diversify their palates has helped micro cuisine franchises with "regionalized" menu options, such as Hawaiian food in California, to gain popularity in recent years. This interest in ethnic cuisine has been cultivated by Generation Z, those born in the early 2000s. Consumers appear to be moving further away from the past "one-Great-American-Meal-fits-all" mentality and increasingly preferring ethnic cuisine. The results of a National Restaurant Association survey show that 80% of US consumers eat at least one ethnic meal per month, and 17% eat ethnic cuisine at least seven times per month. This has caused ethnic food to become a regular part of most American diets, leading to an ever-growing demand for micro cuisine.

There are also notable substitutes in the industry that, despite having low market share, have high growth rates and, are increasingly competitors in the fast food industry. These include street vendors, most notably food trucks, and sushi restaurants. Street vendors were a $2 billion industry in 2016 and had an annual growth rate of 3.7% between 2011 and 2016. Demand for street vendors is increasing because they offer a large variety of foods at even lower prices than do fast food chains. Statistics show that in 2016, street food/food trucks were the 20th hottest food option in the United States. Despite the fact that food trucks are generating revenue of only $870 million per year, the industry had substantial annual growth, 7.9%, between 2011 and 2016. Food trucks are highly desirable for their low-priced, unique, gourmet cuisine. Their revenue expansion outperformed that of broader food-service sectors by more than double, and this trend was predicted to continue during the next three years. Sushi restaurants also comprise a $2 billion industry. Although the annual growth of sushi restaurants is not as impressive as that of food trucks, at 3.3% between 2011 and 2016, revenue is expected to rise as operating conditions are forecasted to improve. Like the Tex-Mex industry, sushi restaurants gained popularity with the introduction of American-influenced versions of sushi, such as the California roll. Sushi has now become part of the mainstream food service, providing both an ethnic and a healthy meal choice.

Fast Casual Competitors

Fast casual restaurants, like fast food chains, do not offer full table service and are considered a quick-service option; however, they pride themselves on offering higher quality food than do fast food chains. The most notable examples of fast casual food include Chipotle, Panera Bread, Jimmy John's, Panda Express, Five Guys, and Chick-fil-A. Despite fast casual being the smallest segment in the restaurant industry, accounting for only 7.7% of total market share, it is growing rapidly and gaining market share, mainly from fast food restaurants. Its growth far exceeds that of the full- and limited-service foodservice segments. Between 2014 and 2015 alone, fast casual restaurants had a 10.4% ($33.4 billion) growth in revenue. The segment's sales growth rate almost doubled that of any other dining segment. Panera Bread had the largest 2015 sales, with $4.8 billion; Chipotle was second, at $4.4 billion, and Panda Express was third, with $2.6 billion.

Most fast casual restaurant chains are relatively new but are continuing to expand throughout the country at a rapid rate. For example, after its first day of trading on January 30, 2015, Shake Shack's stock grew 123%, increasing from $700 million to a market cap worth $1.5 billion in February 2015. Currently, there are over 11,000 stores among the Top Eight fast casual chains in the United States and a total of over 21,000 fast casual establishments. Out of the Top Ten fastest growing restaurant chains in 2015, seven were fast casual. Jersey Mike's Subs, which opened 800 new locations in the past three years and had annual sales growth of $402 to $675 million from 2013 to 2015, was at number one. Chipotle, which opened 229 new restaurants in 2015, was the second fastest growing chain. The fast casual industry continues to grow as fast food giants downsize. McDonald's had closed hundreds of stores in the past two years, and Burger King had been steadily closing stores for the past five years. Burger King's worldwide revenue dropped dramatically in recent years, most notably in 2013, when it dropped to $1.15 billion from $1.97 billion in 2012. It fell further in 2014 ($1.06 billion) and rose slightly in 2015 ($1.1 billion).

Fast casual options better meet consumer preferences than do fast food chains, as they are more desirable due to their higher quality and healthier variety of items. They also provide more dynamic menus, catering to the consumers' evolving tastes, and a more upscale atmosphere while still providing food quickly on site. These factors appear to make up for the slightly more expensive food and slower service. The average receipt price at a fast casual establishment can be up to 40% higher than that of fast food restaurants, yet fast casual establishments are still preferred over fast food restaurants. This can be explained by consumers' preference for healthier food options, for which there is an inelastic demand; i.e., they are not sensitive to changes in price or income. Foods labeled as fresh, organic, or local will always draw consumers, no matter the cost. Statistics show that, in 2016, 10 out of the 20 leading food item options on menus were healthier, fast casual options.

Competitive Convenience Stores

Convenience stores were a $204 billion industry in 2017, with 7-Eleven having the largest market share. The industry roughly doubled in size over the previous three decades, with annual growth slowing down to less than 1% between 2012 and 2017. Nevertheless, convenience stores remain an important choice of fast food for many consumers, particularly Millennials. In the past five years more work hours had reduced leisure time, causing full- time employed Americans to search for quicker (time-saving) food options that were still healthy. Further, convenience stores are perceived by consumers to have fresher and healthier options than do fast food chains, which allows them to compete with fast casual restaurants. These factors have the potential to make convenience stores more appealing than fast food and fast casual restaurants. The greater variety of food and beverage options attracts a more diverse consumer base, cutting into fast food and fast casual chains' sales. Of convenience store customers, 26% reported that they would have spent their purchase on fast food if they had not bought from the convenience store. Like fast food establishments, these stores provide convenience and inexpensive food but at higher quality than some fast food places, with more customizability, and at much lower prices. In response to the increased demand for convenience store foodservices, the industry operators have opened more stores and expanded into new markets, which resulted in increased sales. The number of convenience stores increased 28.7% between 2000 and 2015, and in-store foodservice had $31.2 billion in sales in 2014.

In addition, the decline in gas sales has led operators to look into convenience store foodservices to increase revenue. Storeowners have found that offering more foodservice options as in-store products is more profitable than gasoline sales. In 2015, convenience stores in gas stations accounted for 20.8% of in-store sales and 33.7% of gross profit. Gas station foodservices have become increasingly popular with Millennials and Generation Z, who do not have a negative perception of buying food at a gas station, as do older generations.

Building a Competitive Advantage

The fast food industry is highly competitive, and competition only seems to be increasing with the newfound popularity of fast casual restaurants and convenience stores in recent years. The fast food industry will lag behind, however, if restaurants do not evolve to match fast casual offerings. Fast casual outlet sales increased 10.5% in 2014, whereas fast food chain sales increased only 6.1% during the same year. It is becoming increasingly difficult for burger industry giants to be a consumer's first choice, even though they still take up most of the market share. Both McDonald's and Burger King have raced to diversify their menu options to keep up with competitors. Both chains have added a spicy hamburger option to compete with Chipotle; Burger King capitalized on the burrito and introduced a "Whopperrito." Nevertheless, this did not offset Burger King's decline in the year it was introduced. McDonald's took a different route, taking advantage of its already existing food options and expanded its menu according to consumer demand to remain competitive. For instance, it started to offer an all- day breakfast menu in October 2015. This strategy proved to be successful, as McDonald's saw an increase of 0.9% in store sales in that same quarter.

Fast food chains also have attempted to compete with up-and-coming fast casual operators by including healthier options on their menus. In addition to offering vegetables as a main course, they are using fresher ingredients with fewer additives. Nevertheless, it is difficult for consumers to associate fast food with freshness when looking for a healthy meal. For example, McDonald's salads accounted for only 2–3% of sales in 2013, as opposed to hamburgers and hash browns, which accounted for 13–14%. Burger King also failed in their attempt to provide healthier options, discontinuing their lower-calorie "Satisfries" less than a year after introducing them.

The best strategy for fast food restaurants to build their competitive advantage appears to be to incorporate new trends. Major chains will fight for public attention by quickly responding to any new successful trend. Burger King introduced the Mac 'n' Cheetos after Taco Bell had great success with its Doritos Locos taco. Customizability also has become a key preference of consumers. Research shows that 61% of consumers prefer to have customizable toppings on their sandwiches, and 43% prefer to build their own burger, options long offered in fast casual restaurants. Five Guys offers more than 250,000 ways to order a hamburger. To keep up with the competition, fast food restaurants began looking into customized burgers. McDonald's introduced a more upscale dining experience with "Create Your Taste" in 2014. In addition, fast casual chains, such as Chipotle, are trying to capitalize on hamburger demand. The company opened a new branch,

Tasty Made, in 2016, specializing in burgers and fries. The restaurant reported strong sales and favorable reviews.

Competition in the burger industry intensified in 2015. Top competitors began announcing price promotions and new menu items. All three major players took part: Wendy's introduced the "4-for-$4"; McDonald's, the "McPick 2-for-$2; and Burger King offered two spicy menu items. Burger King's introduction of the Big King sandwich put it in direct competition with McDonald's' Big Mac. Burger King also introduced a $1 BBQ rib in response to McDonald's bringing back the McRib. Unfortunately, in an attempt to be more competitive in the fast food industry and, specifically, to compete with fast casual restaurants, fast food chains have slowed down service through increased drive-through wait time. The new options interfered with the already optimized quick service of burger and fries. McDonald's even acknowledged the problems caused by its overcrowded menu.

Millennials as a Target Market of the Fast Food Industry

Millennials are changing the restaurant game, affecting greatly the fast food and fast casual industries, especially as these consumers move into their prime spending years. These 20- and 30-something consumers have a more health-conscious and ethnically diverse palate than do their parents and grandparents. These newfound consumption habits make fast casual restaurants a more attractive option. As noted, fast food chains made multiple failed attempts at healthier menu offerings, including McDonald's creative salad, Wendy's Frescata (healthy sandwich), and Pizza Hut's fresh spinach option, to name a few. Fast food chains are overcrowding their menus and decreasing efficiency with few or no results when it comes to healthy menu items. Fast casual restaurants, however, from the beginning have advertised themselves as healthier, fresher food options and do not have a negative image to repair, as do fast food chains.

Food Consumption

Millennials eat out much more often than do previous generations, making them a prime target of most foodservice segments. Of Millennials, 53% eat out at least once per week and comprise 51% of fast casual consumers. In 2006, fast casual accounted for only 3.1% of Millennials' food and beverage consumption, but this figure almost doubled, to 6.1%, in 2014 and continues to grow. Technomic.com reported that, between 2011 and 2014, there was a 12.9% decrease in monthly visits to McDonald's from consumers aged 19 to 21. During the same period, fast casual monthly visits increased by 2.3% for the same age group, and the monthly visits of consumers aged 22 to 27 to fast casual restaurants increased by 5.2%. It is clear that fast food consumption is largely decreasing due to the rise of fast casual restaurants.

Fast casual food is not the only threat to fast food operators. Millennials reportedly prefer convenience stores at twice the rate as fast casual restaurants. A marketing research group, NPD, reported that in 2006, convenience stores accounted for 7.7% of Millennials' food and beverage, increasing to 11.1% in 2014. Further, with the nearly half of Millennials aged 18 to 37 who eat ethnic cuisine four times per month, fast food establishments are losing business and are scrambling to attract Millennials. Even the largest fast food chain worldwide, McDonald's, does not rank among the Top Ten restaurant chains preferred by Millennials.

This generation's consumption habits took a toll on fast food sales, as seen in the final quarter of 2014, when McDonald's reported a 21% decrease in net income.

With these figures in mind, it is no wonder that those in the quick- and limited-foodservice industry aim to capitalize on marketing strategies that will attract Millennials, specifically targeting health-conscious Millennials and college students. Sheetz and 7-Eleven expanded their menu options to include nutritionally balanced salads, wraps, and sandwiches. In addition, McDonald's targeted their McWrap sandwiches to attract consumers in their mid-teens to mid-thirties.

Purchases via Digital and Mobile Technology

Technology has become a key aspect of daily life, and companies must keep up with the ever-growing technological advances and consumer dependence on technology or lag behind their competitors. The fast food industry is no exception. In recent years, fast food chains have largely invested in mobile apps for customer purchases. Apps are an easy and convenient way to reach a much larger customer base, as, in 2017, 77% of Americans owned a smartphone (compared to 35% in 2011), and in the prior year, 78% owned a laptop. By 2020, over 10% of quick-service restaurant orders are expected to be placed via smartphone. At this rate, with the help of mobile ordering, the quick-service restaurant industry will realize revenues of $38 billion, with a five-year compound annual growth rate of 57%. The increased convenience, easier payment method, and faster fast food mean that mobile apps can significantly increase store sales of any fast food chain.

Mobile apps cater easily to individual consumer demand. Customers can take their time browsing menu options and track a step-by-step process of their transaction. For in-store pick-ups, apps make for much quicker service. Customers simply purchase food ahead of time, using the app, and pick up their order without waiting in line. Taco Bell has seen 20% higher average-per-order sale from the use of this innovation. Taco Bell is part of Yum! Brands Inc.'s "easy beats better" strategy, in which the company is focusing more on convenience than on quality. This proved to be highly successful for Taco Bell, and the chain saw a 30% higher average-per-order value from mobile purchases compared to in-store. Taco Bell has one of the most convenient mobile apps in the industry, with 46% of delivery orders' coming from digital channels. Pizza Hut is also part of Yum! Brand's mission of convenience. It derives 46% of its sales from digital channels and saw an 18% increase in spending on the average pizza order in 2015.

Pizza parlors have distinguished themselves with continually advancing technology seen in their more sophisticated web ordering system. Approximately half of Domino's and Papa John's sales are made through digital channels. Domino's has become a leading innovator in mobile ordering systems. In April 2016, the chain debuted its "no click" ordering app, which allows the user to order a pizza simply by launching the app. Papa John's has seen a steady 5% annual increase in orders made through digital channels, from 40% in the first quarter of 2013 to 55% in the first quarter of 2016.

Almost all of the giant fast food chains have created online and mobile platforms for customers to place purchases. Starbucks was one of the first fast foodservice chains to see great success in digital purchases, incorporating mobile sales in 2010. Of Starbucks' orders, 24% were made using the mobile app in the first quarter of 2016 (compared to 21% in 2015). Other technological innovations include kiosk orders (self-ordering system) and digital menu boards in the store and for drive-thru. The boards can emphasize promotions and high-profit offers by rotating menu options. This way, more menu items can be communicated to the customer. They also speed up orders, increasing sales. These strategies boost operational efficiency and increase order frequency and customer retention, which, in turn, increase profit margins.

Burger King Operation and Franchisees R. & K. J.'s Background

Burger King remains a force in the burger industry; however, it has been struggling in recent years, most notably when it lost its position as the second largest burger chain in the United States in 2011. The company's revenue began to slowly decline in 2009, and it saw a massive decrease in 2013, with revenues of $1.15 billion, down from $1.97 billion in 2012. The company's rigorous refranchising strategy in recent years proved effective, however, as it resulted in a $2.8 billion increase in revenue between 2014 and 2015 (compared to a $52 million increase between 2013 and 2014 after a reported loss of $0.82 billion between 2012 and 2013). Now, almost 90% of Burger King establishments are franchisee owned, allowing Burger King to focus on building its image and menu to better meet consumer demand. In 2003, fast food chains began to focus their marketing strategy on developing new products rather than on price promotion, and Burger King was no exception. This can still be seen today, as its menu has become more competitive in many aspects, offering healthier and more ethnic- inspired food options. Although Burger King does take advantage of social media and digital marketing, as its competitors do, their competitors make better use of technology. The little technological innovation that Burger King uses, such as online ordering and a mobile app, is common practice among its competitors. The company permits its franchisees to use these methods of technology to reach new consumers. To ensure consistency among its various locations, however, Burger King does not allow much flexibility when it comes to brand messaging and store image.

Franchising gives small business owners a unique opportunity to enter a multibillion-dollar industry with a pre- established, loyal customer base. Burger King offers its franchisees three methods of ownership: individually/owner-operated, entity, and corporate. The franchise agreement sets forth specific standards, procedures, restrictions, and specifications by which the franchisee must abide. Burger King specifies everything from required products to be sold, offered menu items, and food preparation methods to customer service and delivery (if authorized). This provides franchisees with Burger King's successfully proven products and methods. Franchisees also receive ongoing support from the franchisor, with some offering financing opportunities. For example, Burger King offers "next generation kitchen equipment" and remodeling agreements.

However, there are many limitations and difficulties that come with being a franchisee. To start, there is a large initial franchise fee of $50,000 for a 20-year agreement under Burger King. Then, the franchisee must account for location costs, and acquiring and improving the desired real estate could cost over $2 million. There are also royalty fees; Burger King's monthly charges are 4.5% of gross sales. Notably, food costs are problematic for franchisees. To ensure consistency across locations, the franchisor requires all raw materials be purchased from the same supplier. The franchisor has a special relationship with the supplier, earning rebates on franchisee orders, which means franchisees must pay higher costs, 5–10% above prevailing market value. The franchisor may even cause greater competition by attempting to fit as many locations in an area as possible. Franchising is a very restricted operation. Those who want to improve their stores products and services or décor and employee uniforms would be violating their agreement, and any minor violation could have large consequences. Under Burger King, franchisees who do not finish remodeling on time are charged late payments and increased royalty fees until completion.

The R. & K. J. franchise operates several Burger King establishments. Figure 1 (see Appendix A) shows the business structure of an R. & K. J. franchise, which indicates that this Burger King franchise has two owners. One of them, R. J., is the managing owner. A vice-president oversees the operations, maintenance, and financials of the owned stores. A district manager is the liaison between the vice-president and the regional managers who directly oversee the day-to-day operation of the stores in their region. Each store has a store manager who reports to the regional manager. A financial controller, who reports to the vice-president, is in charge of financial operations and oversees the payroll and office management.

The R. & K. J. franchise has seen great success with stores located in urban areas; however, it is struggling financially with stores located in suburban areas. Two establishments in particular, Store A and Store B, are a major concern. It has become increasingly difficult to attract new customers and to operate at a comfortable profit. The franchisee has yet to specifically target Millennials, a profitable market to attract, through advertisements. Continued operation at the current state could leave both locations in a long-term financial slump.

Franchises: Store A and Store B

Traffic, Customers, and Competition

Traffic. Both Burger King franchise locations are situated in high-traffic areas. Store A is located on a main route in its town, and Store B is located off Main Street. In this respect, there are many consumers to attract with minimal effort, especially for Store A, whose route sees heavy traffic throughout the day. Many potential customers are already in the area and will not have to travel far to reach the Burger King. However, there are many other restaurants that also take advantage of the ideal location, creating various competitors for the franchise stores.

Despite the stores' ideal locations, store traffic is light. Store A has faced setbacks in recent years; a nearby mall shut down, significantly slowing traffic. The major problem for the store appears to be a lack of advertising, which makes it difficult to find the Burger King. The store's entrance only becomes more confusing to locate with a large advertisement for Popeye's located within the same building. The drive-thru is also lost with the inconvenience of the parking lot structure. Store B, inversely, sees most of its traffic from the drive-thru. Unfortunately, this means that the store is left practically vacant, as most customers do not enter the store.

Customers and interior design. Both Burger King stores are located in suburban areas, making it challenging to attract middle- and upper-middle class customers who prefer healthier meal options. Nevertheless, stores in both areas have the potential to attract younger customers. A university and two high schools are within less than a 3- mile radius of Store A and over 15 other schools in the area. Store B is located within 2 miles of the town's high school, and there are eight other schools within 3 miles of its location. Thus, both locations have the opportunity to increase customer flow if they focus on targeting Millennials, high school and university students, and employees on lunch breaks. According to the Food Institute (www.foodinstitute. com), 44% of Millennials spend more of their food dollars on eating out than do Generation X and Baby Boomers; and, thus, Millennials should be a prime target for fast food chains. Further, this percentage is growing each year, as Millennials age and see an increase in annual income. Millennial consumers eat out 10 times per month and visit six different fast food restaurants every 90 days. In the town in which Store A is located, 15% of the population is between the ages of 18 and 34 years, while, in the town in which Store B is located, 6.1% of the population is between the ages of 18 and 24 years, and 21.5% are between 25 and 44 years.

In addition to educational institutions, there are many businesses that surround both stores. For example, Store A is located near two libraries and 14 small businesses. This is a rich target market to tap into. Notably, Millennials' eating-out habits do not include lunchtime. Lunch breaks are becoming fewer for many American workers, with only 1 in 5 workers' eating out during lunch. Employees are also taking shorter lunch hours, making it more difficult to leave the office for a meal. Unfortunately, neither Burger King franchise store has a means of online ordering to reach these potential consumers, which makes it difficult for workers to view Burger King as a meal option during lunch hour.

As can be seen, changes need to be made to both stores to get potential customers (e.g., Millennials, small business employees) in the door. The menus lack innovation that would attract Millennials. For example, Store A's promotions include Grilled Dogs, Chili Cheese Dogs, and Bacon Cheeseburgers, which do not meet the needs of Millennials, as they fail to appeal to their concern with healthy food choices. Store A has major interior design issues, as it includes only the bare essentials, making the store appear outdated and uninviting. Conversely, Store B has a more modern, welcoming interior; however, the space is not well used, as most customers prefer the
drive-thru.

Competition. High competition in both areas is also a concern. Store A has seven direct competitors within a 2- mile radius that offer healthier options and direct substitutes for Burger King's items. These competitors include Muscle Maker Grill and Hot Bagels & Café, which provide fresher options, and McDonald's and Wendy's, which dominate the fast food burger industry. There are 10 indirect competitors within a 2- to 8-mile radius, including another Burger King, owned by a different franchisee. This store not only has an ideal location but also is newly renovated and easily accessible, with a comfortable environment. Store B also faces considerable competition; there are nine competitors within a one-mile radius. Even though none is a direct substitute for Burger King, the competitors, including Panera Bread and Subway, offer healthier, more preferred options. There are also two sushi restaurants, providing the ethnic cuisine option. Other competitors include two pizza places and a Bagels & Deli. Such competitors appeal more to consumers, especially Millennials. Finally, these competitors also have a more inviting atmosphere than do the Burger King franchise stores.

Reviews and Customer Satisfaction

Reviews. The Burger King franchisees should take note of their online reviews, as they influence consumers' choice of restaurants. Millennials especially, who rely on technology more than do previous generations, use customer reviews to guide them where to eat. Store A does not have many online reviews; the 19 on Google, 18 of which were within the past year, score it a 2.8/5, and the six on Yelp over the past five years give a 2.5/5. This is compared to the Popeye's next door, which had six Google reviews within the last year that score it a 1.6/5. The store also scores higher than does its substitutes, McDonald's and Wendy's, on Yelp; however, it scores lower on Google. It's important to note that McDonald's has far more customer reviews than does Store A, 38 in total over the past seven years, a clear indication that it is more frequented. Further, the Burger King performs terribly, compared to the healthier options of Muscle Maker Grill and Hot Bagels, which score 4.3/5 and 5/5 respectively on Google, and 3.3/5 and 3.8/5 on Yelp.

Store B performs very poorly in terms of online reviews. Its eight Yelp reviews over the past six years give it a 2/5, while its 22 Google reviews over the past five years score it a 2.5/5. This is very low compared to its competitors Panera and Subway, which have a Google score of 3.8/5 over the past five years and 4.6/5 within the last year, respectively. The restaurants in the shopping center next door, a sushi restaurant and a Bagels & Deli, also have high Google review scores, 4.7/5 and 3.7/5, respectively.

Customer satisfaction. Like online reviews, customer satisfaction surveys provide insight into a business's operational performance from the customer's perspective. The American Customer Satisfaction Index for Limited-Service Restaurants places Burger King at the lower end of the index, with a score of 76. This may seem reasonable, compared to the index benchmark, 79, and the scores of direct competitors, Wendy's at 76 and McDonald's at 69; however, it is poor compared to fast casual competitors Chick-fil-A at 87 and Panera at 81. A customer satisfaction survey was conducted for Store A, with 36 students of a nearby university at which 70% of participants were between the ages of 18 and 30. Unfortunately, participants preferred McDonald's' and Popeye's
to Burger King, at 58% and 64%, respectively. Despite the fact that 95% of survey participants stated that they eat fast food in general, 42% had never eaten at Burger King. This is of even greater concern when considering that only 14% of respondents indicated that they had never eaten at McDonald's. Store B was praised for location convenience, flavor, and price in an online survey of 13 participants. Customer dissatisfaction included food quality and customer service. A survey conducted for Store A made it clear that Millennials prefer healthier food options, as 61% preferred Panera Bread over Popeye's. When asked about fast food consumption on a weekly basis, the results indicated that only 3% ate at McDonald's weekly and 0% ate at Burger King weekly.

Use of Technology

As noted, online and mobile ordering have become important tools for many foodservice operators, as the use of technology is an effective strategy to reach consumers, especially Millennials. With Millennials' purchasing power rising, it has become imperative for restaurants to target them via mobile technology. US Internet users view online reservation services, free-wi-fi and online/mobile ordering as important. Fast food chains need to incorporate technology, as 34% of participants in a 2016 survey on restaurant technology indicated that they order food once per month via smartphone. Restaurant communication and information provided through online means also are features that Millennials value. Further, discounts and special offers appear to be a top priority for consumers, as 80% of US restaurant goers would like to receive them, and 49% of Millennials view them as among the most important feature of a restaurant's website. Unfortunately, the Burger King franchises do not fare well in this segment. Store A does not offer online promotions, and, although Store B does engage in online advertising, they also use outdated methods, such as newspaper ads and flyers.

Both Burger King franchise locations are lacking in even the simplest technological innovation. Store A has old soda machines and no online ordering services. Store B has no method of mobile payment or online interaction with customers. Making food ordering an easier process should be a key focus of the Burger King franchisees, as boxed-meal delivery services were expected to become a $3 to $5 billion market within the next decade. These franchise stores even lag behind other Burger King franchise locations in technology in offering online ordering, use of mobile apps, and more updated technology in-store. The franchisees' other competitors also are far more technologically advanced. Panera Bread adopted mobile apps and online ordering, catering, and delivery systems. McDonald's and Wendy's also have mobile apps and other innovative technology. McDonald's has a nutrition calculator offered on its website, a very useful tool for the health-conscious Millennials of today.

Stores' Revenues, Costs, and Profits

This Burger King franchise's menu and offerings are not compatible with Millennials' demands. The inability to attract this rich market leaves the stores suffering financially; the business is barely making its debt payments and lacks liquidity (see Exhibit 1). The debt-to-asset ratio is a measure of the company's financial leverage (risk), indicating the percentage of assets financed by debt, creditors, and liabilities. This ratio is problematic for Store

A, which had debt nearly five times higher than its assets in 2016 and nearly two times higher for the franchise as a whole in the same year. The times interest earned and fixed payment coverage ratios indicate doubt in the company's ability to make its interest expense and fixed payments. Store A cannot afford to make either payment, while Store B and the franchise as a whole are barely making their fixed payments. The franchise as a whole and both stores are in poor financial health, as indicated by the current ratio, which is below 1, which means that current liabilities exceed current assets, rendering the franchisee unable to convert its assets into cash if necessary to meet its short-term obligations.

	Ratios	Franchise		Store A		Store B	
		2015	**2016**	**2015**	**2016**	**2015**	**2016**
Debt	Debt to Assets	2.06	2.36	5.79	6.09	5.79	2.54
	Times Interest Earned	1.11	1.25	-1.31	-1.15	2.31	2.01
	Fixed Payment Coverage	0.31	0.27	-0.37	-0.24	0.36	0.40
Liquidity	Current Ratio	0.20	0.61	0.10	0.09	0.10	0.21

Exhibit 1: *Debt and Liquidity Ratios of Burger King Franchise, Store A, and Store B*

Store A saw a 5.57% decrease in revenue between 2015 and 2016. Fortunately, the store was able to decrease the cost of goods sold and reduce expenses during that same period, decreasing net loss by about 37%. However, gross profit still declined by 4.56% from 2015 to 2016 (see Exhibit 2).

	2015	**2016**
Revenue	$987,782	$932,765
Cost of Goods Sold	328,516	303,597
Gross Profit	659,266	629,167
Top Expenses		
Wages	216,017	226,429
Rent & Real Estate Taxes	212,685	212,685
Interest Expense	101,271	68,450
Other Expenses	337,342	252,787
Net Profit (Loss)	$(208,050)	$(131,183)

Exhibit 2: Store A Statement of Revenue and Expenses

Store B is more financially stable than is Store A. Store B managed to increase revenues by 2.63% and decrease the cost of goods sold by 5% between 2015 and 2016, increasing gross profit by 25% (see Exhibit 3). Net profit also increased during this period but only by about 17% due to the high increase in expenses, of about 29%. Most notable is the store's unusually large management fee in 2016. It is difficult, however, to pinpoint the correct allocation of costs and resulting profits. It would be more accurate to analyze the store based on revenue.

	2015	**2016**
Revenue	$1,234,916	$1,267,392
Cost of Goods Sold	934,801	892,028
Gross Profit	300,115	375,363
Top Expenses		
Management Fees	69,500	128,000
Advertising	43,287	52,997
Royalties	46,058	44,127
Other Expenses	47,756	40,426
Net Profit (Loss)	$93,512	$109,812

Exhibit 3: Store B Statement of Revenue and Expenses

The losses of Store A and low profits of Store B barely justify the continued operation and prime locations of both stores. The financial struggle is seen in the company's gross and net profit margins, which are the percentage of revenue after deducting the cost of goods sold and after deducting all expenses, respectively. They indicate management efficiency and measure how much money is available after accounting for expenses. Each store has its own major problem: Store B had only 28% of revenue after subtracting their cost of goods sold in 2016, while Store A had a negative profit in 2016, and the franchisee had the same revenue as costs in 2016, with a 0% profit margin (see Exhibit 4).

Profitability	Ratios	Franchise		Store A		Store B	
		2015	2016	2015	2016	2015	2016
	Gross Profit Margin	0.860	0.870	0.840	0.840	0.290	0.350
	Net Profit Margin	0.012	0.000	-0.260	-0.170	0.025	0.025

Exhibit 4: *Profitability Ratios of Burger King Franchise, Store A, and Store B*

Being a franchisee of Burger King has associated limitations for implementation of marketing strategies. The owners, R. & K. J., have serious concerns regarding the viability of their two stores' operation. They need to rethink their marketing strategy and tactics to turn around the two stores and to see revenue growth. They realize that, to make the stores more profitable, they should answer the following questions:

1. What are the strengths, weaknesses, opportunities, and threats of the two Burger King stores?
2. How can the stores stay competitive in their respective local markets?
3. How should these stores attract more Millennials? What strategies and tactics should they use to be attractive to this cohort?
4. How should these stores attract small business employees? What strategies and tactics should they use to be attractive to this cohort?

Appendix A
Figure 1: Business Structure of Burger King Franchisee

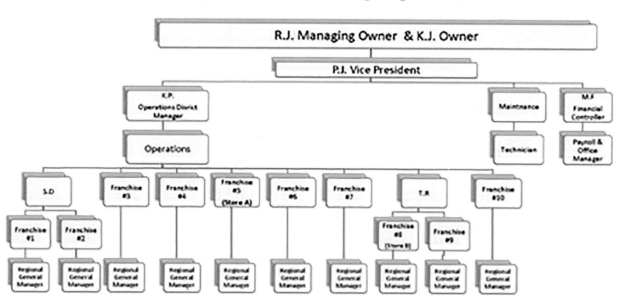

Exhibit 1: *Rosemary Trible, President and Founder, Fear 2 Freedom*

References

1. IBISWorld industry report NAICS 72221a. Fast Food Restaurants in the US: Market Research Report. Retrieved March, 2017 from IBISWorld database.
2. Brand value of the 10 most valuable fast food brands worldwide in 2016 (in million U.S. dollars). In *Statista – The Statistics Portal.* Retrieved 2016, from https://www.statista.com/statistics/273057/value-of-the-most- valuable-fast-food-brands-worldwide/
3. Mike Nudelman &Ashley Lutz. (2015, April 15). 12 facts about McDonald's that will blow your mind. Retrieved from http://www.businessinsider.com/12-facts-about-mcdonalds-that-will-blow-your-mind-2015-4
4. Matt Sena. (2017). Fast Food Industry Analysis 2017 - Cost & Trends. Retrieved from https://www.franchisehelp.com/industry-reports/fast-food-industry-report/
5. Rising beef prices driving burger industry innovation. (2015, August 12). Retrieved from https://www.technomic.com/rising-beef-prices-driving-burger-industry-innovation
6. Leslie Patton. (2014, September 5). Have We Reached Peak Burger? Retrieved from https://www.bloomberg.com/news/articles/2014-09-04/fast-food-chains-growth-in-u-dot-s-dot-may-have-peaked
7. Kate Taylor. (2015, May 5). McDonald's to Refranchise 3,500 Restaurants Worldwide. Retrieved from https://www.entrepreneur.com/article/245809
8. Euromonitor International. (2016, May). Fast Food in the US. Passport database. Retrieved from http://www.euromonitor.com/fast-food-in-the-us/report
9. Daily Mail Reporter (2012, March 19). Wendy's dethrones Burger King to become second biggest burger chain in U.S. (but their combined sales still lag behind McDonald's). Retrieved from http://www.dailymail.co.uk/news/article-2117295/Wendys-dethrones-Burger-King-2nd-biggest-burger-chain- US-McDonalds-1st.html
10. IBISWorld industry report NAICS OD4320. Pizza Restaurants: Market Research Report. Retrieved January, 2017 from IBISWorld database.
11. CHD Expert. (2015, March 19). CHD Expert Evaluates the Pizza Industry in the United States: Any Way You Slice It, Pizza is Popular, and When Looking at The Landscape, Independents are Making a Statement. Retrieved from https://www.chd-expert.com/blog/press_release/chd-expert-evaluates-the-pizza-industry-in- the-united-states-any-way-you-slice-it-pizza-is-popular-and-when-looking-at-the-landscape-independents- are-making-a-statement/
12. IBISWorld industry report NAICS OD5550. Sandwich & Sub Store Franchises: Market Research Report. Retrieved December, 2016 from IBISWorld database.
13. IBISWorld industry report NAICS OD4305. Mexican Restaurants: Market Research Report. Retrieved October, 2016 from IBISWorld database.
14. Leading trends in food items on restaurant menus in the United States in 2017. In *Statista – The Statistics Portal.* Retrieved 2017, from https://www.statista.com/statistics/293885/leading-trends-in-food-items-on- restaurant-menus-us/
15. Roberto Ferdman. (2015, February 3). Asian food: The fastest growing food in the world. Retrieved from https://www.washingtonpost.com/news/wonk/wp/2015/02/03/the-fastest-growing-food-in-the-world/?utm_term=.4999a2a39028
16. Bret Thorn. (2015, September 11). Survey: Consumers rely on restaurants for Chinese food. Retrieved from http://www.nrn.com/consumer-trends/survey-consumers-rely-restaurants-chinese-food

17. Leading trends in breakfast/brunch items on restaurant menus in the United States in 2017. In *Statista – The Statistics Portal*. Retrieved 2017, from https://www.statista.com/statistics/293928/leading-trends-in- breakfast-brunch-items-on-restaurant-menus-us/

18. New Research Finds Americans are Embracing Global Cuisines on Restaurant Menus. (2015, August 19). Retrieved from http://www.restaurant.org/Pressroom/Press-Releases/New-Research-Finds-Americans-are- Embracing-Global

19. IBISWorld industry report NAICS 72233. Street Vendors in the US: Market Research Report. Retrieved October, 2016 from IBISWorld database.

20. IBISWorld industry report NAICS OD4322. Food Trucks: Market Research Report. Retrieved November, 2016 from IBISWorld database.

21. IBISWorld industry report NAICS OD4308. Sushi Restaurants: Market Research Report. Retrieved June, 2016 from IBISWorld database.

22. Leading trends in culinary themes on restaurant menus in the United States in 2017. In *Statista – The Statistics Portal*. Retrieved 2017, from https://www.statista.com/statistics/293972/leading-trends-in-culinary- themes-on-restaurant-menus-us/

23. Fast Casual Industry Analysis 2017 - Cost & Trends. (2017). Retrieved from https://www. franchisehelp.com/industry-reports/fast-casual-industry-report/

24. Top 40 Fast-Casual Chains. (2016, May 21). Retrieved from http://www.restaurantbusinessonline. com/operations/sales-finance/top-40-fast-casual-chains#page=32

25. Trevir Nath. (2015, March 13). Shake Shack And Chipotle: A Financial Comparison. Retrieved from http://www.investopedia.com/articles/active-trading/031315/shake-shack-and-chipotle-financial-comparison.asp

26. Felix Gillette. (2016, August 23). America's Fastest-Growing Restaurant Is On a Roll. Retrieved from https://www.bloomberg.com/news/articles/2016-08-23/america-s-fastest-growing-restaurant-is-on-a-roll

27. Chipotle Mexican Grill, Inc. (2016, February 2). Retrieved from http://ir.chipotle.com/phoenix. zhtml?c=194775&p=irol-newsArticle&ID=2134993

28. Trevir Nath. (2015, February 5). Fast Food Versus Fast Casual. Retrieved from http://www. investopedia.com/articles/investing/020515/fast-food-versus-fast-casual.asp

29. Revenue of Burger King worldwide from 2004 to 2016 (in billion U.S. dollars). In *Statista – The Statistics Portal*. Retrieved 2016, from https://www.statista.com/statistics/266462/burger-king-revenue/

30. IBISWorld industry report NAICS 44512. Convenience Stores in the US: Market Research Report. Retrieved March, 2017 from IBISWorld database.

31. In-store sales of convenience stores in the United States from 2011 to 2015, by format (in billion U.S. dollars). In *Statista – The Statistics Portal*. Retrieved 2015, from https://www.statista.com/statistics/308778/in-store-sales-of-the-us-convenience-store-industry-by-format/

32. Total number of stores of the convenience store industry in the United States from 2011 to 2015. In *Statista – The Statistics Portal*. Retrieved 2015, from https://www.statista.com/statistics/308769/number-of-stores-of- the-us-convenience-store-industry/

33. FPMA. (2016, June 28). FPMA Announces Four Winners of Its Annual Industry Scholarships. Retrieved from http://www.fpma.org/index.php/government-affairs2/2017-legislative-agenda/itemlist/category/6- media?start=14

34. Fast-casual boom continues, finds Technomic. (2016, March 24). Retrieved from https://www. technomic.com/fast-casual-boom-continues-finds-technomic

35. Rich Duprey. (2015, October 28). 3 Reasons McDonald's Corp.'s 1st Sales Increase in 2 Years Isn't a Big Deal. Retrieved from https://www.fool.com/investing/general/2015/10/28/3-reasons-mcdonalds-corps-1st- sales-increase-in-2.aspx

36. Sara Monnette. (2015, August 12). Rising Beef Prices Driving Burger Industry Innovation. Retrieved from https://blogs.technomic.com/rising-beef-prices-driving-burger-industry-innovation/

37. Ashley Lutz. (2013, November 5). Burger King's New Sandwich Could Kill The McRib. Retrieved from http://www.businessinsider.com/burger-king-just-released-a-mcrib-killer-2013-11

38. Ashley Lutz. (2015, March 25). 5 ways millennials' dining habits are different from their parents'. Retrieved from http://www.businessinsider.com/millennials-dining-habits-are-different-2015-3

39. Millennials Coming of Age. Retrieved from http://www.goldmansachs.com/our-thinking/index.html

40. Bruce Horovitz. (2015, February 4). Millennials crave convenience stores most of all. Retrieved from https://www.usatoday.com/story/money/2015/02/04/millennials-convenience-stores-fast-food-restaurants/22872685/

41. Chicago Tribune. (2014, August 31). Why McDonald's has trouble attracting millennials. Retrieved from http://www.chicagotribune.com/news/opinion/editorials/ct-mcdonalds-millennial-chipotle-restaurant-edit-0- 20140829-story.html

42. Roni Robbins. (2014, August 25). McDonald's Not So Golden With Millennials. Retrieved from http://www.adweek.com/brand-marketing/mcdonalds-not-so-golden-millennials-159710/

43. Kate Taylor. (2016, May 1). The biggest change in fast food isn't about food — and it should terrify chains that can't keep up. Retrieved from http://www.businessinsider.com/mobile-orderings-major-fast-food-impact- 2016-4

44. Pew Research Center. (2017, January 12). Mobile Fact Sheet. Retrieved from http://www.pewinternet.org/fact-sheet/mobile/

45. Evan Baker. (2015, July 29). Quick-service restaurants like Taco Bell are using mobile commerce apps to drive higher order values and boost sales. Retrieved from http://www.businessinsider.com/fast-food-chain- mobile-order-ahead-apps-2015-4

46. Evan Baker. (2016, March 16). This is how Taco Bell, Starbucks, and other fast-food chains are using mobile to boost order values Retrieved from http://www.businessinsider.com/mobile-order-ahead-market-forecasts- top-adopters-and-key-trends-for-quick-service-restaurants-next-big-opportunity

47. Kate Taylor. (2016, April 21). Why 'Easy Beats Better' is the new motto at Taco Bell and Pizza Hut .Retrieved from http://www.businessinsider.com/taco-bell-says-better-food-isnt-worth-it-2016-4

48. Brad Gibson. (2014, February 13). Burger King Reports Strong Fourth Quarter Profit And Underlying Revenue Growth. Retrieved from http://www.invests.com/burger-king-reports-strong-fourth-quarter-profit- and-underlying-revenue-growth

49. Burger King 2015 Annual Report. Retrieved from http://www.rbi.com/Cache/1001217621. PDF?O=PDF&T=&Y=&D=&FID=1001217621&iid=4591210

50. Sam Mattera. (2014, September 29). Top Franchises: Investing in Burger King. Retrieved from https://www.fool.com/investing/general/2014/09/29/top-franchises-investing-in-burger-king.aspx

51. Franchisee Disclosure Document – Burger King Corporation

52. Alexandra Talty. (2016, October 17). New Study Finds Millennials Spend 44 Percent Of Food Dollars On Eating Out. Retrieved from https://www.forbes.com/sites/alexandratalty/2016/10/17/millennials-spend-44- percent-of-food-dollars-on-eating-out-says-food-institute/#443887433ff6

53. Most US Restaurant-Goers Order Takeout via Mobile . (2016, November 18). Retrieved from https://www.emarketer.com/Article/Most-US-Restaurant-Goers-Order-Takeout-via-Mobile/1014746

54. Christine Blank. (2014, October). What Millennials Wan. Retrieved from https://www.qsrmagazine.com/exclusives/what-millennials-want

55. Tina Reed. (2016, August 24). The latest player in dinner delivery? MedStar Health. Yeah, that MedStar. (Video). Retrieved from http://www.bizjournals.com/washington/news/2016/08/23/the-latest-player-in- dinner-delivery-medstar.html

56. Revenue of the quick service restaurant (QSR) industry in the United States from 2002 to 2020 (in billion

U.S. dollars). In *Statista – The Statistics Portal.* Retrieved 2016, from https://www.statista.com/statistics/196614/revenue-of-the-us-fast-food-restaurant-industry-since-2002/

57. Market share of leading brands in the United States fast food industry in 2015. In *Statista – The Statistics Portal.* Retrieved 2015, from https://www.statista.com/statistics/196611/market-share-of-fast-food- restaurant-corporations-in-the-us/

58. Allison Aubrey. (2015, September 17). About A Third Of U.S. Kids And Teens Ate Fast Food Today. Retrieved from http://www.npr.org/sections/thesalt/2015/09/17/440951329/about-a-third-of-u-s-kids-and- teens-ate-fast-food-today

Fear 2 Freedom: An IMC Campaign to Enhance Campus Safety Nationwide

By

Lisa D. Spiller, Christopher Newport University
Carol Scovotti, University of Wisconsin-Whitewater

"Oh my! That was our biggest and best Celebration Event yet!" Rosemary's eyes welled with tears as she and Amanda walked across the University of Virginia campus toward the parking lot. The campus was alive with students on that warm October afternoon.

"It sure was," replied her marketing assistant, Amanda. "In fact, the Dean of Students was so pleased that he wants to schedule another event for the spring semester. He realizes the importance of being proactive in everything related to our cause."

Rosemary stopped suddenly, gently tugged on Amanda's arm. "Our cause is now *everyone's* cause. The dean understands that once others know the shocking statistics for sexual assault across our nation's college campuses, they'll jump on board too."

Every two minutes, someone is sexually assaulted in the United States. More than 17.7 million women and 2.8 million men nationwide are victims of sexual assault. Sexual violence is especially prevalent in college communities. In fact, nationwide, 1 in 5 female and 1 in 19 male students will experience sexual assault during their four years in college.

Fear 2 Freedom (F2F), is a global 501(c)3 non-profit organization formed in 2011 to combat sexual assault on college campuses nationwide. If you haven't heard of Fear 2 Freedom, you are not alone. Until now, it hasn't done much marketing. However, with your help, that will change. As a business case, it will challenge you to craft solutions for F2F's many marketing issues. But beyond a class assignment, consider "being the change" and "restoring the joy" on your college campus. Visit www.Fear2Freedom.org to learn more.

Introduction

Rosemary Trible, seen in Exhibit 1, is the wife of a former

Exhibit 1: Rosemary Trible, President and Founder, Fear 2 Freedom

Senator and current university president. Rosemary was violently raped at gunpoint when she was 25 years old. Back then she was a rising talk show host at a Richmond television station. She had just finished filming a show at a location more than an hour from home. It had been a long day and she was too tired to make the drive. Instead, she headed to a nearby hotel for the night. Hiding behind the hotel curtains of her room was a man with a gun. He had seen a recent show where Rosemary had interviewed sexual assault victims. That program made him furious for daring to discuss the topic in public. He fixated on teaching Rosemary a lesson.

In an instant, Rosemary's life was turned upside down. Left with mental and physical scars, her life became filled with fear, pain and embarrassment. For 40 years Rosemary waged a silent, internal war. But silence is the demon of healing in cases of sexual assault.

In 2009, Rosemary broke her silence with "Fear to Freedom," a book about the experience and its aftermath. (Exhibit 2) "I began my own journey from fear to freedom. I always said he not only tore my body, he stole my joy."

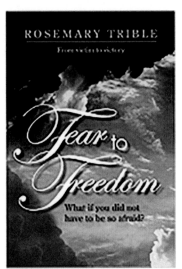

Exhibit 2: Rosemary Trible's book "Fear to Freedom"

The book recounts her struggles with the physical pain and emotional anxiety of the assault. It chronicles her path to overcoming fear and provides advice to victims. Two years after its publication and numerous speaking engagements, Rosemary heeded the call to dedicate her life to being a voice for the voiceless. In 2011, she launched F2F.

Fear 2 Freedom – A Lean Organization

F2F is a non-profit organization located in a small office complex in Newport News, Virginia. It rents two adjoining offices—one for ongoing business operations, the other for volunteers and supplies. The organizational chart is featured in Exhibit 3.

Rosemary serves as President, executive leader, strategic partner, main fundraiser and voice of Fear 2 Freedom. She is also its chief volunteer, opting to donate her time and energy to the cause. Others in the organization include:

- *Executive Vice President*: leads the rollout of F2F's National Campaign; assists with strategic marketing plan development; fundraiser.

- *Chief Operating Officer:* maintains all legal filings and financial documents; supervises new program and resource development.

Exhibit 3: *Fear 2 Freedom Organizational Structure*

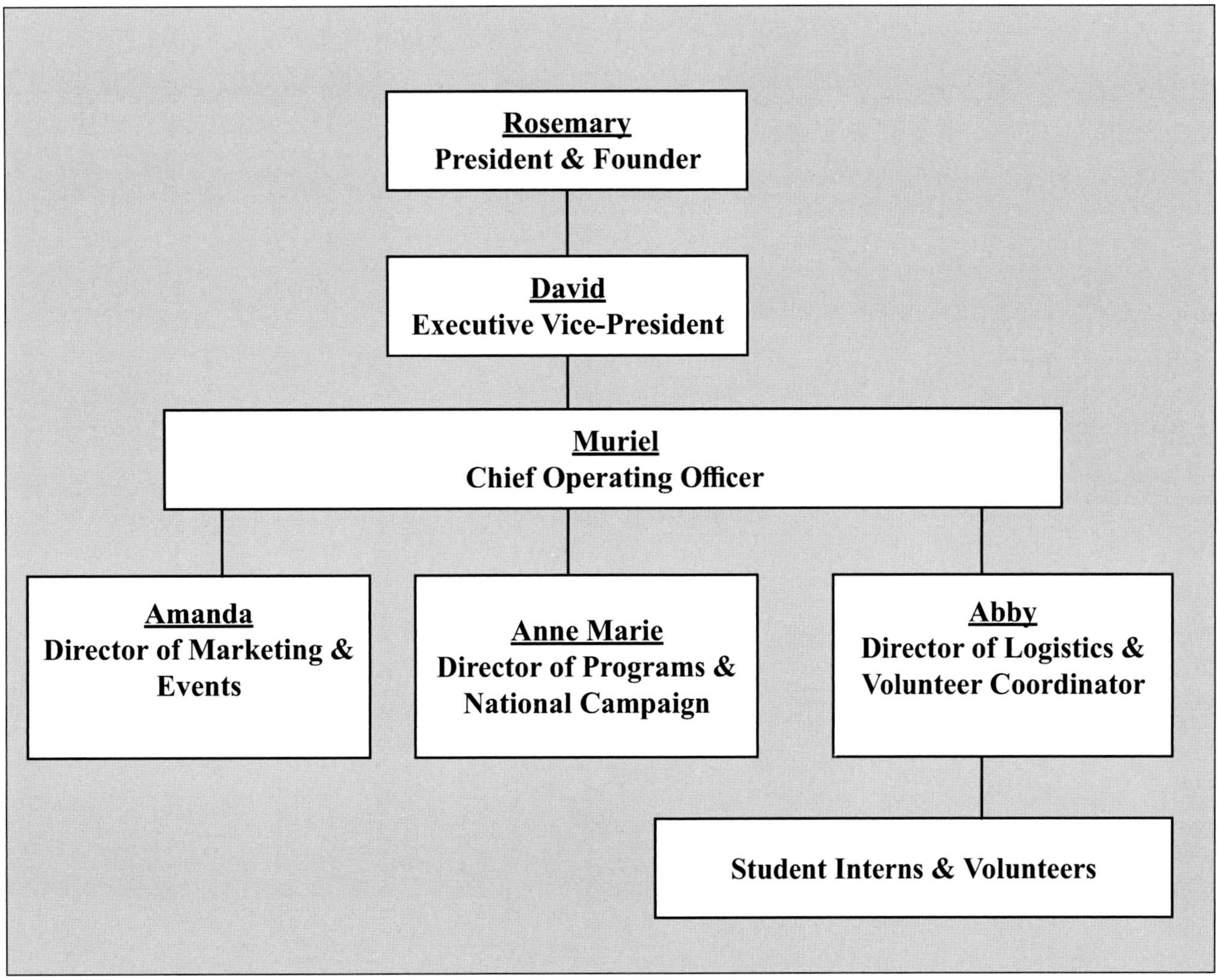

```
                    ┌─────────────────────────┐
                    │        Rosemary         │
                    │   President & Founder    │
                    └─────────────────────────┘
                                 │
                    ┌─────────────────────────┐
                    │          David          │
                    │  Executive Vice-President│
                    └─────────────────────────┘
                                 │
      ┌──────────────────────────────────────────────────────┐
      │                      Muriel                           │
      │               Chief Operating Officer                 │
      └──────────────────────────────────────────────────────┘
         │                     │                      │
┌──────────────┐     ┌──────────────────┐   ┌─────────────────────┐
│   Amanda     │     │   Anne Marie      │   │        Abby          │
│ Director of  │     │  Director of      │   │   Director of        │
│ Marketing &  │     │  Programs &       │   │   Logistics &        │
│   Events     │     │ National Campaign │   │ Volunteer Coordinator│
└──────────────┘     └──────────────────┘   └─────────────────────┘
                                                        │
                                          ┌─────────────────────────┐
                                          │ Student Interns &        │
                                          │     Volunteers           │
                                          └─────────────────────────┘
```

- *Director of Marketing & Events*: coordinates multiple annual F2F Celebration Events; develops all of Fear 2 Freedom's marketing materials; manages marketing campaign activities; distributes direct mail packages.

- *Director of Programs & National Campaign*: implements the National Campaign project; also coordinates multiple annual F2F Celebration Events at colleges, universities and military bases.

- *Director of Logistics and Volunteers:* coordinates materials for F2F Celebration

Events; plans and implements community outreach programs; manages volunteers and interns.

F2F is a lean organization. Everyone chips in to keep costs low. Visitors receive a warm welcome with smiles, hugs, cookies and coffee cake. Its mission is to redeem and restore the lives of those hurt by sexual assault, bringing them hope and healing. It also seeks to empower college students to "Be the Change" and "Restore the Joy" on their campuses and in their communities.

When someone seeks medical attention after sexual violence, the victim's clothes are often kept as evidence. Too often, the victim has to leave the hospital in paper scrubs. A fresh change of clothes in the right size, some toiletries, and a cute and cuddly Freedom Bear stuffed animal make a world of difference. A primary function of F2F is to assemble and distribute After-Care Kits like the one shown in Exhibit 4. F2F relies on funding from grants, corporate sponsorships, foundations, hospitals and charitable donations. Its revenue

stream is shown in Exhibit 5. It also receives in-kind contributions from area merchants for some of the supplies that go into the After-Care Kits. The cost of the contents in the After- Care Kit is about $30.

Volunteers and students assemble kits either at the office or at events held on campuses and military bases. After assembly, kits are transported to a local hospital or community partner. The kits are then given to victims when they seek medical attention after the trauma of sexual assault. The majority of the hospitals cover the cost of the kits. Community partners however, typically don't pay.

Exhibit 4: *F2F After-Care Kit*

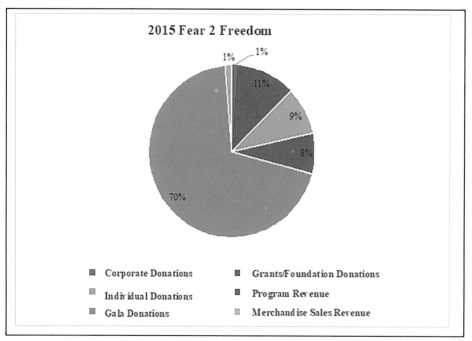

Exhibit 5: *Fear 2 Freedom Current Revenue Stream*

The Network

Dealing with the aftermath of sexual assault requires the work of a well-coordinated network of individuals and non-government organizations (NGOs). As shown in Exhibit 6, F2F partners with hospitals, national organizations, community groups, government, universities and the military to achieve its mission. Each partner serves a vital, distinct role in the healing process.

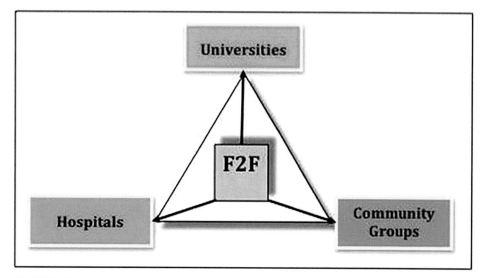

Exhibit 6: *Fear 2 Freedom Partners*

Hospitals

F2F partners with hospitals that have forensic or Sexual Assault Nurse Examiner (SANE) programs. Hospitals provide the F2F After-Care Kits to victims of sexual assault, child abuse, domestic violence and sex trafficking when they come in for treatment. Hospitals designate a member of their SANE team to interface with F2F. When a university or community partner hosts a "Celebration Event" where Kits are assembled, the students load the completed Kits in the hospital supplied ambulance for transportation to the hospital.

The need for these kits is steady and substantial. Since 2012, F2F has supplied more than 12,000 After-care Kits to 30 hospitals and community partners in four states and Washington DC. Please see Exhibit 7 for a breakdown. Internationally, F2F has sent 500 F2F kits to Thailand to women and children coming out of sex trafficking, as well as to Honduras, Nicaragua, Guatemala, Peru and Costa Rica. However, to date, F2F has focused the majority of its efforts on serving victims in the U.S.

State	Partner	State	Partner
Alabama	YWCA of Birmingham	Virginia (continued)	Latisha's House
			Loudon Abused Women's Shelter
Colorado	Western Slope Center for Children		Mary Washington Health Care
			Norfolk General Hospital
Ohio	Cleveland Clinic		Orphan Helpers
	University Hospital		Orphan's Promise
			Portsmouth Naval Hospital

Texas	Midland Rape Crisis Center			Project Horizon
				RCASA
Washington, DC	Children's National Medical Center: Child Advocacy Center			Riverside Hospital
				Riverside Doctor's Hospital
Virginia	Augusta Health			Safe Harbor
	Avalon			Sentara Williamsburg
	Carilion Clinic			SHE
	Central Lynchburg General			Shelter House
	Chesapeake Forensics			St. Mary's Hospital
	Doorways for Women and Families			The Arbors
	Gray Haven			Transitions
	Henrico County Victim Witness Services			Virginia Beach Justice Initiative
	HER Shelter			Virginia Health Systems
	Inova Health System			YWCA of Central Virginia
	James House			YWCA of South Hampton Roads

Exhibit 7: F2F Hospitals & Community Partners

National NGOs

National non-government organizations (NGOs) provide vital resources that also help F2F accomplish its mission. They include:

The Rape, Abuse & Incest National Network – The nation's largest anti-sexual violence organization. As a non-profit NGO, it operates the National Sexual Assault Hotline, and offers free, confidential services to victims. It also manages the Department of Defense (DoD) Safe Helpline, the source of help for the sexual assault victims in the military. RAINN educates the public and advocates for public policy to protect victims of sexual assault (RAINN, 2016).

Promoting Awareness Victim Empowerment – Established in 2001 by a University of Wisconsin-Madison student who was kidnapped and sexually assaulted at age seventeen. PAVE is also a non-profit NGO that focuses on educating high school and college students, military audiences, and members of the Hollywood entertainment industry. Its mission is to "shatter the silence" and prevent sexual assault. It also provides professional development training for law enforcement, therapists, and other professions that help survivors (PAVE, 2016).

Community Partners

Hundreds of local crisis centers across the country provide professional education, individual and group counseling, as well as criminal justice system advocacy.

Women Organized Against Rape (WOAR) - Philadelphia-based WOAR is one of the oldest community advocacy groups with which F2F has partnered. Founded in 1971, it is one of the first rape crisis centers established in the country. WOAR and others like it provide a 24-hour hotline and free counseling to children and adult victims of sexual assault in a limited geographic area. Volunteers often go with victims to the hospital or court. It provides training programs for schools, social service and city agencies on issues of sexual violence (WOAR, 2016).

Universities & Military

F2F focuses its efforts primarily on college and university campuses. However, it has recently reached out to the military, naval academies, and athletic teams. As Exhibit 8 reveals, F2F 17 university partners at the time of this writing, most of which are in its home state of Virginia. The majority of schools had worked with F2F for one to three years.

	No. of years
Alabama --Birmingham Southern University	1
Colorado – Colorado Mesa University	1
Ohio – Case Western Reserve University	2
VIRGINIA	
Christopher Newport University	5
Virginia Commonwealth University	4
College of William and Mary	4
University of Mary Washington	4
Jefferson College	3
Liberty University	3
Regent University	3
University of Virginia	3
George Mason University	2
Old Dominion University	2
Tidewater Community College	2
Washington & Lee University	2
Radford University	1
Hollins College	1

Exhibit 8: *F2F University Partners*

Government Involvement

While hospitals, NGOs, and community partners educate stakeholders and counsel victims, government limits its involvement to creating policy and enforcing laws. In 2013, President Obama signed new regulations into law related to the Violence Against Women Act. After decades of confusion and legal loopholes, new sexual violence incident classifications were established. These definitions help local law enforcement agencies identify offenses. Sexual violence now includes:

- □ **Domestic Violence**: Includes felony or misdemeanor crimes of violence committed by a current or former spouse of the victim, by a person with whom the victim shares a child in common, by a person cohabitating with or who has cohabitated with the victim as a spouse, or by any other person against an adult or youth victim who is protected from that person's acts under the domestic or family violence laws of the jurisdiction.

- □ **Dating Violence**: Includes violence committed by a person who is or has been in a social relationship of a romantic or intimate nature with the victim. The relationship's length, type, and the frequency of interaction between the persons determine whether an action is classified as dating violence.

- □ **Stalking**: Involves conduct that causes a reasonable person to fear for his or her safety, the safety of others, or causes substantial emotional distress. Stalking is also defined as intentional behavior directed at a specific person, which frightens, intimidates, or harasses that person, and serves no legitimate purpose. The revised definition also includes behavior directed toward a member of that person's immediate family and may cause a reasonable person to experience fear, intimidation, or harassment.

Laws pertaining to campus sexual assault violations have intensified as well. Changes to Title IX and the Clery Act are dramatically affecting policies on college campuses nationwide.

Title IX

Title IX is a Federal civil rights law that dates back to 1972. This law prohibits gender discrimination in educational programs or activities by institutions that receive federal financial aid. Originally designed to address scholastic and athletic opportunities for young women, in 2011 its scope expanded to student-on-student sexual harassment and violence.

Title IX applies to more than 16,000 school districts and 7,000 post-secondary institutions, as well as charter schools, for-profit schools, libraries and museums. It requires that those that receive federal financial aid create and publish policies against sexual discrimination, as well as investigate, address, and publish data on sexual violence (U.S. DoE, 2016).

The Jeanne Clery Act

Closely related to Title IX, the Jeanne Clery Act of 1990 requires that colleges and universities whose students receive Federal Title IV Student Financial Aid collect and report campus crime data. The Clery Act has three specific mandates. First, schools must submit an annual security report to federal authorities. Second, everyone in the campus community must be notified when crimes occur. Data comes from local law enforcement as well as campus security authorities, such as resident assistants, dean of students, and coaches. Anyone with significant responsibility for student and campus activities is obliged to provide data. Third, the Clery Act requires that institutions offer support for victims and rights within their campus disciplinary policies (Clery, 2008).

The Clery Act specifies an extensive list of crimes that must be reported, including sexual offenses. Universities must disclose information about crimes that occur both on and off campus. Off-campus offenses include those that occur in different states and countries. If a victim is a member of a campus community and is somehow involved in school-related activity, any crime must be reported.

Recent changes to Title IX and the Clery Act require universities to establish specific policies for handling and reporting violent acts. Institutions with existing policies are compelled to re- examine them to ensure they comply with Federal requirements. The new regulations help to create awareness, interest, and ultimately participation for causes like F2F.

F2F Combats College Sexual Violence

To support its mission to redeem and restore those wounded by sexual assault, F2F seeks to change the cultural understanding and empower university students to "Be the Change" and "Restore the Joy." Rosemary wants to extend the reach of the organization to college campuses nationwide. She needs a targeted integrated marketing communications campaign to achieve this mission.

F2F has four specific objectives for its university campaign.

1. Restore joy by showing compassion and helping alleviate suffering.
2. Educate students about sexual abuse, date rape, and sex trafficking.
3. Motivate students to be part of the solution by assembling F2F After-Care Kits.
4. Empower students to make a difference in the lives of those wounded.

F2F defines its value proposition to university administrators as follows:

Defining your campus campaign to prevent sexual assault takes a coordinated and fully integrated campus strategy. Fear 2 Freedom provides you with the resources needed to foster a culture of intervention, prevention and awareness. It's time to begin a positive conversation with students that empowers and encourages them to be the change and combat assault on campus. F2F provides the program resources you need to meet your Title IX campus training and reporting requirements.

To accomplish its objectives, F2F offers three different levels of programs for colleges and universities. Exhibit 9 details the features and prices for each tier, which are based on college or university student enrollment size. Tier 1 uses videos, discussion, and marketing collateral to educate students on sexual assault, child abuse, and sexual violence on campus. Students are challenged to recognize the impact of sexual assault and the importance of consent and bystander intervention. The content can be used for freshman orientation and by student organizations as well.

Program Feature	Tier 1	Tier 2	Tier 3
"Be the Change" Video	A 30-minute educational video with testimonials from male and female victims, as well as statistics on university sexual assaults, child abuse, and sexual violence. Students hear the courageous journeys of healing from survivors intent to make a difference by sharing their stories. This documentary supports the education and training for students, faculty, and staff within Title IX requirements.		
University Discussion Panel	Guidelines support a formal discussion around topics of campus sexual abuse, intimate partner violence (IPV) and rape. Also includes suggested university procedures and resources.		
Statistics and Fact Sheet	An administrative resource tool that includes the latest figures, facts, and definitions of sexual abuse, sexual violence, IPV and rape.		
The Pledge	An oath that challenges and unified students to combat sexual assault on their college campuses.		
Resource Card	A *pocket-sized* reference guide for students with information on counseling, health related resources, and The Pledge. Cards are customized to each university.		
Survey Assessment Tool	An efficient electronic assessment tool to evaluate and survey the effectiveness of Title IX programming and campus climate on sexual violence and abuse.		
Empowerment Video	An inspiring collection of stories from student survivors who are to be the change through their own journeys of healing.		

The Shadow Event		A restorative 60-minute event to support the healing of campus abuse survivors. It increases awareness, prevention, and intervention. Survivors share their stories in a safe, anonymous environment. Audience members respond with written words of encouragement. The event helps students learn the realities of abuse from one of their peers.	
"Lesson Plan" with Event Checklist		A full lesson plan and event checklist for the shadow event is available to support each campus.	
The Celebration Event			F2F connects universities with local hospitals and community groups. After-Care Kits are assembled by attending students.

Price (based on # of students)	$ 800	$1,300	$2,300	
< 1,000	$1,000	$1,500	$2,500	
1,000 – 5,000	$1,200	$1,700	$2,700	
> 5,000				

Exhibit 9: *F2F Three-Tiered University Programs*

Tier 2 offers all the program features of Tier 1, plus The Shadow Event and lesson plan. An advantage to this level is additional student interaction. The F2F Shadow Event is a unique, transformational university experience to highlight the personal testimonies of sexual assault victims and their journey of restoration and healing. This allows survivors of sexual assault (women and men) to anonymously share their stories with their peers. Students hear from their fellow students on their experience of abuse behind a screen in a safe and confidential environment. Those attending the event have an opportunity to express their personal support and compassion to the survivors by writing a note to the survivor. See Exhibit 10 for Shadow Event photos.

Exhibit 10: F2F Shadow Event Photos.

F2F believes that this generation of college students is the key to changing the shame and stigma of sexual assault. In Tier 3, students get even more hands-on experience with Celebration Events. Students, community partners, and hospitals join forces to combat sexual assault and assemble the After-Care Kits. Students hear from university administrators, survivors, and forensic nurses in this 90-minute interactive program. See Exhibit 11 for Celebration Event photos.

Exhibit 11: *F2F Celebration Event Photos*

Black-Tie Fundraising Gala

Recently, the organization hosted its first Gala to raise both awareness and resources for its cause. Country singer Lee Ann Womack was the featured entertainer for this inaugural fundraiser. Companies and individuals sponsored tables for eight to 10 people. Individual tickets were also available. Despite many not being familiar with the efforts of F2F, the event sold out by word of mouth before any invitations were distributed. See Exhibit 12 for photos from the F2F Gala Celebration.

Rosemary shared her vision about Fear 2 Freedom. Special guest Gil Harrington, founder of Help Save the Next Girl organization, also spoke about her daughter. Morgan. Morgan was kidnapped, assaulted, and murdered after attending a concert at University of Virginia. F2F raised $56,000 from a "paddle raise" auction of six items. By the end of the evening, the Gala raised almost $500,000 for the cause. F2F plans to host more Galas every three to four years.

Competitors

The battle against sexual violence takes the cooperation of many businesses, agencies and organizations. No one group can do it alone. However, as most involved in the battle are non- profits, there is also a battle for funding among the collaborators. F2F must be able to balance the competitive/collaborative dynamics as it expands to more college campuses. It must, "know when to compete fiercely and when to partner" (Brenner, 2011). Expansion means that F2F must compete with organizations not only at the national, but also at the local level too.

Exhibit 12: *F2F First Gala Event Photos*

F2F is not the only organization that focuses its attention on college campuses. Universities have a range of choices to fulfill the mandates of Title IX and Clery Act. Competitors also include those videos or programs on sexual assault topics that are available for college and university campuses. A few of the more popular options include:

- **The Hunting Ground Film** – Universities pay $395 for the Institutional & Public Viewing Edition of the film. This includes an unlimited, site-specific public viewing license.

- **Bringing in the Bystander** – Offers college administrators one 90-minute session or several sessions over the course of a week. Costs are $1,600 plus $350 for training.

□ **Haven** – A 45-minute online program that college students complete at home over the summer followed by a 15-minute follow-up session on campus in the fall. Currently about 600 campuses use the program and pay between $10,000 and $20,000 a year, depending on the size of the university. Haven maintains a record of when students complete the online program.

While videos and online training programs help make communities aware of the problem, many are skeptical about their long-term value (Howard, 2015). Universities committed to battle sexual assault proactively seek more organized approaches. If F2F can effectively reach decision makers at universities with a compelling message, it can achieve its mission of being the source for hope and healing across campuses nationwide.

Target Markets

F2F must make college and university administrators aware of F2F programs. Its ultimate objective is to secure formal partnership agreements for one of the tiered university programs. In addition to gaining administrative "buy in," it must also encourage students and student groups on each campus, such as sororities, fraternities, athletic groups and student organizations, to participate.

To be successful, F2F must effectively target both organizational (B2B) and college student (B2C) prospects. Colleges and universities across the U.S. are its primary target market.
However, no single administrator is responsible for making decisions. F2F must communicate with multiple targets involved in the decision. These typically include:

□ **University Presidents/Chancellors** – While they may difficult to reach, university leaders have the power to make things happen on campus. Regardless of whether presidents and chancellors themselves or their secretaries read the information, F2F has found that when the leader becomes a champion for a cause, the campus community soon follows.

□ **Title IX Coordinators/Officers** – Title IX Coordinators and Officers are the easiest to reach with sexual assault subject matter. Their job is to foster safety on campus, so they actively seek the programs and opportunities that F2F offers.

□ **Deans of Students** – Deans of Students (and similar roles) deal with sensitive student matters. Along with Title IX Coordinators and Officers, personal safety is part of their holistic well-being concern for students.

□ **Student Life Offices** – Offices of Student Life provide funds for campus programs. Their purchasing power makes them important players in decisions about programs like F2F.

Beyond the campus community, F2F must continue to broaden its hospital and community network so the triad (Exhibit 6) is in place to support on-campus programs and events. Every new university that signs up requires the development of a supporting network. The specific target within hospitals is the SANE team of nurses that care for the victims.

While administrators, hospitals, and community partners provide the infrastructure, the primary focus of all that F2F does is the safety and well-being of students. In addition to making students aware of what is considered sexual assault, F2F strives to alert them to its signs and persuade them to take action. In the past, individuals that intervened risked personal assaults on their credibility. Studies have shown that promoting bystander intervention on campus effectively encourages students to act when they see risky situations unfolding (Howard, 2015). While a small percentage of sex offenses on campus involve the "stranger in the bushes," the vast majority is with a perpetrator who is also an acquaintance. In these cases, the victim lets his or her guard down and may not even initially recognize that a sexual assault has occurred. In fact, non-consensual intercourse is a common form of sexual assault on college campuses.

Current Marketing Efforts

Rosemary recently distributed the first national campaign email blast to a targeted audience. F2F compiled a list of presidents, Title IX Coordinators, and heads of counseling for each of the schools in the 26 states in Phase 1 of the F2F Strategic Plan. The same three levels of administrators at 50 Christian schools across the U.S. were also sent the email. A total of 559 outbound emails were sent to launch the F2F National Campaign. Exhibit 13 details the email blast statistics for a subject line test.

Email	Sent	Opened	Bounces	Opt-Out	Clicks
1st email with subject line:					
"New Title IX Campus Assault Film & Programming"	139	43	7	2	4
1st email with subject line: "New Film Addressing Campus Assault & Title IX"	144	56	0	0	14
2nd email with subject line: "New Film Addressing Campus Assault & Title IX"	276	81	17	1	13
Totals	**559**	**180**	**24**	**3**	**41**

Exhibit 13: *F2F National Campaign E-mail blast statistics*

The email blast, shown in Exhibit 14, was distributed via Constant Contact. The content included sexual assault statistics, a quote from Rosemary, an invitation to contact F2F to learn more, links to view the "Be the Change" film trailer, as well as links to contact F2F via its website and social media networks. The results to date showed that 14 college administrators visited the F2F website, 17 administrators viewed the video trailer, four administrators completed and submitted the F2F interest form, and one administrator visited the F2F Facebook page.

Exhibit 14: *F2F National Campaign E-mail blast*

Specific Case Challenges

Rosemary and the F2F staff realize that their marketing efforts to date have been reactive to opportunities and locally based. If the organization is to grow nationally, its needs a scalable marketing approach that effectively persuades university administrators, area hospitals, community partners, and students. Here are several challenges F2F faces.

Challenge 1 – Formulate a comprehensive plan to market F2F to colleges and universities nationwide.
F2F needs a marketing plan that effectively reaches both its B2B and B2C target markets. It must make each target aware of its services, stimulate interest and convert prospects into partners. Each target has distinctive interests and needs, making this challenge especially difficult. Your plan should include both media and message to be communicated to each target. To date, Rosemary has only used outbound email blasts (Exhibit 14) in her limited marketing efforts. So far, results from these blasts have been lackluster (Exhibit 13).

Challenge 2: Determine the most effective methods to target college students nationwide. Technology and
smart phones now impact safety efforts on college campuses. Recently, more college campuses adopted mobile apps to help combat sexual assault. These apps provide access resources for sexual assault victims. Rosemary has contemplated creating a F2F mobile app, however the initial development cost is quite high. She wonders if instead of developing a proprietary app, should F2F partner with one of the existing mobile apps that address sexual assault on college campuses.

Many apps are proactively focused on protecting students and preventing sexual assault from occurring. They include elements such as GPS, emergency contacts, automated messages, and features to ensure a safe walk home. Other apps offer reporting systems and resources to victims of sexual assault such as access to support groups, campus police, Title IX coordinator on campus and at clinics. Some popular sexual assault apps currently used on college campuses include:

- **Circle of 6 U**   http://www.circleof6app.com/

- **Here For You** https://itunes.apple.com/us/app/loyola/id389224172?mt=8

- **LiveSafe**   http://www.livesafemobile.com/

- **UAsk**   https://itunes.apple.com/us/app/ask-dc/id666073950?mt=8

Rosemary needs to assess the value of each available app. Ultimately, she needs a recommendation as to which mobile app is best aligned with the F2F mission for college campuses. If F2F partners with an existing mobile app, how should it be promoted on campus? Is a social media marketing campaign the most effective way to generate buzz among college students? Should the parents of college students be targeted as well? Rosemary has many questions.

Challenge 3: Develop a plan for F2F to become more financially solvent.

F2F needs to better organize its fundraising efforts. The fundraising plan can include any methods you think are appropriate for the organization. Rosemary is open to any idea, such as creating a 5K or 10K race to raise both awareness and funds for the F2F cause, as long as the fundraising events and/or methods are logical and fully detailed.

Challenge 4: Identify other on-campus events F2F could offer to promote its cause and empower students.

Let your imagination go wild as you brainstorm for other activities and events F2F could offer in the university program. For example, the F2F Freedom Bear, seen in Exhibit 15, could be used in many ways to generate buzz and stimulate on-campus excitement.

Ultimately, Rosemary wants all university students to join the F2F cause and be the change to restore joy and help alleviate suffering caused by sexual assault. She wants all students to be educated about sexual abuse and become motivated and empowered to make a difference on their own college campus. So, if Freedom Bear can become an effective part of the university program, then suggest ways to put the little guy to work on college campuses. Start with brainstorming how Freedom Bear could be introduced on your college campus to help achieve the F2F mission and goals. This marketing case can become a life-changing campus project for you to join the F2F movement and "be the change" in restoring hope and bringing joy to those students who have endured sexual assault on your own college/university campus.

Exhibit 15: *F2F Freedom Bear*

References

Brenner, S. (2011, July 7). Why competitive advantage matters: Even for nonprofits. *Community Wealth Partners*. Retrieved from http://communitywealth.com/competitive-advantage- matters-for-nonprofits/

Clery. (2008). Jeanne Clery Act Text Clery Center for Campus Security. Retrieved June 1, 2016. http://www. clerycenter.org/jeanne-clery-act.

Howard, B. (2015, August 28). How colleges are battling sexual violence. *U.S. News*. Retrieved from http:// www.usnews.com/news/articles/2015/08/28/how- colleges-are-battlingsexual- violence

PAVE. (2016). Promoting Awareness Victim Empowerment. Retrieved June 1, 2016. http://www. pavingtheway.net.

RAINN. (2016). Rape, Abuse & Incest National Network. Retrieved June 1, 2016. http://www.online.rainn. org.

U.S. DoE. (2016). Title IX and Sex Discrimination, US Department of Education. Retrieved June 1, 2016. http://www2.ed.gov/about/offices/list/ocr/docs/tix_dis.html.

WOAR. (2016). Women Organized Against Rape: Philadelphia Rape Crisis Center. Retrieved June 1, 2016. http://www.woar.org.

Flowers for Dreams: A Blooming Experiential Brand

By

Stacy Neier Beran, Loyola University Chicago With Ashley Hasty, Indiana University

This case is dedicated to Dr. Kitty Dickerson, Emerita Professor, University of Missouri

Stephen Dyme and his Flowers for Dreams (F4D) digital team were hundreds of images deep as they scrolled through the brand's Instagram account. They were hypnotized, and they were not the only ones. F4D's visual aesthetic captivated nearly 41,000 followers; the account's use of angles, lighting, and consistent filters cut through clutter associated with other brands' Instagram accounts, thus showing what it meant to create "Instagrammable" moments. F4D's account, after all, was constantly named one of Instagram for Business' six brands to follow.

This Instagram search served a role greater than getting lost in a rabbit-hole of boundless beauty: to Stephen, the vibrant thumbnail images provided data. He looked for evidence in the form of comments, hashtags, and even emojis to identify who experienced what F4D offered. He needed insights about who passively followed F4D on social media but also who actively posted images of floral arrangements they had *purchased*. The popularity of F4D social media accounts, including Instagram and Snapchat, meant consumers in and around Chicago clicked with F4D as a brand. No other Chicago flower retailers - independent florists, grocery stores, or e-commerce sites – offered modern, hand-crafted arrangements with same day delivery. Coupled with the promise to donate one-fourth of profits to a rotating roster of local non-profit organizations, Flowers for Dreams became a relevant brand for both its product and its commitment to social good.

Yet, the digital F4D team, led by Stephen as F4D's founder and CEO, observed a developing disparity between who *posted about* F4D and who *purchased from* F4D. Followers who posted images closely aligned with influencer traits associated with Generation Y (Born 1977-1995; slightly older than the Millennials born 1982-2002). Yet, from internal sales data, customers of F4D – those who actually purchased F4D products – did not match psychographic assumptions about Generation Y. F4D customers instead fit behaviors associated with Generation X, particularly single women ages 35-45.

With plans to expand F4D into new markets and introduce new products, Stephen recognized the need to maintain existing relationships with Generation X customers. Yet, he began to favor the nascent opportunity to deepen the F4D's relationship with Generation Y. Assuming substantial differences between these two consumer segments, what marketing plans did Flowers for Dreams need to dream up in order to convert Generation Y influencers to buyers? What solutions might activate an abstract dream into a profitable reality? Stephen needed to identify an effective mix of experiential marketing tactics that would persuade Generation Y to buy more flowers. After all, increased flower sales equaled increased funding donated to charitable organizations and ultimately allowed F4D's "do good" vision to sprout in well-deserving communities.

A Budding Background

When Stephen designed F4D, he never imagined he would become the go-to "flower guy" upon which his family depended for traditional flower-gifting occasions. What blossomed into a $3 million annual revenue business was at first a way for Stephen and his friends to make money during their summer breaks from college. Stephen, in partnership with his co-founder Joseph Dickstein, staged flower sales tables at local high school graduations. These tables provided common bouquets of artificially-colored carnations and roses wrapped in clear plastic sleeves and rubber bands. Stephen primarily wanted to earn income as a flexible summer job. He also planned to use half of the money earned to purchase backpacks and school supplies for children he and his friends tutored. Looking back, the simple model Stephen established expressed his early desire that business and social good could co-exist. His dream to be a social entrepreneur was born.

Stephen and Joe increased the number of school graduations they attended through word of mouth referrals within their community. While Joe's skills aligned with operational efficiencies, Stephen's role developed to address marketing decisions. Buzz about high school graduation sales quickly led to selling flowers at university graduations, including DePaul University and Northwestern University.

Every graduation celebration provided Stephen with a test market: each flower sale afforded Stephen first-hand encounters with what customers wanted when they purchased bouquets. He suddenly appeared as an expert for everyone who bought flowers at graduations, but he realized the need to build knowledge about the florist industry if he wanted to grow graduation pop-ups into more than a side project. He commonly heard his initial customers complain about buying flowers as a "stale," "uninspiring," "outdated," and expensive transaction. As Stephen continued to learn about industry drivers and growth opportunities, he also commissioned a website to build digital presence, thereby reaching beyond graduation celebrations. The initial website allowed F4D to digitally communicate its key selling points - modern bouquets, honest prices, and local non-profit support - to a broader audience.

After nearly five years of operations, F4D had donated almost two hundred thousand dollars to local charities. Moreover, F4D's most recent fiscal year achieved more than 28,000 deliveries composed of roughly 42,500 bouquets. More than 4,000 mini bouquets were distributed throughout Chicago to publicize local events and build F4D brand awareness. F4D also hired approximately twenty full-time employees and contracted other part-time roles, including bike couriers for delivery.

"Do Good" As a Social Enterprise

F4D grew its operations during a significant economic shift to social entrepreneurship. Brands across many industries and consumers within multiple target markets expected purposeful marketing activities as a means to achieve good in society. Social Enterprise Alliance defined a social enterprise as, "an organization or initiate that marries the social mission of a non-profit or government program with the market-driven approach of a business."[36] An estimated 3.5% of the U.S. GDP was attributed to social enterprises, and one in three U.S. consumers increased how often they purchased socially responsible products.[37] Tapping into the zeitgeist of conscious consumerism, F4D met required criteria to establish itself as a dynamic social enterprise.

However, recognizing that the failure rate for small businesses exceeded the success rate, evidence-based growth decisions were now more important than ever for F4D to deliver the impact it promised to consumers and non-profit partners. F4D applied a simple model to identify its social enterprises activities. When Stephen probed into *what, how,* and *why*[38] of F4D's marketing strategies and tactics, each response confirmed F4D's tight positioning as a social enterprise. With that identity intact, Stephen committed to developing F4D as a brand that met the needs of both Generation X and Y consumers. See Exhibit 1 for a model to identify social enterprise core competencies.

Exhibit 1: *Questions to Identify a Social Enterprise*

Question	F4D Rsponse
What does the social enterprise provide as a good or service to solve a social problem?	Modern floral designs with honest pricing that includes bike courier delivery and natural, sustainable packaging; "Every bouquet benefits an amazing charity!"
How does the social enterprise provide the solution?	25% of profits shared monthly with 12 local charities; F4D as a brand becomes the spokesperson for the charity, using all owned media channels to aid in awareness of the charity's mission and populations served
Why does the social enterprise attempt to solve social problems?	Constant representation of a "do good" business within a society that demands funding to solve infinite problems. F4D turned flowers into social capital; it attempts to take the best attributes about Generation Y to substantiate its giving mission e.g. the "power of integrative giving"

---

[36] http://socialenterprisecensus.org/
[37] http://www.goodmustgrow.com/ccsindex/downloads/gmg-info-2016.pdf
[38] http://www.huffingtonpost.com/ben-thornley/social-enterprise_b_2090144.html

Generational Cohorts and Social Enterprise

Maintaining a social enterprise vision strongly suggested that F4D held potential to simultaneously satisfy the needs of both Generation X and Y consumers. Generation X consumers generally made their buying decisions based on thorough product research. Generation X consumers also self-reported to be savvy, skeptical, and self-reliant.[39] Therefore, Generation X required promotional messages from social enterprises to clearly connect to the value offered by the product. Generation Y generally preferred to review blogs to determine purchasing preferences; advertising, therefore, was not seen as a credible source to learn about a company's offerings. Importantly, Generation Y expected "brands to give back to society." Generation Y consumers enthusiastically avoided brands they perceived as greedy for financial gains. For Generation Y, showing support for local community endeavors differentiated social enterprise brands from "business as usual."[40]

Stephen recognized the nuanced distinctions between the two generations. The subtle differences motivated Stephen to see that both markets might be authentically engaged by F4D's social enterprise status. Stephen was also encouraged by industry statistics that showed each generation accounted for 10 to 11 percent of florist industry sales.[41] He did not want to underestimate the importance of sending an impactful message to both Generation X and Y. That message needed to convey that selling flowers was secondary only to the experience of improving communities that mattered to both consumer segments.

The Florist Industry and Competitive Positioning

Competing for the market share of the 20% total sales generated by Generation X and Y presented a sizeable opportunity for F4D. The florist industry in the United States boasted annual revenue of $6.6 billion and produced profits of nearly $200 million. Sales of arranged cut flowers generated approximately one-third (30.4%) of the industry's total revenue. Additional product segments including unarranged cut flowers, potted plants and giftware each contributed between 20-30% of industry revenue, resulting in a consolidated industry with limited product mix.[6] Florists therefore focused their retail strategies on a narrow assortment that offered a depth of choices amongst each category. For example, florists typically supplied popular flowers including cut roses, carnations, gerberas, chrysanthemums, tulips, and lilies, yet each type of cut flower came in countless varietals featuring distinct colors, petal size, and fragrances. Botanists have catalogued more than 400,000 types of flowering plant species,[42] and evolving consumer preferences required florists to provide a diversity of choices within each species. As consumers frequently purchased flowers for occasions ranging from weddings to funerals, florists matched consumer demand for freshly cut flowers and supporting services including delivery and custom arrangements.

[39] http://www.pewresearch.org/fact-tank/2014/06/05/generation-x-americas-neglected-middle-child/
[40] https://www.forbes.com/sites/danschawbel/2015/01/20/10-new-findings-about-the- millennial-consumer/2/#48c62e9c1474
[41] Cohen, A. (2016) IBISWorld Industry Report 45311. Florists in the US. Retrieved May 19, 2017 from IBISWorld database.
[42] https://www.quora.com/How-many-types-of-flowers-are-there-in-the-world

Stephen's journey to disrupt the current florist industry through social enterprise came at an ideal time. The existing florist industry forecast showed a 2.3% decline over five years,[6] yet e- commerce sites anticipated an 11% uptick within the same period. Therefore, F4D's online model provided a promising channel in the midst of an otherwise dismal outlook. Also encouraging to Stephen was how the florist industry was defined. Selling arranged and unarranged cut flowers, potted plants, and giftware required a traditional, brick-and-mortar retail presence; this definition entirely excluded ecommerce. The exclusion resulted from ecommerce florists' practices that bypassed local florist shops to source cut flowers directly from flower farms. Such disintermediation was not unique to the florist industry, especially as consumers' lives become hyper digital and mobile across industries. Online shopping was the norm for Generation X and Y: some studies concluded no differences existed between the generations' preferences for brands' ecommerce and brick-and-mortar stores.[43] As an ecommerce florist, the F4D framework shook apart industry parameters. Furthermore, Stephen had not uncovered another ecommerce florist that accurately translated consumers' intentions to both brighten their lives with flowers and brighten the philanthropic endeavors of local charities.

Nonetheless, Stephen closely monitored competitive alternatives that might prompt consumers to purchase flowers from other venues. Although industry market share belonged to no major brands, supermarkets and grocery stores notably expanded their cut flower sections in order to offer consumers a "cash-and-carry" option. Instead of depending on traditional delivery services such as Florists' Transworld Delivery (FTD), 1800Flowers, or Teleflora, consumers conveniently purchased inexpensive, freshly cut flowers along with other household commodities during frequent grocery shopping trips. As such, the experience of buying flowers for use at home or for gift-giving occasions had been reduced to a low-involvement, routine buy that was empty of experiential attributes. To counter the competitive threat grocery stores posed, distinguishing F4D beyond commoditized blooms at a low prices become critical to persuade

A Marketer's Guide to Reach Each Consumer Generation. (2017, June). *Yes Lifecycle Marketing.*

Generation Y to purchase.

Stephen perceived that F4D possessed a unique alternative compared to traditional florists and grocery stores. Yet, F4D's social media engagement also allowed Stephen to observe competing ecommerce brands as they entered the market. Relatively light regulations governed the florist industry, so new competitors also found barriers to enter to generally remain low.[6] It was no surprise, therefore, when brands like Farmgirl Flowers and The Little Posey quickly garnered devoted social media followers. Farmgirl Flowers, based in San Francisco, California, explained that its purpose was to innovate within the traditional florist industry via purchases of flowers exclusively supplied by American farms. In doing so, its mission connected to creating employment opportunities for farmers and floral designers. Farmgirl Flowers heavily promoted its points of differentiation to include designer quality, burlap packaging, fast ordering, and honest transparency. Recent delivery expansion to 48 states amassed a social media following that engaged 160,000 Instagram followers. See Exhibit 2 for details about Farmgirl Flowers.

Although attracting 53% fewer Instagram followers than Farmgirl Flowers, The Little Posey delivered bouquets within Austin, Texas. For a flat price of $35, The Little Posey provided same- day delivery of simply designed floral arrangements. Like F4D and Farmgirl Flowers, The Little Posey also leveraged its brand identity through minimalist packaging. While F4D and Farmgirl Flowers each emphasized burlap as a natural vessel to hold bouquets, The Little Posey endorsed a "going vase-less" design. Arrangements thus arrived to customers in hand-tied bunches secured in brown parchment paper. The Little Posey also offered a subscription service that mirrored F4D's subscriptions. Still, with nearly 41,000 Instagram followers in a broader geographic market, Stephen needed no convincing that F4D competed not solely on brand aesthetics that fueled colorful Instagrammable moments. F4D competed to "do good" for the charities it represented. See Exhibit 3 for additional information about The Little Posey.

Exhibit 2: *Farmgirl Flowers*
For additional information about Farmgirl Flowers, including its mission, press, and customer testimonials, visit https://farmgirlflowers.com/

Farmgirl Flowers' "The Farmgirl Way" standards

Designer Quality

Burlap Wrapped

Super Fast Ordering

Ethically Grown, Honestly Transparent

WYSWYG

Rave Reviews

Farmgirl Flowers Instagram account

Exhibit 3: *The Little Posey*

For additional information about The Little Posey, including its concept and subscription options, visit https://www.thelittleposey.com/

The Little Posey "mood booster" standards

The Little Posey Instagram account

Core Product Offering

F4D differentiated its marketing activities on three core offerings. Each of these competencies – locally crafted, modern bouquets, honest pricing, and support for local charities – not only substantiated the "what, how, and why" (See Exhibit 1) that made F4D a social enterprise, but also authenticated brand standards for content creation.

Modern Bouquets

First, modern bouquets provided the core of F4D's product mix. As Stephen reinforced, "We wanted to make flowers cool." F4D's floral designers prided themselves in sourcing locally grown flowers in order to design unique arrangements. In particular, F4D's attempt to disrupt the florist industry manifested through the craftsmanship of each bouquet. The designers limited selection to only six bouquet designs. Each design included a variety of colors yet depended on the quality of the flowers available in market each day. The six designs changed each season, and each design was offered in four sizes, ranging from small to extra-large. Design descriptions referenced popular culture to reinforce F4D's commitment to offer a contemporary, on-trend experience. For example, "The Glorious B.I.G. Celebratory, boastful, and loaded with color" attributed its design to music embedded in popular culture. Offering a limited selection enhanced how consumers participated with F4D as a brand. F4D sought a curated, edited brand experience that enabled consumers to enjoy maximum satisfaction from their purchases. Providing a scrambled assortment - typical of the traditional florist industry - forced consumers to spend too much time choosing flowers instead of enjoying the experience of nurturing the flowers or the moment of giving the bouquet.

To create modern bouquets, F4D practiced its social enterprise values by fostering relationships with local flower farms. For example, Farmhouse Flowers, located only thirty minutes outside of Chicago, identified with F4D's social, community-driven practices. Farmhouse Flowers supplied fresh blooms to compose F4Ds designs, yet it also supported educational opportunities within its community: it hired local students across grade levels to provide jobs and essential knowledge about the role of agriculture in the U.S. economy. Farmhouse Flowers described itself as a "family affair;" as a family-run business, its mom-and-daughter team connected to F4D's eagerness to promote gender equality. Next, Brightflower Farms provided nearly 20,000 flowers to retailers throughout the Chicagoland area. Yet, its owners also provided apprenticeships to support small business expansion in the agriculture sector. Furthermore, The Roof Crop, located only ten minutes from F4D's workspace, established "green roofs" as eco-friendly environments within the urban Chicago landscape. As such, the relationship between F4Ds and Roof Crop reinforced the importance of sustainable farming practices within high-pollution zip codes.

Finally, F4D sourced two to three flower species from the Cook County Jail's urban farm, thus tasking inmates with the charge to improve their lives through community-based jobs. Farms like Farmhouse Flowers, Brightflower Farms, Roof Crop, and Cook County Jail met F4D requirements twice over: (1) values aligned between F4D and the flower supplier and (2) keeping local wholesale relationships guaranteed bouquet designs would exemplify the Instagrammable F4Ds brand aesthetic.

Packaging for bouquets and arrangements also showed F4D's commitment to simplifying the florist industry. Bouquets were wrapped in burlap and tied with raffia string. These materials created a consistent aesthetic that identified the F4D brand; the simplicity of the packaging served both to highlight modern floral design and also to eliminate synthetic, environmentally harmful materials (like plastics) extensively used by the florist industry. F4D recently expanded packaging options for each seasonal design. In addition to burlap and raffia, bouquets could be arranged into aspidistra, bark, birch, and tin containers. Customers also had the option to include a free, hand-written card that explained and personalized the mission and values of the monthly charity. The card provided another visual expression of F4D's brand standards that also attempted to create an emotional connection amongst consumers, the local charities, and F4D. Specifically, F4D knew Generation Y valued intense brand loyalty yet simultaneously perceived flower purchases as utilitarian rather than emotional. An enhancement as uncomplicated as a personalized note enriched the experience F4D sought to deliver.

Exhibit 4: *F4D Modern Bouquets and Workshop Space*
Featuring locally-grown flowers and sustainable packaging options
For more about personalized cards,
visit https://www.flowersfordreams.com/blog/category/flower-messages/

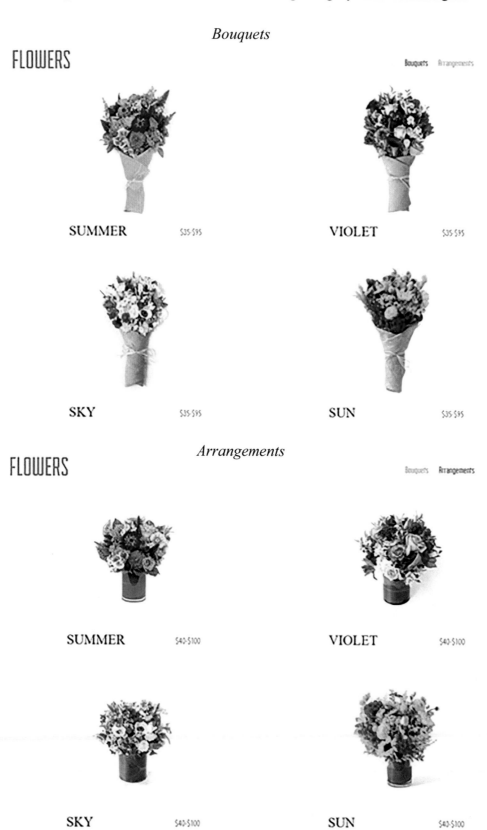

Breadth and Depth of Packaging Options:
Aspidistra (top left), Bark (top right), Birch (bottom left), Tin (bottom right)

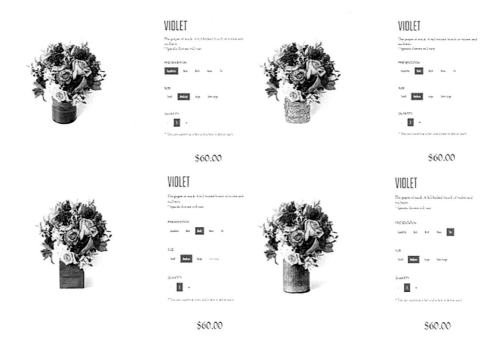

F4D Studio and Workshop Space, West Town Chicago

See Exhibit 4 for additional information about the breadth and depth of the floral design mix as well as the bread and depth of packaging options.

Honest Pricing

Stephen's audit of the florist industry revealed that its complex pricing structure did not represent F4D's social enterprise vision. The traditional florist industry inflated prices to oftentimes include giftware and miscellaneous add-ons that customers did not necessarily need. F4D's passion for designing modern bouquets, for example, excluded overhead associated with chocolates, stuffed animals, and other goods, so F4D sincerely emphasized "honest prices" for cut flowers. To guarantee simple pricing, F4D practiced a "no waste" model: minimizing how much spoilage occurred during the construction of bouquets kept prices low. Prices ranged from $35 for a small bouquet packaged in burlap to $100 for an extra-large arrangement in a tin vase. Additionally, the price line model included free same-day delivery for online orders placed before

2pm. Next-day delivery and $10 same-day delivery was offered within Chicago; $10 next-day delivery was offered within Milwaukee and most suburbs of Chicago and Milwaukee.

F4D also offered a subscription service to customers who desired pre-scheduled delivery of F4D arrangements. Weekly, bi-weekly, and monthly subscriptions provided customers with arrangements to regularly enjoy as home or office decor. The flexibility of the subscriptions also presented customers with an unexpected option for gift-giving occasions. Because Generation X consumers viewed gifting flowers as an activity that aroused their emotions, F4D priced subscriptions to represent both Generation X's emotional connection and its higher household income. Monthly subscription prices ranged from $180 for a weekly subscription to $45 for a monthly delivery. Exacting brand standards applied to each bouquet no matter the subscription period, so subscription recipients repeatedly engaged with F4D's tagline that "Every bouquet benefits an amazing charity!".

Exhibit 5: *Delivery areas included in F4D's honest pricing*

CHICAGO SUBURBS WE DELIVER TO

ARLINGTON HEIGHTS	EVANSTON	OAK PARK
AURORA	GLEN ELLYN	ORLAND PARK
BARRINGTON	GLENCOE	PARK RIDGE
BERWYN	HIGHLAND PARK	RIVER FOREST
BOLINGBROOK	HOFFMAN ESTATES	SCHAUMBURG
BUFFALO GROVE	JOLIET	SKOKIE
CRYSTAL LAKE	LAKE FOREST	ST. CHARLES
DEERFIELD	LAKE ZURICH	VERNON HILLS
DES PLAINES	LIBERTYVILLE	WAUKEGAN
DOWNERS GROVE	NAPERVILLE	WHEATON
ELGIN	NORTHBROOK	WILMETTE
ELMHURST	OAK BROOK	WINNETKA

SEE ZIP CODES

MILWAUKEE SUBURBS WE DELIVER TO

BROOKFIELD	MEQUON	RIVER HILLS
CALEDONIA	MUSKEGO	SHOREWOOD
COLGATE	NEW BERLIN	SILVER LAKE
ELM GROVE	OAK CREEK	WAUKESHA
FRANKSVILLE	PEWAUKEE	WEST ALLIS
GLENDALE	PLEASANT PRARIE	WHITEFISH BAY
HUBERTUS	RACINE	WIND POINT
KENOSHA	RICHFIELD	YORKVILLE
MENOMONEE FALLS		

SEE ZIP CODES

Bike courier delivery service also enhanced the value of F4D's honest pricing. In order to ensure same-day bike delivery, a customer needed to place his/her online order before 2 p.m. on the day intended for delivery. When an online order was received, bouquet designers crafted the design by hand and placed it on a baker's rack in the workshop area (See Exhibit 4). The bouquets were then placed in wooden crates affixed to the fronts of bikes. The wooden crates showcased the F4D logo, thus branding otherwise plain details, similar to minimalist burlap packaging. Upon delivery, the purchaser received an email confirmation to close the full sales cycle from online order to receipt.

Fixing the cost of bike courier delivery into pricing also showed how F4D played into Chicago's existing bike culture. The city of Chicago readily invited its citizens to use bikes as a collective attempt to decrease harmful emissions generated in an urban environment. Chicago's bike network – zig-zagging almost 300 miles – earned the city recognition as the most bike-friendly city in the United States.[44] Rain, snow, or shine, bike couriers pedaled through downtown and surrounding neighborhoods secured with blooming wooden crates. F4D wanted customers to associate the cost for buying bouquets with the humbleness of bike delivery, not with opaque fees that otherwise plagued the florist industry. See Exhibit 5 for delivery areas covered by F4D's honest pricing.

Local Charities

Modern bouquets and honest pricing allowed F4D to represent local charities. Annually, the F4D team accepted and reviewed hundreds of applications to select 12 local charities. Selected charities rotated monthly during the following year. The applications required non-profits to demonstrate their missions, values, and fortitude to solve problems impacting Chicago communities. Since it started operations, F4D provided monetary support to more than 40 charities. Maintaining honest prices enabled F4D to award 25% of its profits to the charities. These monetary donations fully supported F4D's mission as a social enterprise, yet implementing what Stephen referred to as "the power of integrative giving" meant more than signing over a donation check. F4D acted as a new promotional channel for each charity. Each charity benefited from targeted messages on owned F4D media. Followers of F4D's blog, for example, saw F4D employees volunteering at the selected non-profits' events. Email, social media, and the F4D's website all conveyed unified messaging to convey the charity's mission, tell its story, and highlight solutions from the non-profit's work. Bouquet packaging also included a small tag - approximately the size of a business card - that shared details about the charity including its website, social media, and logo. The promotional collateral served to expand awareness and activate unique visits to non-profits' digital medias. Although the donations received from F4D's bouquet sales enhanced the charities' bottom lines, the active collaboration between the charities and F4D established how the F4D's model could "do good" for all stakeholders involved.

Exhibit 6: *F4D's Charity Support*
Twelve logos of charities supported by F4D

---

[44] http://www.chicagotribune.com/news/local/breaking/ct-bicycling-magazine-rating-20160917-story.html

Email announcement to encourage charities' applications to F4D

See Exhibit 6 for a selection of local charities chosen by F4D and email communication announcing application availability.

Strategic New Product Offerings

Combining modern bouquets, honest prices, and non-profit donations created F4D's cash cow, largely stabilized by Generation X customers. Yet, given 73 million Generation Y consumers in the US, F4D needed to design engaging new offerings that kept branded experiences as fresh as the daily-cut blooms. Stephen therefore prioritized three product expansions: (1) weddings & events (2) a flower truck, and (3) geographic expansion. The objective of each new offering was twofold (1) to convert Generation Y influencers into F4D customers through relevant, participatory experiences and (2) to enhance consumers' associations with F4D as a "do good" brand.

Weddings

The first F4D product expansion emphasized floral arrangements for weddings and other special events. Although Generation Y consumers waited longer to marry than Generation X traditionalists, 86% reported future intent to marry.[45] Consequently, Generation Y drew upon higher household incomes for wedding planning and simultaneously demanded personalized details to wow their guests.[46] Floral services for weddings were also expected to grow, driven by higher spend per wedding. F4D engaged wedding customers by building an experiential profile that invited participation through prospective brides' selection of appealing floral arrangement images and phrases to describe coveted wedding themes (including additional references to pop- culture with phrases like *Downton Abbey*). F4D wedding planners shared each phase of consultations, follow-up appointments, and day-of services. Customers also subscribed to *One Fourth*, a community-based bridal magazine. The experiential nature of the wedding process needed to be as meaningful as the actual flower arrangements.

To integrate its honest pricing, F4D chose not to charge for initial consultations on weddings or events with a budget of $1,000 or more. Contrary to a "less is more" strategy when it comes to limited options for modern bouquets, F4D believed each wedding should be treated uniquely and therefore did not offer wedding packages. Instead, a F4D wedding designer created new and inspiring pieces for every bride. These one-of-a-kind wedding arrangements also generated engaging content for F4D's social media channels. To further accentuate its wedding experiences, F4D secured a supplementary Instagram account (@f4dbrides) to exclusively promote its customized approach. See Exhibit 7 for a screenshot of the @f4dbrides Instagram account.

Exhibit 7: *Weddings*
@f4dbrides Instagram account

---

45 Euromonitor Passport, retrieved June 2017
46 http://www.gallup.com/poll/191462/gallup-analysis-millennials-marriage-family.aspx

Email promotion of One Fourth magazine

We're giving away free copies with every Friday delivery.

one Fourth
BY FLOWERS FOR DREAMS

LOCAL FARMS | CHICAGO'S FIRST FLOWER TRUCK | TRAINING REFUGEES
ISSUE 01 | 2017

INTRODUCING

ONE FOURTH MAGAZINE

We got tired of the same old bridal magazines so we decided to create our own. A millennial-driven, community-focused publication with floral editorials, charity features, and a neighborhood guide.

Receive one of the first 100 issues when you order flowers for delivery tomorrow.

Also of note, F4D supported the flourishing acceptance of same-sex marriages. F4D's blog and video featured a same-sex couple's journey in a series entitled *Chicago Love Stories*. This again represented F4D's constant support of local charities: the couple's story was posted during the month that F4D's highlighted Equality Illinois, a local nonprofit aimed to enhance social justice initiatives within the LGBTQ community. See Exhibit 8 for more information about the *Chicago Love Stories* blog series.

Seasonal Workshops

Seasonal workshops also aimed to encourage Generation Y participation in the brand. Similar to wedding services, these active, participatory events plugged into Generation Y's interest to spend more money on intangible experiences than tangible goods. For example, F4D scheduled flower crown workshops to spotlight Lollapalooza, an annual concert attended by more than 400,000

Exhibit 8: *F4D's Chicago Love Stories blog, including embedded video content*

CHICAGO LOVE STORIES: EQUALITY ILLINOIS

FEBRUARY 8, 2017

To celebrate love, happiness, and flowers here in Chicago, we at Flowers for Dreams are bringing you another year of Chicago Love Stories. In the past, we have looked at couples with small businesses and even your favorite Instagram pairs, but this Valentine's Day, we're featuring those involved with non-profits.

people each year.[47] In conjunction with the workshop, F4D offered a social media contest with a grand prize of two free workshop tickets and Lollapalooza Sunday passes. One thousand entries were received via Instagram and Facebook; Snapchat announced the lucky winner. Other small local businesses with cult followings in Chicago – Antique Taco and Koval Distillery – provided workshop participants' food and cocktails.

Two wreath-making workshops provided winter holiday entertainment. A Christmas wreath workshop invited participants to wear ugly Christmas sweaters and indulge in gingerbread cookies and spiked hot chocolates while designing personalized wreaths. Wreath materials included leafy evergreens, pine, red berries, and pinecones, which overcame assumptions that F4D's modern designs were limited to brightly colored Spring/Summer bouquets. A brunch- themed rustic workshop also engaged participants in wreath-designs, yet a marked difference between workshops was noted. The Christmas wreath participants fit a culturally cool "hipster" vibe, while the brunch wreath workshop suited Generation X interests.

Building on the Winter Workshop successes, F4D offered Spring bouquet workshops. Participants had the opportunity to build individual Spring bouquets. F4D again partnered with local shops to provide food and beverage. Sweet treats from BomboBar, seasonal cocktails from Rhine Hall, and fresh roasted coffees from Metric Coffee amplified the workshop experience.

Tickets to each workshop cost participants $75. The premium ingredients for the experience - all natural flowers and foliage, food, drink, and endless Instagrammable moments - positioned F4D as the brand that connected attendees to share wholesome, down-to-earth moments. See Exhibit 9 for promotional messaging about workshops.

Free Flower Fridays

F4D dreamed Free Flower Fridays to be another experience - similar to a neighborhood block party - that shook up the staid floral industry in Chicago. F4D arranged mini-bouquets and invited consumers through owned media to visit the F4D studio after work on Friday afternoons. Attendees learned more about F4D and enjoyed complimentary gifts from local small business. Most importantly, F4D donated to their nonprofit partners for each free bouquet taken. On the first Free Flower Friday, more than forty bouquets generated non-profit donations, and attendees expressed how much fun they had through user generated content, namely via Instagram tagging. For the second Free Flower Friday, F4D partnered with local food trucks - La Boulangerie, Eastman Egg, Da Lobsta, Pint, and More Cupcakes - to provide food and juices. See Exhibit 10 for email promotion and an Instagram image from a Free Flower Friday participant.

[47] http://www.nbcchicago.com/news/local/400k-attend-25th-annual-lollapalooza-in-chicagos-grant-park- 388797742.html

Flowers for Dreams: A Blooming Experiential Brand

Exhibit 9: *Workshops*
Email promotion for Spring Workshops

DESIGN YOUR OWN SPRING BOUQUET.

Join us for a weekend of workshops. Build your very own Spring bouquet while enjoying sweet treats from BomboBar, seasonal cocktails from Rhine Hall, and fresh roasted coffees from Metric Coffee. All for just $75/guest. Grab a friend and grow your skills.

Select a date + time.

˅

Email promotion for Wreath Workshops

It's wreath season.

For the first time ever, we're offering wreaths for <u>delivery anywhere in Chicagoland</u>. From Naperville to Lake Forest, Elgin to Downtown, you can now have a wreath hand delivered for the holidays.

HOLIDAY

WINTER

ORDER NOW >

185

Want to build your own instead?

You're in luck. We're hosting three workshops this weekend.
Each with custom Koval Distillery cocktails and delicious Bang Bang Pie.

GRAB A FRIEND & SELECT A DATE

v

December 9th @ 7pm   December 10th @ 12pm   December 11th @ 11am

SIGN UP HERE >

The Flower Truck

F4D next combined innovative distribution and promotion to transform influencers to loyal customers. F4D designed, licensed, and mobilized a Flower Truck. As a nod to the popularity of food trucks popularized by Generation Y "foodies" in urban settings (and integrated during Free Flower Fridays), F4D scaled delivery patterns from its bike couriers to excite customer interactions through a "walk-up window" truck. To make this dream flower truck come alive, Stephen first tirelessly worked to overturn Chicago's seven decade long flower peddling ordinance. The Flower Truck became Chicago's first mobile florist since 1943.

With regulations finally favoring F4D,[48] the Flower Truck mobilized an interactive brand experience that overcame geographic constraints for many potential consumers. F4D's West Town studio and office space was not meant to experience foot traffic as a retail trade area; West Town was not a shopping district like Chicago's celebrated Magnificent Mile and State Street. Bouquets could be purchased from the West Town studio, but F4D's sales overwhelmingly leveraged ecommerce ordering. Therefore, the Flower Truck acted as a mobile pop-up shop that simultaneously decreased risk associated with traditional store operations and increased one-on- one experiential interactions. Parked during lunch breaks by curbs zoned for food trucks, the Flower Truck staged sales of mini bouquets designed to brighten office settings and showcase F4D's modern aesthetic. Accordingly, the Flower Truck enabled F4D to engage busy Generation X and Y professionals who escaped downtown high rises during the workweek grind and thus generated awareness within a heavily-populated central business district.

---

[48] http://www.chicagotribune.com/bluesky/originals/ct-flowers-for-dreams-truck-bsi-20160606-story.html

The Flower Truck appeared in professional districts during the workweek, but it was highly visible during weekends as well. Chicago residents celebrated summer with attendance at more than 400 outdoor festivals, farmers' markets, and neighborhood block parties.[49] Each community event gave the Flower Truck a test market to explore times, days, and available merchandise for the truck's inventory. Fifteen dollar mini bouquets and $30 small bouquets became popular impulse buys that enhanced attendees' event experiences. The Flower Truck also stocked F4D t- shirts and branded "swag" (buttons, bottle openers, and canvas bags). The Flower Truck popped- up in Logan Square, Wicker Park, and other trendy Chicago neighborhoods. Annual festivals like Renegade Craft Fair integrated the Flower Truck into an artisan and maker culture that overtly valued small batch manufacturing and handcrafted goods.

At larger events like Lollapolloza, the Flower Truck sold concert-goers flower crowns, a symbol of a free-spirited, bohemian vibe. The Flower Truck activated the F4D's brand beyond a single bike-to-residence delivery and exposed it to countless attendees of these events. Using its own Instagram account (@f4dtruck), each event appearance was tracked via social media updates through Instagram Stories and Snapchat. The Flower Truck seamlessly communicated the modern message F4D aimed to promote amongst influencers and customers alike. See Exhibit 10 for images of the Flower Truck.

On the move to Wisconsin: #HelloWisco!

The Flower Truck built brand awareness, yet its transportation utility also - quite literally - drove the brand into a new geographic market. F4D's initially promoted its trade area as delivering up to fifty miles outside Chicago. Keeping a tight trade area radius allowed for bike courier services to be properly priced and reliably implemented. The Flower Truck allowed increased aided awareness for the brand and increased sales of a limited product line. After four years of steadfast operations and branding in Chicagoland, F4D took the Flower Truck to the interstate to introduce the brand to southwest Wisconsin.

Census statistics positioned Milwaukee as a location with favorable demographics for F4Ds. (See Appendix A for age ranges of Milwaukee, WI residents). Yet Stephen saw southwest Wisconsin as an attractive market for three other reasons. First, Wisconsin was situated close to Chicago, so the streamlined sourcing, design, and distribution logistics were effectively replicated. Thus, F4D retained quality expectations to preserve the brand's reputation as a social

---

[49] https://www.choosechicago.com/events-and-shows/festivals-guide/

Exhibit 10: *Free Flower Fridays*
Email promotion announcing Free Flower Fridays

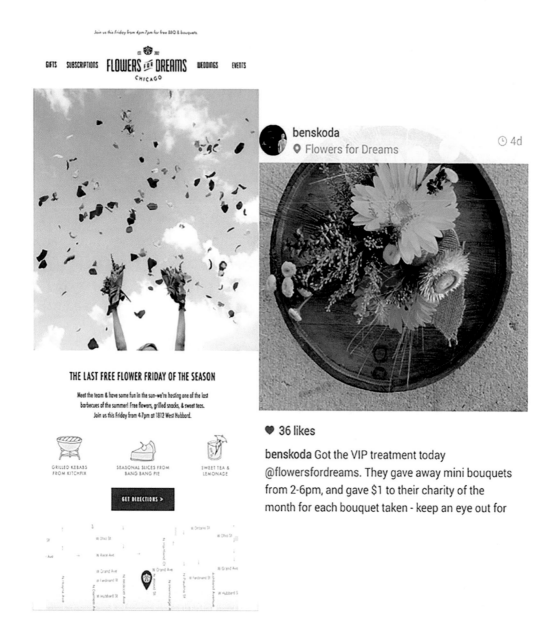

enterprise. Chicago and Wisconsin each boasted local idiosyncrasies that fed the modern visual brand standards F4D represented, yet a Chicago resident experienced the same F4D "look and feel" as a Milwaukee resident. Stephen and the F4D team carefully planned for consistent consumer experiences with F4D branding, particularly via digital and social media. Finally, and perhaps most importantly, Stephen believed the culture of Wisconsin closely aligned with Chicago; he saw Wisconsin to embody the "Midwest niceties" that also characterized Chicagoans.

Exhibit 10: *The Flower Truck*
Email promotion announcing the Flower Truck

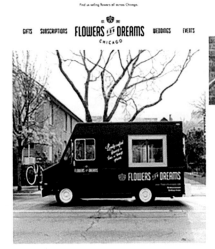

SCHEDULE

TRACK THE TRUCK

@f4dtruck Instagram account

Furthermore, expansion into southwest Wisconsin eliminated the need for distinct promotional messages. Stephen's team anticipated that the strong brand associations developed in Chicago would transfer to Milwaukee. The Wisconsin launch optimized the brand's integrated tactics to highlight local brands and leverage Milwaukee social media influencers. Instagram images teased followers with pictures and captions hinting at the newest location without revealing the specific city. This built anticipation and encouraged interaction within social media channels during the Flower Truck's maiden voyage to Wisconsin. On the first official day of Wisconsin operations, the Flower Truck provided a hub for consumers to experience the brand. F4D essentially expanded its Free Flower Fridays events by offering free mini bouquets at targeted Milwaukee spots, not just for one day but for a full week.

Recipients of the bouquets were encouraged to post images to social media using the hashtag #HelloWisco. Tracking the Flower Truck's location around Milwaukee led social media followers to see it pop-up at local businesses including coffee shops, bookstores, and beloved independent boutiques. Emails to Chicago customers offered $5 credits for referrals of Wisconsin friends. Ultimately, F4D united promotional messaging across each communication channels for an entire Midwest community.

See Exhibit 11 for email communication announcing delivery to Milwaukee and an illustration of the delivery area from Chicago to Milwaukee.

The Decision Problem

With the approach of F4D's first peak summer season to operate in two major markets, Stephen realized how critical timing became to ensure each new product resulted in purchases from Generation Y. Experiential products like weddings and events, the Flower Truck, and new geographic expansion connected customers with the incredible stories of the dreams each floral design supported. Yet, which of these strategies did Stephen need to prioritize? Did too many expansions dilute the value of F4D brand? Could the F4D brand penetrate the Generation Y market with experiential products while maintaining the loyalty of Generation X with its core product? What combination of participatory experiences motivated Generation Y to not only post about F4D but to also purchase? Stephen dreamily let his eyes wander back to F4D's Instagram account for evidence, but he knew he couldn't stop to smell the roses for too long: there were bouquets to sell and charities to support.

Exhibit 11: *Email promotions announcing expansion to Wisconsin*

Email #1

Email #2

Appendix A
Census Data about Milwaukee, Wisconsin (from SimplyMap)

Variable	Milwaukee, WI	USA
% Population, 45 to 54 Years, 2020	10.51%	12.49%
% Population, 45 to 54 Years, 2016		
% Population, 35 to 44 Years, 2020		
% Population, 35 to 44 Years, 2016		
% Population, 25 to 34 Years, 2020		
% Population, 25 to 34 Years, 2016		
% Population, 18 to 24 Years, 2020		
% Population, 18 to 24 Years, 2016		

PG&E: Marketing Energy Efficiency Programs for Businesses

By

Blodwen Tarter, Golden Gate University
Mary Beth McCabe, National University San Diego
Matthew Sauber, Eastern Michigan University
Daniel Shen, State University of New York at New Paltz

Roberta Johnson was excited. Jacobs and Clevenger, the marketing agency for which she worked, had just been awarded a major project for the Pacific Gas and Electric Company (PG&E). And Roberta was the newly named account manager! The kickoff meeting with the account management and creative teams was scheduled for this afternoon.

A Chicago-based firm, Jacobs and Clevenger was well known for its expertise in direct marketing. In fact, Ron Jacobs, one of the firm's founders, had co-authored the classic textbook *Successful Direct Marketing Methods*. The company website described the agency as "The multichannel digital direct marketing agency that provides measurable response."

Independently owned for more than 30 years, this medium-sized agency had been exploring new opportunities for its own growth. In the process of this exploration, Ron Jacobs identified the regulated utilities industry as one that could benefit from well-targeted marketing. By this time, Jacobs and Clevenger had developed quite a specialty in marketing for utility companies.

The roots of the Pacific Gas and Electric Company (PG&E) go back to California's Gold Rush days when the San Francisco Gas Company was founded in 1852. The San Francisco Gas and Electric Company and the California Gas and Electric Corporation merged in 1905 to create the new Pacific Gas and Electric Company.[1] Today, PG&E provides electricity and natural gas to homes and businesses throughout northern and central California, serving more than 5 million customers and generating almost $17[2] billion in revenue. This makes PG&E the largest utility company in the U.S. by number of customers served and the amount of revenue it generates. It has the second highest retail prices in the country, after New York's Consolidated Edison.[3]

With a growing population in California and the ensuing increase in demand for energy of all kinds, people were becoming more aware of the environmental impact of producing and delivering energy. Of course, the rising cost of energy to all consumers was also a concern. Under pressure from regulators and the public, PG&E was increasing its focus on helping businesses and individual households become more aware of energy efficiency. The financial reach of the company and the scope of its service made PG&E a particularly high-visibility utility company for both regulators and its customers. After the 1973 energy crisis, Congress wrote the National Energy Act, to focus on energy conservation and that meant reducing the demand. Decades later, PG&E still struggled to make this happen.

This public policy drive to reduce energy consumption is seemingly in conflict with what one normally expects from a business – an effort to increase consumption of its goods and services. Yet, because of the regulatory mandate, PG&E had no choice: regulators required a tangible, sustained, and substantive effort to reduce consumption. In addition, the high profile of the company suggested that any positive efforts to be a good corporate citizen might help PG&E mitigate negative consumer perceptions in other areas of its business.[4]

As a regulated industry, with a virtually captive audience, marketing to its customers was not PG&E's strong suit. Most businesses and individual households had to buy their energy from PG&E so the company did not have the same depth of expertise in marketing as most other companies of a similar size. Frankly, PG&E needed help-- and the company recognized it.

The utility turned to Jacobs and Clevenger to find a way to educate small and medium businesses about PG&E's energy efficiency programs and to increase the businesses' participation in these programs. The project was only one of many efforts to reduce energy consumption among PG&E customers but, as typical

---

[1] http://www.pge.com/en/about/company/profile/hist ory/index.page

[2] 2015 operating revenues for PG&E Company http://www.sec.gov/Archives/edgar/data/75488/000100498016000065/ form10k.htm#_Toc443485795 3"Electricity - Energy Explained, Your Guide To Understanding Energy - Energy Information Administration". www.eia.gov. Retrieved 2015-12-05.

[3] "Electricity - Energy Explained, Your Guide To Understanding Energy - Energy Information Administration". www.eia.gov. Retrieved 2015-12-05.

[4] In 2010, a deadly gas line explosion in San Bruno, CA killed eight people, injured scores of others, destroyed 38 homes, and exposed numerous failures in PG&E's record-keeping and maintenance of critical infrastructure. Some lawsuits against the company were settled for $565 million dollars in 2013. http://www.huffingtonpost.com/2013/09/11/pge-san-bruno- settlements_n_3903832. html Other suits were subsequently settled for undisclosed sums. http://www.sfgate.com/bayarea/article/PG-E- settles-more-San-Bruno-suits-3742194.php In addition, the Public Utilities Commission, PG&E's local regulator, levied a record-breaking $1.6 billion fine for corporate errors in a variety of areas. http://www.latimes.com/business/la-fi-puc-fine-20150409-story.html

with many agency assignments, PG&E sought specific expertise that Jacobs & Clevenger offered: targeted marketing experience and an understanding of utility companies.

Roberta called the meeting to order at 2 pm and reviewed the agenda. "I think everyone here is already familiar with PG&E and its basic business. So we will start with a quick overview of the specific situation and then our objectives for this project. After that, let's start brainstorming on how to approach this challenge.

Most business owners and managers consider energy consumption a necessary evil and one over which they have very little control. Energy is a low involvement product category. Yet the cost of energy is increasingly expensive and of greater impact on the environment than ever before. So business operators need to pay attention and take action to reduce or, at least, to control, their energy use. By better focusing on the needs of its business customers, PG&E could provide information that would establish the utility as a helpful partner rather than as an indifferent supplier. Toward this end, PG&E had developed the Business Energy Checkup. This online self-assessment tool had three components: tracking energy use, getting energy- saving recommendations, and creating an energy savings plan. To use it, the business had to first create a "My Energy" account.

Unfortunately PG&E's efforts to get businesses to use the Business Energy Checkup online tool or to set up a "My Energy" account had not been very effective so far.

Telephone research conducted by the Blackstone Group revealed

Low impact: Over 80% of eligible respondents did not recall any direct mail or energy efficiency-related emails;

Low interest: Over 80% of those who recalled the mailings or emails, had no serious interest to enrolling in My Energy or completing a Business Energy Checkup profile;

Little benefit: No more than 10% of recipients that recalled the Pilot program attempted to enroll in My Energy or complete a Business Energy Checkup profile.

PG&E had a vision for energy management and sought to revolutionize energy solutions for customers. Yet businesses that looked to PG&E for help using energy more efficiently were simply unable to find the information and tools available. In its research, Jacobs and

Clevenger discovered that customers don't actively search for energy solutions; they search for answers to specific problems. They want to lower their energy bill. The gigantic commercial refrigerator in their restaurant kitchen no longer works very well and needs to be replaced. The heating or the air-conditioning system is broken. Each of these problems has an energy component for which PG&E could be a resource – if the businesses just knew where or how to seek assistance.

Not surprisingly, the commercial sector uses energy in different ways than home/residential users. Lighting constitutes the largest (19%) use for electricity in the U.S. commercial sector such as retail, office buildings, educational institutions, institutional use, and government buildings. Ventilation (11%), space cooling (10%), refrigeration (8%), office equipment including computers (7%), and space and water heating (6%) are other major commercial uses of electricity. All other uses (39%) of electricity in this sector include powering medical, security, and fire suppression equipment; powering elevators and escalators; and running cooking and laundry equipment.[5] In commercial buildings, the use of natural gas is similar to its use in residences: space heating, water heating and sometimes for air conditioning.[6]

Given the situation, the campaign's objectives were to:

1. Connect PG&E's small and medium business customers with timely and relevant savings information at points when they are looking to solve a problem,
2. Generate "handraisers" and move customers along their energy management journey,
3. Provide engaged customers with new energy management solutions they may not have considered,

Establish PG&E as an innovator and thought leader in cutting edge energy solutions designed specifically for customers.

Roberta reminded the group that, in its pitch to PG&E, Jacobs and Clevenger proposed that "PG&E's extensive energy management resources needed to be mined, rearticulated and disseminated in a way that helped customers self-realize ways they can save and implement solutions." In other words, PG&E had to help customers help themselves. This is all about content marketing. How could the agency create compelling content to start and sustain the conversation between PG&E and its small and medium-sized business customers? She invited the attendees to start throwing out ideas.

The list of possibilities grew quickly.

- We know PG&E has all this great material. How could we reorganize it? Where should it be located? How should it be distributed?
- Let's look at the search engine optimization. It may be relatively easy to make this information more easily "findable" by search engines such as Google and Bing.
- What about an e-book? Or a webinar? Business-to-business marketing uses these tools all the time-- they are great lead generators. We can require an online form be completed before they get the e-book about "easy energy-saving practices" or something like that.
- How do businesses use social media? It's not the same as the business to consumer approach, is it? What role could social media play in this plan? Maybe we should explore how "influencers" could be part of this plan.

---

[5] U.S. Energy Information Administration, Annual Energy Outlook, 2015. Reference Case, Table 5 (April 2015). http://www.eia.gov/energyexplained/index.cfm?page=electricity_use
[6] http://geology.com/articles/natural-gas-uses/

- PG&E knows everything about its customers' energy use. How can we use that information to create customized and attention-getting messages? Auditing and analyzing energy use in a variety of categories such as lighting, air conditioning and heating, office equipment, appliances, and machinery – and then zeroing in on the items in each category might give us the basis for messages individually tailored to each customer.
- Everybody's email inbox is too full. Why not try some good direct mail? That might really stand out from the crowd.
- Do you think businesses look at their statement inserts in their physical bills? What if their bills are all online?
- Perhaps we can use sales promotion techniques or awards and recognition. Gamification tools such as points, badges, and leaderboards can also be helpful to engage and recognize business customers' energy efficiency.
- Some small business owners are rather traditional. Would they respond to other forms of print communications? What publications do they read?

It was almost time to adjourn the meeting so Roberta concluded with "This is a great start, team. We have a week to develop the plan of what we propose to do specifically. First, let's make sure we have the right profile of the target customers and their motivations to save energy. The small and medium business market is huge and quite varied. We know the industry has some bearing on energy usage. Can we segment this market in a meaningful way that goes beyond the size of the business and its industry? (See Appendix A for a list of industries served.) Is there anything we have missed about small and medium businesses in this area?

We should make sure that we consider all forms of marketing communications and remember that this is a business to business solution (See Appendix B.). What are the media habits of our target market? How do we integrate all the messages we create and media we select? We really want PG&E's business customers to control their energy consumption, contain their costs, and benefit from all of the help that PG&E can provide them. I'm sure we can figure out how to do this effectively.

Of course, all of this needs to be measurable. Any marketing efforts have to demonstrate their value. Data collection for future use in further marketing efforts is a high priority. We can't forget that."

APPENDIX A

Industries Served by PG&E[7]

PG&E serves about 800,000 small and medium-sized businesses in Central and Northern California. They are classified in the following categories:
- Agriculture and Food Processing
- Builders
- Food Services
- Health Care
- High Tech
- Hospitality
- Industrial
- Municipalities
- Office Buildings
- Retail
- Schools and Colleges

APPENDIX B

Business to Business (B2B) Marketing Overview

Business to Business (B2B) marketing is the marketing of goods and services to business organizations for production, business operations, or for resale to consumers. For example, an auto maker needs to purchase components and parts such as engines and braking systems from suppliers to be used in producing vehicles. The auto maker also needs to pay for utilities such as electricity and water in order to operate. The auto maker may need to purchase services such as advertising and market research to operate more efficiently. Its final product – vehicles bearing its brands – is sold to dealerships who then resell to consumers.

When companies buy and sell goods or services for their business purposes, they are in business markets. While business markets and consumer markets both involve buying and selling of goods and services, decision making in business markets differs significantly than in consumer markets.
- Business goods and services often have more complicated technical specifications and requirements;
- Business buyers are far fewer in number but most business buyers purchase in much larger quantities;
- Business buying often involves more people in the decision making. This is particularly true for major purchases, when decisions are reached by the joint effort of procurement, technical departments, and even top management;

---

[7] https://www.pge.com/en/mybusiness/save/energyefficiencycontractors/findspecialists/index.page?

- Business buying follows more rigorous procedures from product specification to supplier search and qualification, and from ordering to receiving orders and making payment.

These differences have at least two important implications for B2B marketing. First, business buying is very goal-directed. Business organizations are under tremendous pressure to make the right decisions – meeting technical requirements, price goals, and strategic objectives. Second, the business buying process is often more complex and may take much more time than consumer buying because business purchases are large in quantity, have a major impact on the business organization, involve more people, and may have to follow more procedures. These are exactly the reasons why content marketing has found such widespread use in business markets. Digital content provides highly targeted information in a timely yet cost-efficient manner and plays an important role in helping business buyers move forward in their decision making processes.

APPENDIX C

Content Marketing

Search engines and social networks add powerful tools to the arsenal of marketers. One strategic use of these tools is **content marketing**, the purpose of which is to consistently create and distribute valuable and relevant content to attract and retain a clearly-defined audience and to drive profitable customer action.

Companies can create many types of content to be published on the web and promoted through search engines and social networks. The following content types are commonly used:

- **Ebooks, white papers, research reports, how-to guides, and case studies**: online publications in the formats of books, papers, reports, guides, or cases.
- **Templates and tools**: A template is a file of basic format (e.g., for business letters, charts, graphs) that can be downloaded by users. Tools are computer program applications that perform certain functions (e.g., a web-based calculator to estimate investment returns or to calculate energy consumption or energy savings).
- **Infographics**: graphic representation of information to make the data easily understandable. Many examples are available online.
- **Podcasts:** episodes of audio and video files that subscribers can stream or download. These are analogous to radio broadcasts or short movies.
- **Webinars:** presentations transmitted over the Web using video conferencing software (i.e., a web-based seminar).
- **Videos**: digital video files that can be streamed online or downloaded from a website.
- **Blogs**: informal or conversational writing on a regularly updated website or web page.
- **Landing page**: a web page that appears to a visitor who clicks on a search result, an online ad, or other types of links in emails or social media. Many landing pages contain a specific call-to-action.

Regardless of the format, it is critical to make sure the content is 1) relevant and engaging to the targeted audience and 2) optimized for the media (search engines, social networks, or websites).

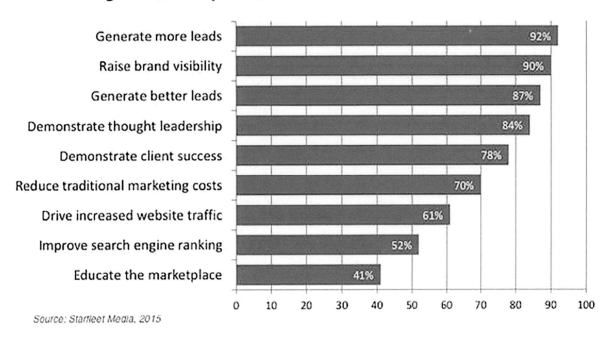

What are your company's primary objectives for investing in content marketing in the first place?

Source: Starfleet Media, 2015

Figure 1: Companies' Objectives for Content Marketing[8]

Before launching a content marketing campaign, or any marketing campaigns, a company should first set clear objectives. B2B content marketers often seek to generate more and better leads, raise brand visibility, demonstrate thought leadership, drive website traffic, or educate its customers. (See Figure 1 above.) Moving on to campaign implementation, a key decision is to determine which media outlets should be used to distribute the content. Media outlets should not work in isolation. Instead, one should select a combination of media outlets (e.g., multiple search engines and social networks) that work together in an integrated fashion to meet campaign objectives.

Finally, how do marketers monitor and assess campaign performance? Key metrics of performance should be used to monitor whether the campaign is on track to meet its objectives. For example, if the objective is to generate leads, the quantity and quality of generated leads may be assessed by monitoring the total number of leads generated and the average sales revenue among those who actually place orders. If the objective is to increase website traffic, increase in the number of unique visitors may be a good metric. Search engines and social networks often provide analytics tools that can be used to facilitate the monitoring and assessment of campaigns (e.g., Google Analytics, Google Adwords, and Facebook Insights). A company can also develop its own applications to customize its interactions with search engines and social networks.

---

8 http://www.starfleetmedia.com/2015/09/03/assessing-primary-objectives-b2b-content-marketing/

APPENDIX D

<u>Search Engine Marketing</u>

Search Engine Optimization and Pay per Click

For a company to drive traffic to its website, search engines such as Google, Yahoo, and Bing can play a big role. To understand why, think about how we visit a website: while we occasionally choose to enter the website address (a.k.a. **direct traffic**), we are more likely to use a search engine to find the website (a.k.a. **search**), or click a referral link from another website. According to some research, organic search accounts for about 60% of web traffic while only 12% of website traffic originates from direct input of the website URL. [9] Search engines are a primary method of navigation on the Web, especially when we are searching for something of specific interest: we search, view the search results, and click on a website link relevant to our search.

Search engines use mathematical formulas known as search algorithms to rank websites based on relevance to the search. Search algorithms are proprietary, so we cannot tell exactly what algorithms are being used by a search engine. Apart from the word(s) used to search, search engines may use other information for its algorithms (e.g., searcher's location, previous search behavior). The more relevant search results are delivered by search algorithms, the more satisfied and loyal we are, the more search share a search engine gets from us. The three most significant search engines in the US are Google, Microsoft Bing, and Yahoo. The shares of the search market owned by each search engine changes frequently and marketers must track those changes to know how to best allocate its resources among search engines.[10]

From a company's perspective, one way to make its website easily found on a search engine is to make its website rank higher by the search engine when certain keywords are used in search queries. On a search engine results page (SERP), a company wants its website to be among the top three presented on the first page of the search results. **Search engine optimization,** or **SEO**, is about improving the search engine ranking of a website by satisfying the requirements of a search engine's algorithms. Although search algorithms are quite complex and change frequently, search engines generally rank websites based on how relevant websites are to a search query (the words that users type into the search box). For example, an algorithm is likely to consider:

- ☐ Words used on the website;
- ☐ Page titles of the website;
- ☐ Links to the website;
- ☐ Reputation of the website.

---

[9] https://searchenginewatch.com/sew/study/2355020/organic-search-accounts-for-up-to-64-of- website-traffic-study , accessed 4/20/2016

[10] For instance, according to ComScore, Google led the U.S. explicit core search market in April 2016 with 63.8% market share, followed by Microsoft sites (Bing) 21.6%) and Yahoo (12.2%). http://www.comscore.com/Insights/Rankings

A company's website ranked higher by search engines is likely to receive more **organic** visitor traffic because it depends on "natural" search results, rather than paid advertising search results as we discuss next.

When organic search results do not bring sufficient visitor traffic, a company can use paid search engine advertising programs, such as Google's Adwords or similar advertising programs of Yahoo and Bing, to feature its ads alongside organic (or natural) search results. Search engines ads are targeted, primarily based on search keywords. Searchers click on relevant ads to go to a landing page on the company's website.

Search engine advertising is also known as **pay per click**, or **PPC**, because a company is charged by the number of times its ads receive clicks. Web traffic generated through search engine advertising is referred to as **paid search**. Well-designed paid search advertising can generate revenue for companies in a variety of ways and quite cost-effectively. For this reason, marketers are spending billions of dollars annually on search engine advertising with no sign of slowing.

SEO and PPC complement each other in promoting the visibility of a company's website to search engine users and are collectively referred to as **search engine marketing** or **SEM**. Driving traffic to websites enhances brand and product awareness and facilitates online transactions, including product purchases, as well as the sharing of information. Search engine marketing is important for marketers for two reasons: quantity and quality. Google, the largest search engine in the world, processes over 40,000 search queries every second, which translates to over 3.5 billion searches per day and 1.2 trillion searches per year worldwide.[11] This has the potential to provide a company enormous exposure.

Less apparent is the quality power of search engines: our psychological mode using search engines has tremendous potential for marketing activities and campaigns. When we search, we are motivated to give out something (i.e., our interest) and to get back something of interest in return (e.g., content, services, goods, information). Our interests, as revealed to search engines, are extremely valuable because they are related to commercial activities, directly or indirectly. For example, if we search for "webcam", we may well be somewhere in a buying process: recognizing a need for a webcam, searching for various models to compare, narrowing down to a few options for close quality/price comparison, making choices, or placing orders. Exposing your product during this search process may spark the searcher's interest, lead him or her to obtaining information, and, eventually, to a sale.

---

[11] http://www.internetlivestats.com/google-search-statistics/

APPENDIX E

Social Media Marketing

Referral links placed on social media sites are particularly noteworthy in terms of directing visitor traffic to a company's website. There are over 2 billion users of social networks worldwide, with a projected increase to 2.72 billion by 2019.[12] Not surprisingly, social media is becoming an ever-increasing source of website traffic. Reports differ on social media's precise share of referred traffic but the trend is clear.[13]

In spite of the large number of users of social networks overall, the market share of different social networks varies widely (and changes frequently), with Facebook and YouTube leading the pack. Social networks differ a lot in their ability to direct traffic to a particular company's website. The quality of traffic also varies, with some social networks generating more valuable visitors who are more likely to be converted into customers.

Social media marketing refers to a company's marketing activities on social media platforms. Similar to search engine marketing, there are organic and paid components in social media marketing. Generally, social networks do not charge companies to use their social networks for marketing activities such as creating company pages (e.g., Facebook Page) or a company channel (e.g., YouTube Channel) that contain marketing messages and informative or entertaining content. Instead, social networks generate revenue by charging for targeted advertising (e.g., Facebook ads, promoted tweets in Twitter), data analytics, and other value- added services.

APPENDIX F

Chart courtesy of Jacobs & Clevenger

---

[12] http://www.statista.com/statistics/278414/number-of-worldwide-social-network- users/
[13] http://www.forbes.com/sites/jaysondemers/2015/02/03/social-media-now-drives-31-of-all-referral-traffic/#48fa17f1aeed

The Re:new Project: Carrying the Story of Refugee Women

By

Kate Schaefer, Columbia College Chicago

The Founder's Story

In July 2001, The Re:new Project's founder, Rebecca, her husband, and baby moved to Nairobi, Kenya where Rebecca's husband was a relief worker. A few months had passed when Rebecca first heard a group of women singing. As she neared the sound, she saw more than 50 women draped in African Kitenge cloth singing Swahili songs. Rebecca quickly learned that the women were refugees employed by Amani Ya Juu, a microenterprise that taught the women to sew. The community of women created a flourishing shop where they sold more than 350 products, ranging from small wooden villages to fabric bags to children's toys. The women designed the products while bonding through singing, sewing, and sharing their refugee stories.

Rebecca spent the better part of her five years in Nairobi at Amani Ya Juu. Amani Ya Juu provided a thriving and peaceful workplace for the refugees. Each day, the refugees made their way to Amani Ya Juu to work within its acre of land that housed a garden, a small café, a sewing room, and a chapel. Here, Rebecca listened daily as the women shared their stories. Some refugee women were animated as they told their stories with dramatic actions and vibrant interpretations. Some sat motionless and spoke softly of what they had been through. Some cried and some expressed anxiety through laughter and nervous giggles. These women experienced some of the worst forms of persecution; they were raped, hunted, and abused.
Their children were killed in front of them or taken from them. They walked hundreds of miles. They almost starved to death. They abandoned all that they had. Many were widows yet took care of ten or more children, including their own children plus nieces and nephews who were orphaned due to war or disease.

Rebecca constantly saw the impact these women had on one another; the connections, sense of community, and support empowered the women. They thrived because they had one another; they created their own community.

After five years in Nairobi, Rebecca's time in Kenya came to a close as her husband's work came to an end. She said goodbye to the women who had become her second family. Rebecca knew that although her family was moving thousands of miles from Nairobi to Illinois, the next chapter in her life would, no doubt, be shaped by her experiences in Nairobi at Amani Ya Juu.

The Re:new Project is Born

After settling in their new home in Wheaton, Illinois, a suburb about 25 miles west of Chicago, Rebecca made a late night Target run. On her way home, between the rain, sleet and snow, Rebecca faintly made out a woman walking on the side of the road, wrapped loosely in an African Kitenge cloth. Rebecca followed her into the apartment complex and knocked on her door.

When the door opened a reminiscent smell of spices greeted Rebecca, along with a smiling woman and the laughter and chatter of gregarious children. And just like that, Rebecca felt like she was in Nairobi again. Upon entering the woman's home, Rebecca said "Jambo sana" (Hello in Swahili) and quickly learned that this family was from Somalia. The woman told Rebecca that she and her family had walked out of Somalia to a refugee camp in Northern Kenya. At the end of their conversation, the woman pleaded with Rebecca, *"You can give me job? You see many kids? You can give me job?"* As Rebecca drove home, she thought back to her time in Nairobi at Amani Ya Juu. The refugee women acquired employable skills and developed meaningful relationships with other refugee women while working at Amani Ya Juu. Rebecca was unaware of a similar service in the Chicagoland area.

Over the next few months, Rebecca visited the woman and her family and listened intently to her stories and experiences in the United States. The stories she shared were so familiar to what Rebecca had heard from the women in Nariobi. Employment was one of the greatest needs for refugees during the resettlement process. Thus, in 2009, Rebecca developed the Re:new Project. Rebecca's goal for The Re:new Project was to empower refugee women to gain valuable skills by offering vocational training, create a safe, supportive and nurturing community of women, and offer a flexible work environment.

The History of The Re:new Project

The Re:new Project was a non-profit social enterprise that employed and educated refugee women who resettled in the United States from all over the world, including places such as Somalia, Uzbekistan, Pakistan, Burma (Myanmar) and The Kingdom of Bhutan. These women survived war, persecution or political conflict. Upon resettlement in the United States to begin a new chapter in their lives, the women were referred to The Re:new Project through a partnership with World Relief or word of mouth from other artisans.

What Does "Refugee" Mean?

Refugees have been forced to flee their home countries. According to the United Nations High Council for Refugees (UNHCR), refugees are people fleeing conflict or persecution. In a recent year, there were 65.5 million people forcibly displaced worldwide; 33,972 people a day were forced to flee their homes because of conflict and persecution ("United Nations High Council"). Refugees resettled in a foreign environment, surrounded by unfamiliar faces, customs and lifestyles. They often felt isolated, lonely and financially stretched. According to Rebecca, her definition for refugee evolved and became three-dimensional: "A refugee is someone who, because of being persecuted for reasons of race, religion, nationality or political opinion, is outside the country of his or her nationality" ("Re:new Project").

The Re:new Project invested in the lives of these women on an economic, social and and spiritual level by providing refugee women with a space to connect with others. The women created handbags and accessory items using upcycled fabrics to sell in The Re:new Project's retail space as part of their social enterprise. This provided the women with sustainable income in a flexible, community-based environment. The opportunities created by The Re:new Project tied closely back to the organizational mission, vision, and manifesto. (See Appendix A.)

What is a Social Enterprise?

Non-profits typically were funded by a combination of donations, corporate contributions, foundation gifts and grants, and interest from investments, among other sources of incomes. (See Exhibit 1.) However, The Re:new Project operated an e- commerce and bricks and mortar retail store to advance its social mission and create financial sustainability for the organization, thus categorizing the organization as a social enterprise.

The Social Enterprise Alliance suggested the following basic working definition of social enterprise:

A social enterprise is an organization or initiative that marries the social mission of a non-profit or government program with the market-driven approach of a business ("Social Enterprise Alliance").

Exhibit 1: *Nonprofit Funding*

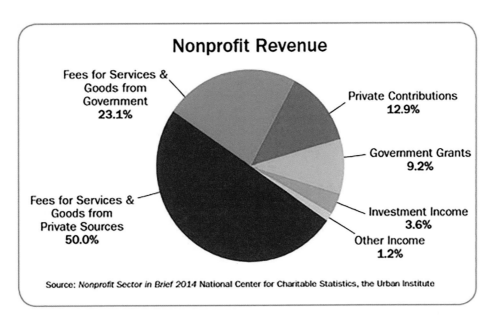

Of particular importance to The Re:new Project was the interest Millennials showed in social enterprises. Millennials responded favorably to social enterprises and social entrepreneurs. A 2015 Cone Communications Millennial Corporate Social Responsibility Study found that Millennials actively pursued products, events, and services that supported corporate social and environmental efforts. For example, 87% of Millennials would purchase a product with a social or environmental benefit (compared to 83% of the U.S. average), and 70% of Millennials were willing to pay more for a product if it impacted an issue they cared about, compared to 66% of the US average ("Cone Communications").

The Re:new Project was well positioned to appeal to the socially conscious Millennial customer as every product sold through the microenterprise had a direct, positive impact on the refugee women. These sales funded the Artisan Development Program that trained The Re:new Project artisans in obtaining marketable skills to help them rebuild their lives in a new country.

The Re:new Project's Workshop and Retail Environments

The Re:new Project began in a 350-square-foot room with five machines and four students and grew to a retail storefront and workspace totaling over 2500 square feet. The Re:new Project provided services such as the Artisan Development Program and Care Services to more than 135 women who have resettled in the US from Somalia, Turkey, Nepal, Iraq, Bhutan, Sudan, and Tanzania, among other countries.

The refugee women who participated in The Re:new Project's Artisan Development Program received free vocational training. They learned sewing skills to use throughout their lives in order to earn a living wage. Some learned sewing skills that were used at home while caring for children; others used the skills learned and launched their own businesses. Others were employed at The Re:new Project, using their sewing skills to earn a fair living wage making handbags and accessories. The Re:new Project's merchandise assortment included messenger bags, totes, wallets, clutches, dopp kits, and key chains. The merchandise sold at The Re:new Project's retail store provided a tangible product that allowed customers to support the organizational mission.

Products were designed and produced in The Re:new Project's studio using upcycled textiles. Textiles were donated by furniture retailers and manufacturers, fashion designers, apparel retailers and fabric stores. Because textiles were donated in different quantities, each product was truly one-of a kind. The handbags and accessory items were then sold in various retail outlets, including The Re:new Project's retail space as part of a social enterprise. Each bag was labeled "Carry the Story" (See Exhibit 2) along with the name of the artisan/refugee woman who sewed the bag. The idea was that "when you carry Re:new products, you carry the stories of the remarkable women who sought refuge here" ("Re:new Project").

However, as The Re:new Project grew, both in programming and product, it became apparent that different platforms communicated different messages. They lacked a cohesive integrated marketing communications (IMC) plan as they were not consistently promoting the social enterprise benefits to philanthropic consumers through touch-points with consumers, including, but not limited to storefront messaging, print and digital media. An effective IMC plan would ensure that The Re:new Project's brand messaging was communicated simultaneously through store interior and exterior displays, print and digital platforms. The Re:new Project's website included highly visible imagery and videos of the refugee women, but this same information was nowhere to be found through social media, the organizational blog, or printed marketing collateral. Customers were unable to "carry the story" because they were unaware of the women's stories.

Although the refugee women recognized the importance of sharing their stories, few were able to publicly tell their story for fear of safety and retaliation. As a result, the stories of their struggles, challenges, and experiences were imperceptible.

Exhibit 2: *"Carry the Story" Product Labels*

The Ultimate Consumers: Identifying Re:new's Target Market

The Re:new Project knew that the e-commerce and bricks and mortar stores reached two different consumer groups: Baby Boomer and Gen X customers visited the bricks and mortar store as they preferred to shop in a physical space with tangible product, while The Re:new Project's web presence was strengthened through key word searches and search engine optimization, social media, and e-commerce to connect with Millennials.

Although Baby Boomers, Gen X, and Millennials all shopped bricks and mortar retail, they did so in varying capacities. According to market research done by The NPD Group, "age seems to determine a shopper's affinity for buying from a real-world store" (Conley). Baby boomers gravitated toward bricks and mortar retail, members of Gen X shopped both virtually as well as in bricks and mortar, and Millennials were interested in bricks and mortar shopping only when it could be done easily. (See Exhibit 5.)

The Re:new Project's bricks and mortar location was not optimal to reach Millennials. Located in downtown Glen Ellyn, IL, the shopping district did not include national or big box retailers but rather independent boutiques, salons, and restaurants. As a conservative shopper, the Millennial customer focused on value rather than convenience; many times the Millennial customer turned to online shopping to maximize value and minimize expenditures. The independent retailers found in the Glen Ellyn shopping district made it difficult for the tech savvy Millennial shopper to utilize apps, shop online, and/or compare price offerings as these retailers didn't have a strong web presence. Customers shopping The Re:new Project's bricks and mortar store generally were local women who happened upon the store window while in the Glen Ellyn shopping district.

This type of shopping environment appealed to the Baby Boomer and Gen X shopper, which aligned with the demographic make-up of Glen Ellyn. The population of Glen Ellyn was comprised primarily of Generation X (30.7%), followed by Baby Boomers (19%), then Millennials (13.3%); the median age of Glen Ellyn residents was 41 years old ("Suburban Stats").

However, targeting Millennials was important to The Re:new Project because of their buying power as well as buying behavior. The buying behavior of Millennials was dramatically different from Generation X and Baby Boomers; the Millennial generation was the most cognizant of supporting social entrepreneurships. More than nine-in-10 Millennials would switch brands to one associated with a cause (91% vs. 85% U.S. average) (See Exhibit 6) and 78% of Millennials at least sometimes considered ethics in their purchasing compared to 61% of Baby Boomers ("Cone Communications").

Connecting with Customers

With growing emphasis on omnichannel retail, cohesive messaging through an integrated marketing communications plan was imperative. Millennial shoppers were not strolling past store windows deciding whether or not to stop in; Millennial shoppers lived online. The NPD Group claimed that 54% of Millennials' purchases were made online. And, because Millennials "believe that profit and purpose go hand in hand", Millennial shoppers were an important demographic for The Re:new Project to target. In order to reach the Millennial customer, The Re:new Project developed an online presence as a companion to the bricks and mortar retail space.

The Re:new Project developed a strong web presence by utilizing an e-commerce site (renewproject.org) as well as several social media sites (blog, Facebook, Pinterest, Instagram,) to connect with digital native Millennials. They developed a series of hashtags that were consistently used (#carrythestory, #renewproject, #refugeeswelcome, #artisanmade) throughout social media posts. These hashtags were developed to create a sense of community and relevancy through social networks; not tied to a specific cause.

When an Executive Order was put in place that banned all refugees from entering the United States, The Re:new Project began a social media campaign to encouragement for the refugee women and provide a glimpse into each woman's journey. (See Exhibit 3.) They used Facebook to show support for the refugees by posting individual messages that introduced each woman by first name, country of persecution and reason for fleeing. The first of its kind for The Re:new Project, this campaign lasted the entire 120 days of the ban. Another 'first' for The Re:new Project was the 100% participation by the refugee women; the refugee women deemed it important to publicly share their stories. There was a level of anonymity since very few personal identifiers were included. Although the messaging was strong on social media, it was nowhere to be found in the bricks and mortar store.

Although The Re:new Project established a presence through various channels, its leaders found that customers were using each platform for different purposes. Customers visited the website for information gathering; they were able to learn about upcoming events, new product launches, and the journeys of the refugee women. Facebook and Instagram were used to see new products and keep tabs on The Re:new Project's activity. After viewing products online, users then visited the bricks and mortar store to view The Re:new Project's full collection and make a purchase. Social media was used to further develop a sense of community, connect with like-minded people, and learn more about how to support refugees. In addition, The Re:new Project found that 60% of traffic to their site was on a mobile device, but their site was not mobile friendly. The Re:new Project's existing website template was outdated, so many of the sub-pages were inaccessible on a mobile device.

The Re:new Project also lacked consistent messaging in the bricks and mortar retail space, the e-commerce site, and the social media outlets. The primary focus of the bricks and mortar store was the merchandise itself; the stories of the refugee women were nowhere to be found, making it difficult for shoppers to draw parallels between merchandise and organization's mission. The digital platforms (website, e- commerce, and social media outlets) heavily focused on the stories of the refugee women through imagery, videos, and personal anecdotes; the selling of merchandise was secondary to storytelling.

Exhibit 3: *Social Media Campaign Spring 2017*

Carry the Story: Store Interior and Exterior Messaging

Visiting the bricks and mortar space showed little evidence of the personal stories of the refugee women. The stories of the women of The Re:new Project were powerful and inspiring as they had overcome obstacles beyond imagination; purchasing The Re:new Project merchandise helped to make a positive, life-changing impact on the lives of the refugee women and their families, yet this message was not conveyed to shoppers. The challenge faced by The Re:new Project was how to communicate the stories and/or experiences of the refugee women to The Re:new Project customers, both the intentional shopper in the store and the unintentional passer-by.

Most people were unaware of the refugees' stories because they were not visible in the window or store interior yet these stories were the differentiator between The Re:new Project's products and other handbags and accessories offered in the marketplace.
Approximately half of the women who participated in The Re:new Project's programming were able and willing to tell their stories in written, oral, and/or visual formats (store interior and exterior, website, and social media) but the other half expressed grave safety concerns. They were fearful of putting themselves and their families in unsafe situations by putting their names, faces, photographs, stories, and/or other personal identifiers in such a visual and lasting platform. The Re:new Project struggled to find a way to tell the stories of all the women, not simply the ones who were able to share their stories in written, oral and/or visual formats.

The refugee women recognized the importance of sharing their stories, so whenever possible, The Re:new Project relied on sales associates to "carry the story" in a safe and respectful way as these stories were important to the sales of The Re:new Projects' products. The sales associates worked with customers to show them the label with the name of the artisan who worked on the bag and share part of her story with shoppers.

Exhibit 4: Generational Spending Habits

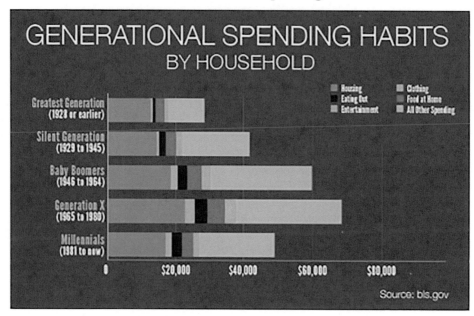

Exhibit 5: Millennial CSR Buying Behavior

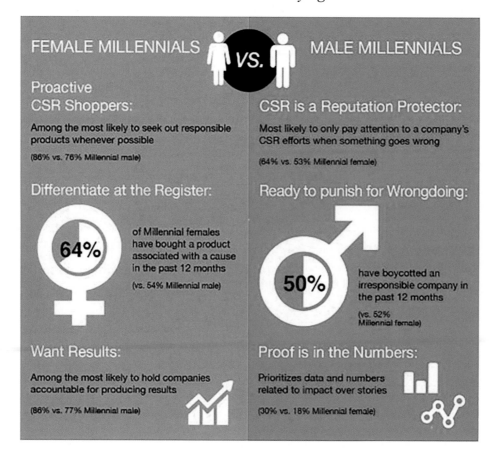

However, sales associates were unable to reach every customer and/or share a variety of stories with shoppers. Therefore, many of the refugee women were not represented because their stories could not be shared or shoppers were not purchasing product they had worked on. The Re:new Project did, however, include subtle messaging throughout the store (See Exhibit 6) to connect the merchandise to the refugee women through in- store signage as well as limited photos of the refugee women, but the powerful stories about the journeys, experiences, and challenges faced by the refugee women were absent from the bricks and mortar shopping experience.

The store exterior was an underutilized space; the exterior street-level window was changed out once a quarter (Spring/Summer, Back to School, and Winter/Holiday as examples) and featured seasonal, trend-appropriate merchandise. (See Exhibit 7.) Product rotated on a weekly basis but window display themes rotated four times a year. Signage was minimal and did not call attention to The Re:new Project's point of differentiation—its mission, the social enterprise, and/or request for shoppers to "carry the story". Passer-bys didn't know the story behind the bags, the challenges faced by the refugee women, or The Re:new Project's sustainable business model. The store front window was not effectively used to marry The Re:new Project's mission with the social enterprise. This was a stark contrast from their website which prominently displayed a series of rotating images, videos and messages pertaining to the organizational mission and participants. The Re:new Project lacked cohesive messaging across the different platforms.

Exhibit 6: *Re:new Brick and Mortar Store Interior*

***Exhibit 7:** Re:new Brick and Mortar Store Exterior*

A Cohesive Marketing Campaign

The Re:new Project's primary promotional tactic was a dynamic, informative website. The Re:new Project's digital presence effectively translated the stories of the refugee women through videos, photographs, and story-telling. (See Exhibit 8.) With rotating images depicting the women, product offerings, upcoming events, and notable press coverage, the website was highly visual. The home page featured a tab entitled 'Our Story', leading visitors to believe they would learn about The Re:new Project's story. As the video began, viewers were introduced to one of the refugee women telling her story. This reinforced The Re:new Project's mission, creating an emotional connection as viewers heard the stories and learned the impact each purchase had on the refugee women. Such an emotional connection worked alongside the rational appeal of The Re:new Project's product offerings, including product quality and value benefits. This messaging was incredibly important to directly tie back to The Re:new Project's mission to "create a space for refugee women to thrive" ("Re:new Project").

***Exhibit 8:** Website Messaging*

In order to increase customer loyalty, The Re:new Project built upon the well-developed artisan stories found on their website and invited viewers to connect through other platforms: blog, Facebook, Instagram, and e-newsletter. Inviting viewers to connect (using opt-in techniques) came across as genuine and unobtrusive and reinforced The Re:new Project's messaging, creating a more effective marketing campaign that integrated different mediums. Social media provided a way to develop meaningful connections, build a brand, and initiate thoughtful conversations with users. According to Sprout Social, 88% of 18-29 year olds, 84% of 30-49 year olds, and 72% of 50-64 year olds used Facebook (York). However, the use of social media proved to be an especially effective way to connect with Millennials as two- thirds (66%) of Millennials used social media to engage around corporate social responsibility compared to 53% of the U.S. average ("Cone Communications"). Another benefit of utilizing social media was increased exposure; The Re:new Project was able to create awareness of their organization, mission, and products to a wider audience through their existing followers. However, once users gravitated to other platforms (bricks and mortar, Facebook or Instagram), the messaging changed. The bricks and mortar store and social media platforms focused on the social enterprise rather than the organizational mission; the focus was on The Re:new Project's product offering rather than the refugees' stories.

The Re:new Project's mission was not emphasized across other mediums; there was a disconnect across digital and bricks and mortar outlets as the messaging was inconsistent. A united message would more effectively reiterate The Re:new Project's mission and vision. The emotional connection successfully created on the website between the merchandise and social enterprise was absent in the brick and mortar retail space.

The Decision Problem

As The Re:new Project's marketing efforts evolved to incorporate new and different platforms (exterior window, e-commerce, website, social media, mobile, e-newsletter), the organizational mission became more and more challenging to incorporate consistently for both The Re:new Project and the artisans. The simple request to "carry the story" of the refugee women became much more complicated given the exposure and global accessibility of digital content, making it difficult for The Re:new Project to develop an integrated marketing communications plan that was effective but still protected the artisans.

Several questions arose for Rebecca and The Re:new Project team:

- How can The Re:new Project tell a cohesive story, encouraging customers to "carry the story" across the various platforms?
- Is there a way to tell the stories of all the refugee women, not simply the ones who are able to share their stories in written, oral, and visual formats?
- How can The Re:new Project market their point of differentiation (cause marketing) to passer-bys in the brick and mortar space?

Works Cited

"About—Social Enterprise". Social Enterprise Alliance, 1 June 2017, www.socialenterprise.us/about/social-enterprise/.

Blumenthal, Eli. "Millennials drive spike in online shopping." *USA Today*, 8 June 2016, www.usatoday.com/story/money/2016/06/08/survey-more-than-half-purchases-made- online/85592598/. Accessed 1 June 2017.

Conley, Paul. "Winning Millennials, Gen X, and Boomers with the Five Ws." *The NPD Group,* www.npd.com/wps/portar/npd/us/news/tips-trends-takeaways/winning- millennials- gen-x-and-boomers-with-the-five-ws/.
Accessed 15 June 2017.

Duggan, Maeve. Greenwood, Shannon. Perrin, Andrew. "Social Media Update 2016". *Pew Research Center*. 11 Nov. 2016. http://www.pewinternet.org/2016/11/11/social- media- update-2016//. Accessed 28 June 2017.

Loudenback, Tanza. "Millennials are rapidly changing today's business landscape—here are 6 reasons for it." *Business Insider*, 18 April 2016, www.businessinsider.com/jason- haber- millennials-best-social-entrepreneurs-2016-4/#-1. Accessed 28 June 2017.

Martin, Emmie. "Goldman Sachs says millennials didn't inherit a spending habit companies have capitalized on for years." *Business Insider*, 12 Jan. 2017, www.businessinsider.com/goldman-sachs-millennials-spending-habits-2017-1.

"New Cone Communications Research Confirms Millennials as American's Most Ardent

CSR Supports", *Cone Communications,* 23 Sept. 2015, www.conecomm.com/news- blog/new-cone-communications-research-confirms-millennials-as-americas-most-ardent- csr- supporters. Accessed 25 May 2017.

Pilcher, Jeffry. "Say It Again: Messages Are More Effective When Repeated." The Financial Brand, 23 Sept. 2014. www.thefinancialbrand.com/42323/advertising-marketing-messages-effective-frequency/. Accessed 30 June 2017.

"Population Demographics for Glen Ellyn Village, Illinois in 2016 and 2017." *Suburban Stats*, www.suburbanstats.org/population/illinois/how-many-people-live-in-glen-ellyn- village.

Sabrina, Danielle. "Rising Trend: Social Responsibility is High on Millennials' List" *The Huffington Post,* 3 Feb. 2017. www.huffingtonpost.com/danielle-sabrina/rising-trend-social-respo_b_14578380.html. Accessed 25 May 2017.

Social Enterprise Alliance. www.socialenterprise.us. Accessed 1 June 2017.

The Re:new Project. www.renew.org. Accessed 1 June 2017.
The UN Refugee Agency. www.unhcr.org. Accessed 1 June 2017.

York, Alex. "Social Media Demographics to Inform a Better Segmentation Strategy."
Sprout Social, www.sproutsocial.com/insights/new-social-media-demographics. Accessed 1 June 2017.

Appendix A: Re:new's Mission, Vision and Manifesto

MISSION

Re:new creates a space for refugee women to thrive.

VISION

To foster a society that values and seeks out flourishing relationships with its refugee neighbors.

MANIFESTO

We believe that all people are made in the image of God and are therefore valuable and worthy of the highest honor and respect.

We believe in the value of coming alongside those in our community who are in need, regardless of religion, race, or nationality.

We believe that the act of creating things of value is a powerful exercise in restoring hope to broken lives.

We believe that loving and serving one another transforms lives.

We believe that we are stronger when we are joined together in our common humanity.

Save the Redwoods League: Take a Walk in the Redwoods-- On Us!

By:

Blodwen Tarter, Golden Gate University

The Magnificent Redwoods

The redwoods, once seen, leave a mark or create a vision that stays with you always. No one has ever successfully painted or photographed a redwood tree. The feeling they produce is not transferable. From them comes silence and awe. It's not only their unbelievable stature, nor the color which seems to shift and vary under your eyes, no, they are not like any trees we know, they are ambassadors from another time.
- John Steinbeck, *Travels with Charley In Search of America, 1962*

To John Steinbeck and many others, redwood forests symbolize the essence of nature that must be preserved for now and the future. Poets and authors have waxed eloquent about these wonders of the natural world. They inspire awe for their natural beauty, for their sheer size, and for their unparalleled age. Two of the world's three species of trees commonly called redwoods are found primarily in California: the coast redwood (*Sequoia sempervirens*) and the giant sequoia or Sierra redwood (*Sequoiadendron giganteum*). The coast redwood is the world's tallest tree and the giant

Sequoia is the largest, most massive tree. The tallest known coast redwood is 379 feet tall-- as tall as a 37-floor skyscraper. The largest known giant Sequoia weighs 642 tons. Both species can live for hundreds, even thousands, of years. Redwoods were once found throughout the northern hemisphere. By the 1850s, coast redwoods covered about 2 million acres along the California coast, from just over the Oregon border to south of Big Sur. Further inland, the giant sequoia hugged the western slope of the Sierra Nevada mountain range. Widespread destruction began when gold was discovered in California in 1849 and hordes of settlers and miners demanded lumber.

The Establishment of Save the Redwoods League

The United States began to realize the value of its diminishing wilderness in the mid-19th century. By the early 20th century, the preservation movement was born. Many Californians focused on protecting the redwoods, those special trees that grow naturally only in California.

Founded in 1918, by a small group of concerned California conservationists, the not-for-profit Save the Redwoods League protects "redwoods by purchasing redwood forests and the surrounding lands needed to nurture them. Another way we protect forests is by acquiring conservation easements or agreements, which grant the League the legal right to safeguard the forest from harmful land use practices forever."[1] But it is not enough to protect the trees and the land. The League's mission now includes restoring logged areas and repairing damage in order to return the redwood forests to a healthy state more like the old- growth forest.

Naturally, and equally important, Save the Redwoods League seeks to connect people to redwoods forests and parks through exposure and education. So-called nature deficit disorder describes "the psychological, physical and cognitive costs of human alienation from nature"[2] and many agree that a walk in the woods is a profoundly healing and enriching experience. The redwoods are still endangered by logging, environmental degradation, and climate change. A mere 120,000 acres remain of the old-growth coast redwood forest. About 23% of the coast redwoods are protected in parks and preserves, while 77% (1.256 million acres) are privately owned. The Sierra redwood has an even smaller range: 48,000 protected acres (the size of Cleveland) in 75 groves scattered along the Sierra Nevada. Only about 3,000 acres of giant sequoias are in private hands.

Since its founding, the League has been instrumental in protecting the last vestiges of these ancient forests by helping purchase and protect nearly 200,000 acres. Dozens of parks, preserves, and conservation easements have been created or extended through the efforts of Save the Redwoods League. The League provides education grants, research grants, and supports citizen science that enlists volunteers to study where redwood forest plants and animals live, and to share the data collected with redwood forestry experts.

But the League does not do this alone. It has a close and long-standing relationship with the California State Parks and National Park Service in whose parks and preserves most of the publicly-protected redwood groves are located. In fact, the League helped establish the California State Park system in 1927. It partners with scientists and supports research about issues that affect the redwoods. Teachers and schools participate. Conservation groups and park cooperating associations work closely with the League. Thousands of individual members support the work of the League.

---

[1] http://www.savetheredwoods.org/our-work/protect/
[2] https://www.psychologytoday.com/blog/people-in-nature/200901/no-more-nature-deficit-disorder

Audience Definition

Like all organizations, Save the Redwoods League must remain relevant to its stakeholders and seeks to expand its reach. It wants to draw more people to the glory of the redwoods, to increase awareness of the precarious state of the forest, to encourage people to visit the redwoods, and to gain loyal and active supporters- people who will donate funds and volunteer.

To better understand its audience, the League commissioned a study that identified four groups or "core audience archetypes," all of whom recognized that redwood forests are something special. [3] These audiences are:

- The **Conservationist**: who desires to protect nature and preserve open space
- The **Steward**: who desires to engage the land respectfully, to not only conserve land but to also care for it
- The **Explorer**: who desires to discover something new, perhaps by hiking, to challenge themselves
- The **Parent**: who desires to provide children with enriching experiences, to nurture children and families. This includes teachers and caretakers.

In addition to these groups (which are not confined to specific demographics and may overlap), the League identified two other audience groups: Latinos and Millennials. The Hispanic/Latino population of California was rapidly growing, accounting for more than 38% of the people living in California. Forecasts suggest that, by 2060, Hispanics will account for 48% of the state's population.[4] A study by the Outdoor Foundation reported that while Latinos "made up a small percentage of total outdoor participants, those who did participate averaged the most annual outdoor outings per person."[5] The League decided to focus some of its outreach on this large minority group in the state.

Millennials, the cohort of people born between 1980 and 2000, now exceed the Baby Boomers (born between 1946 and 1964) in numbers and are rapidly growing in spending power as they mature in the job market.[6]

They are becoming parents with the accompanying influence on their children's attitudes towards the outdoors. Research suggests that Millennials are more critical when it comes to giving funds. They want to know where every single penny of the dollar donated is spent.

Reaching the Audience

The League's ongoing efforts to engage and educate its target audiences involved the standard suite of modern marketing communications methods. The organization had an attractive, easy- to-navigate, and regularly updated website that was mobile-responsive. With rapidly increasing use of smartphones, 40% of

---

[3] 2012 Audience Profile and Targeting Study
[4] http://www.dof.ca.gov/research/demographic/reports/projections/P-1/documents/Projections_Press_Release_2010- 2060.pdf
[5] https://outdoorindustry.org/images/researchfiles/1652_ResearchParticipation2014.pdf
[6] Amid The Stereotypes, Some Facts About Millennials http://www.npr.org/2014/11/18/354196302/amid-the- stereotypes-some-facts-about-millennials

the League's audience visited the website from a mobile device. It communicated to its supporters via opt-in email newsletters and blogs. The organization's president blogged and tweeted regularly. Social media presence on Facebook, Twitter, and Instagram, Google+, Flickr, Pinterest, and YouTube enabled the League to communicate quickly and efficiently with stakeholders who preferred these online channels and leveraged the ease of pass-along for its messages.

Not to be forgotten were more traditional methods of direct mail and personal outreach to key donors and members. Strong relationships with the media, particularly reporters who covered the environment and the San Francisco Bay Area, allowed the League to use the power of public relations effectively. All of these efforts were supported by a small staff of four employees in the Outreach department.

An Unanticipated Opportunity

On October 26, 2015, REI, the Seattle-based outdoor gear company and member-owned cooperative, announced that it would close the day after Thanksgiving. For the first time in its 76-year history, all of REI's 143 stores and its online website would be closed for business on the busiest shopping day of the year. (The previous year 133 million people hit the stores for early holiday shopping and special Black Friday deals. [7])

In the letter to its five million-plus members, REI's CEO wrote "Black Friday is the perfect time to remind ourselves of the essential truth that life is richer, more connected and complete when you choose to spend it outside. We are closing our doors, paying our employees to get out there."[8]

Officially designated #OptOutside, REI's campaign quickly went viral, spreading rapidly by word-of-mouth and a variety of media. In a country saturated with marketing messages to "buy, buy, buy" and often criticized for encouraging overconsumption, the campaign's suggestion to reconnect with people you love and the great outdoors resonated widely. One reporter characterized this as "the green backlash against Black Friday."[9] Before it was over, more than 1 million people across the US had opted outside for the day after Thanksgiving.[10]

A Quick Reaction

Immediately after REI's announcement, Save the Redwoods League decided to join the

#OptOutside movement. The League seized the opportunity to increase awareness of the mighty redwoods and of the California State Parks where ancient redwoods are protected by building on REI's efforts to get people outside on Black Friday, a day more frequently devoted to shopping then to a walk in the woods. What did the League do?

[7] www.thedailybeast.com/articles/2015/11/27/the-green-backlash-agains-black-friday.html
[8 and 10] See Appendix 3
[9] www.thedailybeast.com/articles/2015/11/27/the-green-backlash-agains-black-friday.html

To help people take a walk in the redwoods, they worked with the California State Parks system to offer free park passes for all 49 redwood state parks.[11] Jennifer Benito-Kowalski, Chief Communications Officer and the impetus behind the League's campaign, named it Free Redwood Parks Day. Its hashtag? #OptOutside#IntoTheRedwoods.

This seemingly simple concept was actually an extraordinary effort by small group of people in a very short period of time, leading to unprecedented success. As the first major organization to align itself with REI's campaign, the League led the way for 18 co-operating associations and 49 redwoods state parks to develop creative ways to build on the momentum created by REI. Twelve states in the US eventually joined the movement to get people outside and followed California's lead by offering a free park day on Black Friday.

There was not much time between REI's announcement and Black Friday. Planning an entire campaign in just nine days and implementing an event on this scale in only thirty days demanded focus, careful attention to detail, and rapid decision-making. Here is the timeline of events.

26 October 2015	REI announces #OptOutside to its members via email.
27 October	REI announces #OptOutside widely
28 October	Benito-Kowalski proposed the Free Redwood Parks Day to Save the Redwoods League president and gained approval.
6 November 2015	Benito-Kowalski proposed the Free Redwood Parks Day to the California State Parks chief deputy director.
12 November	Benito-Kowalski outlined the communications plan and directed the Save the Redwoods League Outreach team to begin work on implementation immediately, anticipating formal approval.
16 November	Benito-Kowalski gained California State Parks' cooperation; directed the Outreach Department to complete its tasks in just two business days.
17 November	The Outreach team completed the media advisory, news release, webpages, social messages, emails for members, blog posts, developed the ticket signup process, coordinated with the California State Parks and 18 nonprofit park organizations.
18 November	Free Redwoods Park Day campaign launched at 7 a.m. Benito-Kowalski personally pitched the story to key media and answered their inquiries.
26 November Thanksgiving	Park passes "sold out"; the team directed traffic to other parks offering free admission.
27 November Black Friday	Free Redwoods Park Day!
30 November	Team measured the outcomes through analytics.

---

11 An anonymous donor provided the funds for the passes. There was no marketing budget!

In spite of the immense time pressure, the team established clear and specific objectives for the campaign.

To advance our goal of inspiring the world with the beauty of nature through a network of magnificent redwood parks, we set the following objectives for Free Redwood Parks Day:

A)   *5,000 Free Redwood Parks Day passes (one per vehicle) are downloaded from the League's website from November 18 to November 27, 2015.*

B)   *Assuming two people in each vehicle, 10,000 people visit California redwood state parks on Friday, November 27, 2015.*

C)   *We increase awareness of the League's work. The numbers of unique visitors to the League's website increase by 48 percent; and new Facebook fans and new Twitter and Instagram followers increase by 40 percent from November 18 to November 27, 2015, compared to the same period the previous year.*

A variety of messages were developed to reach each of the six target audiences. They needed to be clear, straightforward, and resonate with the values of the targeted group while driving people to take specific actions: go online, sign up for free passes and encourage others to do the same thing. Then, visit a redwoods park on Black Friday with friends and family!

Examples of two targeted messages follow.

Target: **Stewards**

Message: The day after Thanksgiving, Save the Redwoods League and California State Parks invite all to bring friends and families to explore a beautiful redwood state park.

Why the message is relevant and likely to trigger a response, based on stakeholder analysis: Stewards care deeply about protected land, and they recognize the redwood forests as unique and magical. Stewards have active social lives. The message offers an opportunity for Stewards to enjoy the beautiful redwoods and their friends simultaneously.

Target: **Millennials**

Message: Come to a redwood state park; the shopping and the leftovers can wait.

Why the message is relevant and likely to trigger a response, based on stakeholder analysis: Millennials are deeply concerned about the global pace of consumerism. They hike and backpack. REI is their favorite outdoor retailer. The message validates their concern about consumerism, positioning the event as an alternative to shopping and offering a chance to enjoy the outdoors they love. Because they shop at REI, they are more likely to hear our offer, which is linked to REI's promotion with the #OptOutside hashtag.

"The California conservation story of the decade"

Once the campaign launched, the team had to keep the momentum going with the media and its partners, who were critical to making the event actually work on the Friday after Thanksgiving. Good execution was essential and adjustments had to be made on a moment's notice. Volunteers from 18 groups affiliated with redwood parks, as well as California State Parks staff, welcomed visitors bearing a printed "Redwoods Hike Challenge" pass and tried to count the passes to tally attendance. Turnout was so great that 31 parks "sold out" their allocated free passes while others had problems with adequate parking.

The following Monday, the Outreach team sprinted to evaluate the results. They learned that they had, in every verifiable instance, exceeded their goals! Visitors to the website, new Facebook fans, new Twitter followers, and new Instagram followers increased exponentially. (See Appendix 2.) Unfortunately, the exact number of park visitors could not be counted because California State Parks staff or volunteers were not available for all parks. Nevertheless, the 5176 people who downloaded passes indicated they would bring multiple guests (ranging from 2-10 per pass), probably exceeding the goal of 10,000 visitors.

Upon reflection, media relations were one key to the success of the campaign. Jennifer Benito-Kowalski's pitches to reporters and the distribution of the news release on Cision and Vocus PR service obtained coverage in 328 traditional media. While difficult to compare, this exceeded the total of 301 media placements in the entire previous year by 8 percent! Top outlets covering the story included NBC Bay Area, CNN Wire, Time Online, The Daily Beast, National Public Radio, San Francisco Chronicle, the Los Angeles Times, and Travel + Leisure Online. All in all, Free Redwoods Park Day appeared to be what Sam Hodder, president of the League, called "the California conservation story of the decade."

A Delightful but Intimidating Challenge

Given this tremendous success, how could Save the Redwoods League continue the momentum created by the Free Redwood Parks Day for the coming year? Would there be another #OptOutside campaign, anchored by REI or some other commercial entity, or would every organization be on its own? Jennifer Benito-Kowalski and the Outreach team had their work cut out for them. Should they make the same offer or a different one? What should the communication plan be for this "new tradition"?

> *These kings of the forest, the noblest of a noble race, rightly belong to the world, but as they are in California we cannot escape responsibility as their guardians.*
> - John Muir, *Save the Redwoods*, 1920[12]

---

[12] "Save the Redwoods" by John Muir. Source: Sierra Club Bulletin Volume XI Number 1 - January 1920, pp. 1-4. http://www.yosemite.ca.us/john_muir_writings/save_the_redwoods.html

Appendix 1

Save the Redwoods League Mission and History[13]

Our Objectives

Developed by our founders, our objectives remain essentially unchanged and continue to drive our work today.

- ☐ To **rescue from destruction** representative areas of our **primeval forests**.

- ☐ To cooperate with California State Parks, the National Park Service, and other agencies, in **establishing redwood parks and other parks and reserves**.

- ☐ To **purchase redwood groves** by private subscription.

- ☐ To **foster** and encourage a **better and more general understanding** of the value of **primeval redwood** or **giant sequoia** and other forests of America as natural objects of extraordinary interest to present and future generations.

- ☐ To **support reforestation** and **conservation** of our forest areas.

Our History

For those who have had the chance to stand in a **redwood grove**, there are few **life experiences** that match it. **We can all agree that there are some places on Earth that are so special that they are worth saving.** This shared belief motivated our founders to establish Save the Redwoods League in 1918.

In 1917, the head of the National Park Service, Stephen Mather, inspired our founders — prominent conservationists John C. Merriam, Madison Grant and Henry Fairfield Osborn — to investigate the state of the redwood forests in Northern California. They had heard the new Redwood Highway had opened up the area to more logging, threatening the ancient trees.

Along the Mendocino County coast, they passed long-standing logging operations. Farther north, along the Eel River, they saw practically undisturbed forests. As they continued north, they reached the Bull Creek-Dyerville Flat area in Humboldt County, an area dense with gigantic redwoods reaching more than 300 feet high.

In the presence of such awe-inspiring beauty and serenity, Merriam, Grant and Osborn felt compelled to remove their hats and speak only in whispers. That evening, they agreed that a state or national park was needed to save some part of the north coast redwood forest for future generations.

---

[13] http://www.savetheredwoods.org/about-us/mission-history/

Grant worked with Merriam, Osborn, Mather and others to form Save the Redwoods League in 1918, beginning with an initial donation of $100 toward the effort. Thanks to you, our loyal members and friends around the world, we have achieved much to realize the founders' vision.

But our work is not done.

Unfortunately, today the work needed to protect redwood forests is **harder** and **more complex** than ever before. There are still ancient redwoods slated for **cutting** that need to be protected. Redwood lands already protected in state and national parks also face threats such as devastating government **budget cuts**. These cuts close parks, leaving no personnel to protect redwoods from threats such as **illegal logging and pollution** from marijuana cultivation. Some of these lands are still struggling to recover from years of past damage and **neglect**.

Today, we remain driven by the same objectives our founders established.

Appendix 2

Social Media for #OptOutside#IntoTheRedwoods
Free Redwoods Park Day

From the League's Facebook page

Save the Redwoods League
November 24, 2015 ·

Experience the wonder of ancient giants at Del Norte Coast Redwoods State Park on Free Redwood Parks Day, 11-27. http://bit.ly/1OPo3xg #OptOutside #IntoTheRedwoods

👍 Like   💬 Comment

savetheredwoods @savetheredwoods · 27 Nov 2015
Great reasons to #OptOutside #IntoTheRedwoods today (other than the free admission!): bit.ly/1N8CyFW

↩   ⇄ 5   ♥ 9   •••

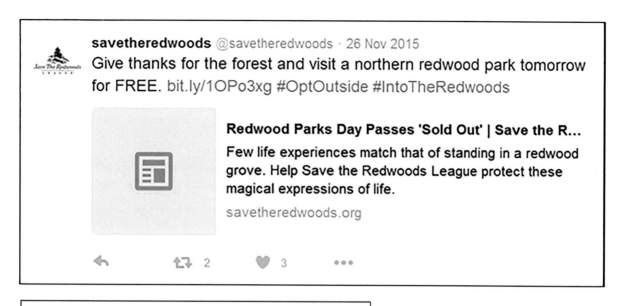

Free Redwood Parks Day Metrics

Website: SaveTheRedwoods.org

Objective: 48% increase

Unique visitors

18-27 November 2014: 10,027
18-27 November 2015: 117,401, increased 1,170%

Facebook

Objective: 40% increase

New fans

18-27 November 2014: 99
18-27 November 2015: 1,396, increased 1,410%

Twitter

Objective: 40% increase

New followers

18-27 November 2014: 13
18-27 November 2015: 80, increased 615%

Instagram

Objective: 40% increase

New followers

18-27 November 2014: 7
18-27 November 2015: 67, increased 957%

Appendix 3

PRESS RELEASE

Contact: Jennifer Benito-Kowalski, Save the Redwoods League | D: (415) 820- 5814 | E: jbenito@ SaveTheRedwoods.org or Patsy Barich, Bon Mot PR | C: (415) 596-5860 | E: patsy@bonmotpr.com

SAVE THE REDWOODS LEAGUE TO PROVIDE FREE DAY-USE ADMISSION FOR ANYONE WHO VISITS A PARTICIPATING CALIFORNIA REDWOOD STATE PARK ON THE DAY AFTER THANKSGIVING
—*Conservation nonprofit and California State Parks invite everyone to start a new Black Friday tradition*

SAN FRANCISCO (November 18, 2015) — **Save the Redwoods League**, the only nonprofit organization in the world dedicated to protecting redwood forests throughout their natural ranges, today announced Free Friday in the Redwoods — **free admission to 49 participating California redwood state parks on Black Friday, November 27, 2015.**

On the day after Thanksgiving, Save the Redwoods League and California State Parks invite everyone to bring their friends and families to explore a beautiful redwood state park. The shopping — and the leftovers — can wait. Thanksgiving is about sharing time with friends and family, and appreciating our many shared blessings. Redwood parks are uniquely suited for both! So come to a redwood state park; free admission sponsored by Save the Redwoods League is the best bargain you're going to find this Black Friday!

"Thanksgiving is a great American tradition," said Sam Hodder, president and chief executive officer of Save the Redwoods League. "This year, Save the Redwoods League wants to make it even better. We are starting a new tradition for Black Friday. We invite everyone to experience the moments of joy, renewal and inspiration that you'll find among our natural wonders, the ancient giant redwoods."

"California State Parks and Save the Redwoods League have worked together for more than 80 years to provide for the health, inspiration and education of the people of California by helping to protect its most valued natural resources," said California State Parks' Director, Lisa Mangat. "Free Friday in the Redwoods continues that tradition, inviting everyone to enjoy one of our greatest treasures, the redwood forest."

EDITORS PLEASE NOTE: All visitors wishing to enjoy Free Redwood Parks Day must go to SaveTheRedwoods.org/freefriday to **download and print a paper Free Redwood State Parks Day- Use Pass,** which must be presented to state parks staff at the entry gate. If no state parks employee is on duty, the pass must be displayed on their vehicle's dashboard. Free admission is good for day-use only. **Day-use hours are typically 8 a.m. to sunset.** Recreational activities at individual parks may vary.
Examples include walking, hiking, biking and picnicking. Please check the California Redwood State Park you wish to visit for hours and activities. Links to each park are at SaveTheRedwoods.org/freefriday.

EDITOR'S ALSO NOTE: Free trip guides and brochures also available on our website. **To access B- roll or redwood state park images please visit our media resources page.**

For more information, visit SaveTheRedwoods.org/freefriday or follow the hashtags #OptOutside #IntoTheRedwoods at facebook.com/SaveTheRedwoodsLeague and at twitter.com/savetheredwoods.

Participating California Redwoods State Parks and Partnering Cooperating Associations/ Friends Groups

SaveTheRedwoods.org/freefriday

Near the Bay Area	Santa Cruz	Monterey
Annadel SP Bothe-Napa Valley SP Jack London SHP Mount Tamalpais SP Samuel P. Taylor SP Partners California State Parks Foundation Jack London Park Partners	Big Basin Redwoods SP Butano SP Castle Rock SP Henry Cowell Redwoods SP Portola Redwoods SP The Forest of Nisene Marks SP Wilder Ranch SP Partners Mountain Parks Foundation Portola and Castle Rock Foundation Sempervirens Fund	Andrew Molera SP Garrapata SP Julia Pfeiffer Burns SP Limekiln SP Pfeiffer Big Sur SP
North Coast Redwoods	**Sonoma-Mendocino Coast**	**Sierra Nevada**
Admiral William Standley SRA Benbow Lake SRA Del Norte Coast Redwoods SP Fort Humboldt SHP Grizzly Creek Redwoods SP Harry A. Merlo SRA Humboldt Lagoons SP Humboldt Redwoods SP Jedediah Smith Redwoods SP John B. Dewitt Redwoods SNR Patrick's Point SP Prairie Creek Redwoods SP Richardson Grove SP Sinkyone Wilderness SP Smithe Redwoods SNR Standish-Hickey SRA	Armstrong Redwoods SNR Austin Creek SRA Fort Ross SHP Hendy Woods SP Jug Handle SNR Kruse Rhododendron SNR Mailliard Redwoods SNR Mendocino Headlands SP Mendocino Woodlands SP Montgomery Woods SNR Navarro River Redwoods SP Russian Gulch SP Salt Point SP Sonoma Coast SP Van Damme SP	Calaveras Big Trees SP **Partners** Calaveras Big Trees Association

Partners	Partners	
Humboldt Redwoods Interpretive Association Redwood Parks Association National Park Service	Fort Ross Conservancy Hendy Woods Community Mendocino Area Parks Association Stewards of the Coast and Redwoods	

SP: State Park | SNR: State Natural Reserve | SRA: State Recreation Area | SHP: State Historic Park

Link to news coverage (see 2015 section): http://www.savetheredwoods.org/about- us/newsroom/save-the- redwoods-in-the-news/

Appendix 4

REI #OptOutside

Email to members announcing the plan

REI IS CLOSING BLACK FRIDAY

This Black Friday the co-op is doing something different. We're closing all 143 of our stores. Instead of reporting to work, we're paying our employees to do what we love most— be outside.

We want you, our members, to be the first to hear—not just what we're doing, but why.

We're passionate about bringing you great gear, but we're even more passionate about the experiences it unlocks for all of us. Perhaps John Muir said it best back in 1901: "thousands of tired, nerve-shaken, over-civilized people are beginning to find out that going to the mountains is going home."

We think Black Friday is the perfect day to remind people of this essential truth.

And don't worry, as a member you'll still enjoy great deals on great gear all holiday season long. But on this one day, we're going to #OptOutside and we want you to join us.

While the rest of the world is fighting it out in the aisles, we hope to see you in the great outdoors. Visit optoutside.rei.com and you'll discover great ways to #OptOutside from coast to coast.

Let's get out there, REI

P.S. If you have friends you want to encourage to #OptOutside, please pass along this invitation. You can also visit optoutside.rei.com to customize your own Black Friday message and share it via social media. There's plenty of room out there for all of us.

The Logo

The #OptOutside Website

Message from REI's President – Search REI
#OptOutside on YouTube for related videos

<u>The Results: From the #OptOutside Website</u>
December 2015

Appendix 5

Outdoor Participation in the US[14]

What Motivates Americans to Get Outside
The majority of Americans participated in outdoor activities to get exercise. The second biggest motivator was the opportunity to spend time with friends and family, which highlights the family-friendly nature of many outdoor activities.

Why did you participate in outdoor activities?
Outdoor Participants Ages 6+

Get exercise	72%
Be with family friends	54%
Keep physically fit	53%
Be close to nature	48%
Get away from usual demands of life	46%
Observe scenic beauty	46%
Enjoy the sounds/smells of nature	44%
Experience excitement/adventure	43%
Develop my skills/abilities	35%
Be with people who enjoy the same things I do	31%
Gain a sense of accomplishment	29%
Experience solitude	26%
Gain self-confidence	24%
Be with people who share my values	18%
It is cool	18%
Talk to new/varied people	12%
Other reason(s)	6%

[14] Outdoor Participation 2014, The Outdoor Foundation found at http://www.outdoorfoundation.org/pdf/ResearchParticipation2014.pdf

Getting Youth and Young Adults Outdoors

Like all outdoor participants, youth and young adult participants were motivated to recreate outdoors by being with loved ones and getting exercise. There were differences in age however. Seventy-six perceent of children cited friends and family as the biggest motivator, but youth participants were less likely to be motivated being with friends and family as they aged. Similarly, 75 percent of young adults said getting exercise was the top reason, which is less of motivator for the younger age groups.

What motivated you to participate in outdoor activities?

	Ages 6-12	Ages 13-17	Ages 18-24
Be with family friends	76%	63%	51%
Get exercise	65%	69%	75%
Experience excitement/adventure	52%	44%	51%
Develop my skills/abilities	48%	50%	43%
It is cool	42%	28%	19%
Be with people who enjoy the same things I do	38%	43%	25%
Keep physically fit	36%	56%	60%
Be close to nature	31%	33%	47%
Enjoy the sounds/smells of nature	26%	26%	39%
Gain self-confidence	24%	30%	35%
Gain a sense of accomplishment	22%	31%	39%
Observe scenic beauty	22%	27%	44%
Get away from usual demands	18%	33%	49%
Be with people who share my values	13%	24%	18%
Talk to new/varied people	10%	13%	12%
Experience solitude	5%	13%	29%
Other reason(s)	7%	5%	5%

Participation in Outdoor Recreation Among Diverse Groups

As minority groups up a larger share of the population, engaging diverse populations in outdoor recreation has never been more critical. Unfortunately, minorities still lag behind in outdoor participation.

As seen in previous years, participation in outdoor activities was highest among Caucasians in all age groups and lowest among African Americans. The largest gap in participation was between Caucasian and African American adolescents. While 65 percent of Caucasian adolescents ages 13 to 17, participated in outdoor recreaction in 2013, only 42 percent of African American adolescents participated.

Although Hispanic Americans had the second-lowest outdoor participation rate, those who did participate tended to get outdoors the most.

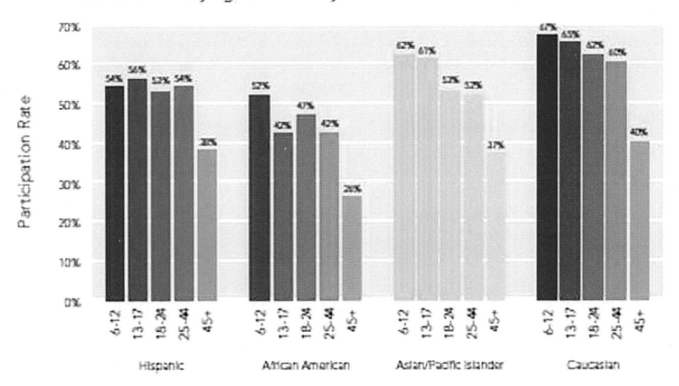

Average Outings per Outdoor Participant

African American	40	Caucasian	43
Asian/Pacific Islander	37	Hispanic	47

SHINOLA
DETROIT

Shinola: What's Next for a Brand Linked to Detroit's Manufacturing Heritage?

By

Matthew Fisher, Golden Gate University Blodwen Tarter, Golden Gate University

Martin Digger had recently applied for a job at Shinola, the Detroit-based company that manufactures consumer products ranging from watches to bicycles. He was excited about the possibility of returning to his hometown to use his new marketing degree as a brand assistant. To prepare for his interview, he walked to the closest coffee shop, ordered an extra-large coffee, and opened his laptop to review the history of the firm and Shinola's products. He was glad to see that the articles overwhelmingly praised the company.

According to the Shinola website,

> Of all the things we make, the return of manufacturing jobs might just be the thing we're most proud of. Shinola is founded in the belief that products should be well-made and built to last. Across a growing number of categories, Shinola stands for skill at scale, the preservation of craft, and the beauty of industry.[i]

Those values resonated with Martin and his hopes for both Detroit and his own work.

However, Martin paused when he came across one article that was critical of the firm.

> *Shinola's entire presence is predicated on its ties to the City of Detroit. The justification for the cheapest men's watch being $550? For bicycles that cost a minimum of $1,950? American manufacturing costs more. Quality materials cost more. American products are inherently worth more. Like buying a pair of Toms helps some poor Third World kid, by buying a two thousand dollar bike you're doing your part to help rebuild a fallen American city. In this way, Shinola reminds us what the American dream actually is: a selling point, nothing more than a sales pitch.*

> *Shinola is using my city as its shill, pushing a manufactured, outdated and unrealistic ideal of America.[ii]*

Martin was proud to have grown up in Detroit. Detroit residents remained resilient in spite of the city's reputation as the epitome of the decline of American manufacturing and crushing poverty after so many auto manufacturers closed their Detroit factories and moved elsewhere. (See Exhibit 1)

Exhibit 1: *The City of Detroit*

Detroit Michigan Map

Map Source: https://www.google.com/maps/place/Detroit,+MI/@42.3523699,-101.0289235,4z/
data=!4m5!3m4!1s0x8824ca0110cb1d75:0x5776864e35b9c4d2!8m2!3d42.331427!4d-83.0457538
See the 2011 Super Bowl ad, "Imported from Detroit," featuring the rap artist Eminem and Chrysler for another
impression of Detroit. https://www.youtube.com/watch?v=SKL254Y_jtc

Martin was reflecting on the challenges facing Detroit and doing business there when he heard his name called. Hannah Rent, a friend from high school, was pleased that Martin was back home. She was even more excited that Martin was interviewing with Shinola. Hannah worked for a local marketing agency and was quite familiar with the brand. Before Martin could say anything more, Hannah pulled out a folder and showed him Shinola's first advertisement (see Exhibit 2).

She said "Check out the classic design of this watch and the picture of the Argonaut building. Isn't that a great use of a Detroit landmark building to tie the brand to Detroit?" She added, "I really like Shinola's story. I also use this ad to show to clients the power of branding both heritage and place." (See Exhibit 3)

Shinola's initial marketing campaign focused on the individuals who assemble its watches, suggesting that purchasing the watch supports jobs and the rebirth of Detroit, thereby emphasizing a social dimension that differentiates the firm. Consumers are not simply buying a timepiece; they are supporting both the revitalization of a city and of American manufacturing. More than 500 employees work for the company, of which almost 400 are located in Detroit.[iii] At least one investor had been convinced of the Shinola story and its value, as Revolution Growth Fund invested a reported $25 million in Shinola's parent company, Bedrock Manufacturing.[iv]

Martin asked, "How does leveraging the connection to Detroit have anything to do with premium priced watches? Hey, I love Detroit but the city isn't exactly known for making watches. Cars, yes-- but watches? I mean, I studied important brands that have been around for years and how they leveraged their heritage to tell a brand story, but how can Shinola, a new firm, do this? After reading some of these articles, I wonder whether Shinola is exploiting the city of Detroit. Is it really a partner in the city's so-called rebirth? Can it pull off this whole approach? Can it really be an authentic brand?"

Hannah and Martin settled in for a longer discussion about Shinola and its connection to Detroit. Where did the company, the Shinola brand, and the image of Detroit intersect? Were they compatible and "true" or simply a fake marketing ploy? Martin wanted to be certain that he could fully engage with the brand and the company with which he was about to interview.

Exhibit 2: *Shinola's First Ad*

First Shinola Advertisement.

Source: http://marketingmag.ca/wp-content/uploads/2016/06/shinola.jpg

Exhibit 3: *Shinola Ad*

GIVE A GIFT
MEASURED IN
MAN-HOURS,
NOT KARATS

SHINOLA
DETROIT

COLLECTION FROM $475

Built in Detroit, Michigan, USA. Here is a storied American brand, and a storied American city. Shinola transformed 30,000 square feet of raw space into a state-of-the-art watch factory inside the College for Creative Studies within the historic Argonaut building. Production combines meticulous hand-assembly with the most advanced technology available to ensure the watches are both beautiful and built to last. Crafted by skilled artisans with a tremendous pride of work to reclaim and define American luxury through American quality.

Source: https://milled.com/hamilton/bTBpEeFLZwoNil9g

The Detroit Heritage: Car Manufacturing and World War II

Detroit is close to Canada, located between two of the Great Lakes (see Exhibit 1). It flourished in the early days of U.S. automobile manufacturing. With the onset of World War II, the scope and scale of Detroit's manufacturing ramped up to support the war effort.

> *Carmakers built everything: tanks, airplanes, radar units, field kitchens, amphibious vehicles, jeeps, bombsights, and bullets. ... Detroit, with 2 percent of the population, made 10 percent of the tools for war.[v]*

Manufacturing employment peaked in the 1950s at roughly 300,000 people, along with a population of 1.86 million residents.[vi] Detroit represented the ideal of American manufacturing and prosperity throughout the first half of the twentieth century.

Detroit's Decades of Decline

A slow erosion of population, employers, and consequent increases in unemployment marked the years that followed the peak in 1950. Riots and civil disturbances, often exacerbated by racial tensions, contributed to Detroit's image as a city in decline.[vii] Several economic and marketing revitalization attempts marked the next two decades, including a famous 1970s slogan of "Say Nice Things About Detroit," that attempted to reverse the negative press about the city.[viii]

By 2013, the city was home to only two car assembly plants.[ix] As residents continued to move to the surrounding suburbs, the city's population dwindled to just under 685,000.[x] Blighted properties numbered over 84,000.[xi] As the cost of maintaining an aging infrastructure increased, the declining population and tax base doomed city finances.

On July 18, 2013, the city of Detroit filed for bankruptcy. In this once thriving city full of middle class jobs and social mobility, a third of the population lived in poverty[xii] and the unemployment rate stood at 22.1%, when the national rate was just 7.4%.[xiii]

Resurgence of the City = Tough, Cool, Resilient

The bankruptcy filing catalyzed the Detroit community, the state of Michigan, creditors and foundations across the nation. A tremendous collaborative effort, "the grand bargain," pulled the city out of bankruptcy somesixteen months after the filing. "Reinventing Detroit" had begun.[xiv] Marketers jumped on the bandwagon of hope and determination. As *The Guardian* newspaper reported, "to an advertiser's eye, Detroit is cool. Gritty. Tough.
Resilient. Authentic in its struggle. True in its American spirit of hard, honest work, ruins and all."[xv]

Shinola Emerges

Tom Kartsotis founded Fossil in 1984 and built the firm into the world's fourth largest watch company. After leaving active management of Fossil, he started another watch company in 2011.[xvi] A Texas native with no prior connection to Detroit, Kartsotis understood the value in associating a brand with a place. Sensing opportunity, he selected Detroit as the city for the new company and resurrected the Shinola brand for a new purpose. While the original brand had no connection to Detroit, the long-defunct Shinola shoe polish (see Exhibit 4) was popular when the city mobilized to help win World War II.

In 2012, Kartsotis signed a lease for 30,000 square feet in Detroit's Argonaut building (see Exhibit 5). Historically significant, the site housed the General Motors Research Laboratory from 1928 to 1956 "where hundreds of patents and products were developed." [xvii] Everyone in Detroit associated the building with the pinnacle of Detroit's manufacturing dominance, creativity, and innovation. Later, Shinola ads and the company's website would feature the Argonaut building to reinforce Shinola's connection to Detroit.

Exhibit 4: *Shinola Polish*

A tin of the original Shinola shoe polish
Source: https://en.wikipedia.org/wiki/Shinola#/media/File:Shinola.jpg

As a starting point for the brand's development, Kartsotis commissioned a study that found people would pay $15 for a pen made in Detroit rather than $5 for a pen made in China or $10 for a pen made in the United States. These results suggested that a product associated with the right place could command a price premium. Of course, Shinola's watches currently retail for $475 and up, definitely a premium price.

The flagship retail location opened in a restored brick storefront that reinforced associations of artisan crafted products (see Exhibit 6). The first brand slogan, "where American is made," directly sought to cement the view that Shinola products are the result of a resurgent manufacturing movement.

The Runwell and Other Watches

Enter the Runwell watch, Shinola's flagship product. Sporting a simple and timeless design with a large round dial face and chunky case, the Runwell's watchband is made from thick leather with visible contrast stitching that implies that it is handmade. The leather for the straps was initially sourced from a tannery in Chicago, while construction is now completed in the Detroit workshop that opened in 2014.[xviii][xix] A "limited lifetime guarantee on every watch" reassures the buyer of the product's quality.[xx]

Exhibit 5: *The Argonaut Building*

The Argonaut Building, Detroit, Michigan.
Source: https://en.wikipedia.org/wiki/Argonaut_Building

The Runwell and Other Watches

Enter the Runwell watch, Shinola's flagship product. Sporting a simple and timeless design with a large round dial face and chunky case, the Runwell's watchband is made from thick leather with visible contrast stitching that implies that it is handmade. The leather for the straps was initially sourced from a tannery in Chicago, while construction is now completed in the Detroit workshop that opened in 2014.[xxi][xxii] A "limited lifetime guarantee on every watch" reassures the buyer of the product's quality.[xxiii]

Foregoing the traditional hinged felt and plastic jewelry box, each Shinola timepiece is housed in a wooden box and accompanied by a small jar of Shinola leather balm. The metal top of the jar is reminiscent of a shoe polish tin, connecting the brand to its namesake shoe polish. A metal plaque in the wooden box names the person who assembled the watch (See Exhibit 7).

Exhibit 6: *Detroit Retail Store*

Detroit retail store.
Source: http://www.adweek.com/brand-marketing/how-shinola-went-shoe-polish-coolest-brand-america-165459/

Exhibit 7: *Watch and Box*

Shinola Runwell 47mm watch and box.
Source: http://www.gmtminusfive.com/shinola-runwell-41mm-review/

Consumers like the watch:

> *"It's expensive for what it is… but it's also undeniable that these watches are well designed and finely crafted. …It's definitely a retro affair, and the model I tested emphasizes that with a brass finish on the metal case. The lugs are similar to those that were once welded to pocket watches to make the first wristworn timepieces, and even the choice of typefaces for the Shinola logo and movement name harken back to a vaguely 30s or 40s-ish time period. All of which is to say, I like the look of the watch very much, but if your taste runs more modern you might not agree."[xxiv]*

Other designs complete the watch lineup and allow the brand to vary shapes, sizes, features, and accent elements. Some watches are sold with additional watchbands to coordinate with clothing.

The Great Americans Series

In 2013, Shinola began offering limited edition watches honoring "Great Americans." The first watch of the series highlighted the Wright brothers, the fathers of modern aviation, with the watch face displaying "The Wright Brothers" printed on it. The brand integrated this theme with a limited edition "Wright Flyer" bicycle. Buyers of either the watch or the bicycle became members of "The Foundry", a private collectors club, offering members early purchase of new limited-edition watches, an annual tour of the Detroit factory and access to exclusive events.[xxv]

Subsequent editions honored Henry Ford, pioneer of auto manufacturing; Muhammad Ali, one of the greatest boxers of all time; Maya Angelou, notable author and poet; and Jackie Robinson, the legendary baseball player who was the first African-American to play in the formerly all-white Major League Baseball. By associating the brand with prominent historical figures, the brand ties its products to reverence for individual accomplishments.[xxvi]

Expanding Product Lines and Categories

While the brand is centered on watches, Shinola continues to add new products, including bound paper journals, bicycles, and record players. Shinola assembles the bicycles, but the journals and record players are built by partners that reinforce the Shinola design aesthetic and use consistent brand elements. Another partnership produced special editions of Randolph Engineering sunglasses, originally built for U.S. military aviators.

As the product lines expand beyond items made or assembled in Detroit by Shinola itself, it raises the question of continued associations with the city of Detroit. Do these new products weaken the link to Detroit's heritage?

Authenticity… We Want It Real

A 2013 Boston Consulting Group survey of 2,500 consumers concluded that "being authentic" was one of the most attractive qualities of a brand.[xxvii] But what does "being authentic" mean? Consumers are well aware that businesses want to sell them something, yet some brands are judged trustworthy while others are dismissed. We naturally judge the authenticity of an individual by the consistency of their words and actions. Brands are similarly judged by consumers.

Gilmore and Pine, in their book *Authenticity: What Consumers Really Want*, offer two questions that help people judge authenticity:[xxviii]

1.) Is it what it says it is?
2.) Is it true to itself?

The first question speaks to the integrity of a brand, while the second is connected to the consistency of the brand's actions. Gilmore and Pine also describe the "Paradox of Authenticity":[xxix]

1.) If you are authentic, then you don't have to say it. 2.) If you say it, then you better actually be it.
3.) It is easier to be authentic if you don't say you're authentic.
4.) It is easier to render offerings authentic, if you acknowledge they are fake.
5.) You don't have to say your offerings are inauthentic, if you render them authentic.

Marketers that apply the following guidance are likely to be judged as authentic by their consumers:[xxx]

Commodities	Goods	Services	Experiences & Referential	Transformation & Influential
Stress materials	Stress your firsts	Be direct & frank	Pay personal tribute	Appeal to personal aspirations
Leave it raw	Revive the past	Focus on the unique	Evoke a time	Appeal to collective aspirations
Be bare	Look old	Go slow	Pick a place	Embrace art
Go green	Mix & Mash	Treat as temporary	Make it matter	Promote a cause
	Anti-conventional	Be foreign	Be realistic	Give meaning

Other researchers, Grayson and Martinic, remind us that "perceived links with a time, person, or place" influence perceptions of authenticity.[xxxi] These perceptions can be very personal and subjective but the marketer seeks links that influence the greatest number of consumers to view the brand as authentic. As competitors copy product features, mass-produced goods become increasingly impersonal and manufactured in far-off places, consumers seek authenticity.[xxxii] Gilmore and Pine sum up the importance of this attribute with, "quality no longer differentiates; authenticity does."[xxxiii]

Authenticity, as a branding concept, is not without its detractors. Brand strategist Constance DeCherney argued, "Defining a brand by authenticity lacks clarity, is open to interpretation, and it's ambiguous" and believes that a focus on defining brand intentions is more important to a brand's success.[xxxiv] DeCherney stated that proponents of authenticity use the concept so loosely that it lacks any real guidance or meaning. Furthermore, she noted that authenticity tends to anchor a brand to the past, "holding us back, keeping us tethered to yesteryear" and advocates that companies should instead "create a brand purpose that intentionally impacts the future."

The Analysis and Decisions

Martin needed to decide if he felt the Shinola brand could grow and thrive, given its current situation. If so, how? Did he believe in its future enough to join the company, if given the opportunity? One journalist reported 2014 sales of this so-called affordable luxury brand of 150,000 – 170,000 watches,[xxxv] up from an initial online sale of 2,500 units in March 2013.[xxxvi] Shinola's future seemed promising but Martin wanted to be sure.

Buying a second cup of coffee, Martin listed his questions and began to try to answer them. He intended to ask some of these questions at his upcoming interview and to see if his interviewer's responses matched his own evaluation.

1. What are the strengths and weaknesses of the Shinola/Detroit association? Of the idea of associating the brand with manufacturing superiority? Of focusing on "handcrafted" products and featuring the people who put together Shinola's goods?

2. What are the opportunities and risks associated with the deliberately constructed brand heritage and the various brand attributes of Shinola?

3. Is the Shinola brand "authentic" and convincing? Does brand authenticity really matter?

4. What product categories fit and which do not fit with Shinola's established vintage brand association?

5. What kinds of marketing actions would support new product introductions and the ongoing marketing of the current Shinola-branded products? Which media and what messages would work best?

6. Which "Great American" would you suggest for the next limited-edition watch in "The Great Americans" series? Why? How would you connect this specific person to the Shinola brand? How would you package the physical product?

---

[i] Shinola.com website (2017) Retrieved from: https://www.shinola.com/
[ii] Moy, J. (March 26, 2014) On Shinola, Detroit's Misguided White Knight. Retrieved from http://www.complex.com/style/shinola-detroits-misguided-white-knight
[iii] Reindl, J.C. (June 17, 2016) FTC tells Shinola: Stop saying 'Where American is made'. *Detroit Free Press.* Retrieved from http://www.freep.com/story/money/business/2016/06/17/shinola-altering- marketing-claims-after-ftc-rebuke/86044878/

iv http://www.revolution.com/bedrock/

v Burgess, S. (Oct. 9, 2015) Detroit's Production Battle to Win World War II. Retrieved from http://www.motortrend.com/news/detroits-production-battle-to-win-world-war-ii/

vi Vlasic, B. (September 22, 2013) Detroit Is Now a Charity Case for Carmakers. *The New York Times*. Retrieved from http://www.nytimes.com/2013/09/23/business/detroit-is-now-a-charity-case-for- carmakers.html

vii Cosgrove, B. (July 22, 2012) Detroit Burning: Photos From the 12th Street Riot, 1967. *Time*. Retrieved from http://time.com/3638378/detroit-burning-photos-from-the-12th-street-riot-1967/

viii Black, A. (August 26, 2015) 'Say nice things about Detroit' creator helps carry on message. *Crain's Detroit Business*. Retrieved from http://www.crainsdetroit.com/article/20150826/NEWS/150829890/say-nice-things-about-detroit- creator-helps-carry-on-message

ix Vlasic, B. (July 15, 2013) Last Car Plant Brings Detroit Hope and Cash. *The New York Times*. Retrieved from http://www.nytimes.com/2013/07/16/business/last-car-plant-brings-detroit-hope-and- cash.html?pagewanted=all&_r=0

x Bomey, N., Gallagher, J., and Stryker, M. (Nov. 9, 2014) How Detroit Was Reborn. *Detroit Free Press*. Retrieved from http://www.freep.com/story/news/local/detroit-bankruptcy/2014/11/09/detroit- bankruptcy-rosen-orr-snyder/18724267/

xi Kurth, J. & MacDonald C. (May 14, 2015) Volume of abandoned homes 'absolutely terrifying'. *The Detroit News*. Retrieved from http://www.detroitnews.com/story/news/special- reports/2015/05/14/detroit-abandoned-homes-volume-terrifying/27237787/

xii Halperin, A. (July 6, 2015) How Motor City Came Back From the Brink…and Left Most Detroiters Behind. *Mother Jones*. Retrieved from http://www.motherjones.com/politics/2015/07/motor-city- after-bankruptcy-and-detroiters-left-behind/

xiii Bureau of Labor and Statistics (2017) 2013 Local Area Unemployment.

xiv Bomey, N., Gallagher, J., and Stryker, M. (November 9, 2014) How Detroit was Reborn. *Detroit Free Press*. Retrieved from http://www.freep.com/story/news/local/detroit- bankruptcy/2014/11/09/detroit-bankruptcy-rosen-orr-snyder/18724267/

xv Hackman, R. (May 14, 2014) Detroit: the bankrupt city turned corporate luxury brand. *The Guardian*. Retrieved from https://www.theguardian.com/money/2014/may/14/detroit-bankrupt-brand-ad- chrysler-nostalgia

xvi Reindl, J.C. (June 17, 2016) FTC tells Shinola: Stop saying 'Where American is made'. *Detroit Free Press*. Retrieved from http://www.freep.com/story/money/business/2016/06/17/shinola-altering-marketing-claims-after- ftc-rebuke/86044878/

xvii Proposed General Motors Research Laboratory/Argonaut Building Historic District (2017) Retrieved from http://www.detroitmi.gov/Portals/0/docs/historicdesignation/Final%20Reports/General%20Motors%2 0Research%20Laboratory%20Argonaut%20Building%20HD%20Final%20Report.pdf

xviii Elejalde-Ruiz, A. (March 6, 2015) Shinola's Detroit story a successful sell. *The Chicago Tribune*. Retrieved from http://www.chicagotribune.com/business/ct-shinola-storytelling-0308-biz-20150306- story.html

xix Perman, S. (April 201) The Real History of America's Most Authentic Fake Brand, *Inc. Magazine*. Retrieved from https://www.inc.com/magazine/201604/stacy-perman/shinola-watch-history- manufacturing-heritage-brand.html

xx Shinola website https://www.shinola.com/introducing-shinola-guarantee.html

xxi Elejalde-Ruiz, A. (March 6, 2015) Shinola's Detroit story a successful sell. *The Chicago Tribune*. Retrieved from http://www.chicagotribune.com/business/ct-shinola-storytelling-0308-biz-20150306- story.html

xxii Perman, S. (April 201) The Real History of America's Most Authentic Fake Brand, *Inc. Magazine*. Retrieved from https://www.inc.com/magazine/201604/stacy-perman/shinola-watch-history- manufacturing-heritage-brand.html

xxiii Shinola website https://www.shinola.com/introducing-shinola-guarantee.html

xxiv Etherington, Darrell. (November 29, 2013) Shinola's Runwell Is A Solid Watch With American Pedigree, But You'll Pay For The Homegrown Factor. *TechCrunch*. https://techcrunch.com/2013/11/29/shinola-runwell-41mm-review/

xxv The Foundry (2017) Retrieved from https://www.shinola.com/the-foundry.html

xxvi Wilson, J. (October 28, 2016) What a stylish way to honor one of the greats. *Essence*. Retrieved from http://www.essence.com/celebrity/maya-angelou-shinola-watch

xxvii Ryder, B. (November 14, 2015) It's the real thing. *The Economist*. Retrieved from http://www.economist.com/news/business/21678216-authenticity-being-peddled-cure-drooping- brands-its-real-thing

xxviii Gilmore, J.H. and Pine, B.J., II. (2007), Authenticity: What Consumers Really Want, (Pp. 97). Harvard Business School Press, Boston, MA.

xxix Gilmore, J.H. and Pine, B.J., II. (2007), Authenticity: What Consumers Really Want, (Pp. 89-90). Harvard Business School Press, Boston, MA.

xxx Gilmore, J.H. and Pine, B.J., II. (2007), Authenticity: What Consumers Really Want, (Pp. 56-77). Harvard Business School Press, Boston, MA.

xxxi Grayson, K. and Martinec, R. (2004), Consumer perceptions of iconicity and indexicality and their influence on assessments of authentic market offerings. *Journal of Consumer Research*, Vol. 31 No. 2, pp. 296-312.

xxxii Beverland, M.B. and Farelly, F.J. (2010), The quest for authenticity in consumption: consumers' purposive choice of authentic cues to shape experienced outcomes. *Journal of Consumer Research*, Vol. 36 No. 5, pp. 838-856.

[xxxiii] Gilmore, J.H. and Pine, B.J., II. (2007), Authenticity: What Consumers Really Want, (Pp. 23). Harvard Business School Press, Boston, MA.

[xxxiv] DeCherney, C. (February 3, 2017) F*ck Your Authenticity. This Should Be the Year of Good Intention, *Adweek.* Retrieved from http://www.adweek.com/brand-marketing/fck-your-authenticity- this-should-be-the-year-of-good-intention/

[xxxv] Schneider, Sven Raphael & Shapira, J.A. (October 20, 2014) Shinola Watches – Made in Detroit? *Gentlemen's Gazette.* https://www.gentlemansgazette.com/shinola-watches-detroit/ [xxxvi] VanderMey, Anne. (July 9, 2013). Think you know Shinola? Think again. *Fortune.* http://fortune.com/2013/07/09/think-you-know-shinola-think-again/

Sporting KC Gets an Assist from SeatGeek Can Sporting KC Score?

By

Deborah Cowles, Virginia Commonwealth University
Jan Owens, Carthage College
Matt Sauber, Eastern Michigan University

Executive Summary

Sporting KC is an American professional soccer club based in the greater Kansas City metro area with the actual matches played at Children's Mercy Park in Kansas City, Kansas. Beginning in 2017, the club sells tickets through SeatGeek, an online ticket platform as its primary ticketing distributor. Jake Reid, Sporting KC's President, sees this relationship as the next generation of online ticket sales. As the popularity of professional soccer expands, Millennials will become the largest demographic segment of sports fans. Moreover, as consumers increasingly make purchases in a digital -- largely mobile -- environment, Sporting KC expects the SeatGeek relationship to be a strategic partnership for growth and profitability for both entities. Now, the challenge is for Sporting KC's marketing team to take advantage of SeatGeek's – *and* the team's – strengths and to ride the momentum of positive trends.

The Case Study

The Scene

Sporting Kansas City President Jake Reid [1] leaned back in his desk chair, elated yet aware of new challenges. It had just been announced "that ticketing industry leader SeatGeek will become the club's official ticketing partner starting in 2017".[2] This was an outcome of a ground-breaking multi-year initiative between SeatGeek and Major League Soccer (MLS), which made SeatGeek the official ticketing partner of MLS. The new open-ticketing system sought to enhance fan satisfaction with the ticketing process, and open up a myriad of opportunities for fan engagement. Jake and decision-makers at Sporting KC had spent some time comparing a number of competitors in the ticketing industry (see Appendix A.) In the end, Jake and his team members were convinced that this new SeatGeek-MLS ticketing agreement represented the future of the online ticketing industry, not only for Sporting KC and other MLS teams, but for other sporting and entertainment venues.

Jake felt certain that the SeatGeek partnership would create exciting new opportunities for the club and its supporters, but now Sporting KC had to figure out how to make the most of SeatGeek's unique ticketing platform. Just like Sporting KC, SeatGeek always strived to be an advocate for ticket buyers, customers, and fans[3] -- it seemed to be a marriage made in heaven. Moreover, because "Sporting KC has a championship legacy, a loyal fan base, and a reputation for innovation on and off the pitch,"[4] it was seen as a showcase for the potential power of using the SeatGeek platform. Both the team and SeatGeek co-founders Jack

Groetzinger and Russ D'Souza were counting on Sporting KC to serve as an example for other MLS teams. Along with technology partner TopTix, SeatGeek would make all Sporting KC and Swope Park Rangers (of the United Soccer League) home matches as well as other ticketed events at Children's Mercy Park available for purchase.

Jake knew it was time for his marketing team to get to work. They had to develop and implement strategies that would live up to the expectations of the team, MLS, and SeatGeek.

Background

Digital Disruption. At the foundation of the SeatGeek-Sporting KC partnership was the knowledge that it wasn't just the ticketing industry that had been -- and continues to be -- disrupted by digital and mobile technologies. "Digital disruption is the change that occurs when new digital technologies and business models affect the value proposition of existing goods and services."[6] At one point, Jake had wondered, "How did the ticketing industry get to where it is today?"

The ticketing industry for live events had changed dramatically over a number of decades. In the 60s and 70s, tickets for concerts and sporting events were sold at venues and organizer/promoter/agent ticket offices. Promoters helped organizers with lining up local sponsors, booking venues, and selling tickets. Typical contracts had a fixed fee for the venue, and promoters would receive 15% of the proceeds. Managers could receive 10% to 25%, leaving organizers with 60% to 75% of the profit.[7]

In the 80s, TicketMaster Entertainment Inc. changed the ticketing industry. It became a primary ticket outlet by selling and fulfilling tickets for most U.S. venues on behalf of event promoters. TicketMaster successfully convinced venues to outsource ticket sales to it, and in return TicketMaster paid them for each ticket they sold. TicketMaster also applied their preparatory technology and organizational expertise that venues lacked, to the operation of selling tickets globally. The distribution strategy was overwhelmingly successful, and TicketMaster became the official ticket office of the majority of venues in the United States.

With the advent of the Internet and digital technologies, online ticketing increasingly became the primary method of issuing, marketing, selling, and processing live events. Digital communication also created instant access to ticket holding data, including the level of supply and demand for live event tickets. In live sporting events, any ticket holder (e.g., sports club, ticket agent, individual customer) could be a *de facto* supplier of tickets. By the early 2000s, digital technology platforms such as Stubhub created secondary marketplaces where people engage in buying and selling sports (and other) tickets at market prices.

Although Jake knew that SeatGeek's mobile-centric vision set it apart from its online ticketing competitors, he was also curious about the digital disruption that has occurred in other industries, including media, telecom, consumer financial services, retail, technology, insurance, consumer products, nonprofit, business and professional services, and education.[8] Were there any lessons to be learned from industry disruptors like Uber, Skype, Spotify, WhatsApp, Netflix, Airbnb, and others?[9] Just as Jake was aware that SeatGeek was a primary disruptor in the ticketing industry, he felt it might be possible for Sporting KC to become the disruptor among sports properties as a result of its SeatGeek partnership.

One Problem, Two Solutions. It was no secret that for many years, consumers had become increasingly dissatisfied with the online purchase of tickets for sporting events, concerts, and other venues. Ironically, it was former TicketMaster CEO Nathan Hubbard who commiserated: "Fans have known for decades that, whenever they buy tickets for concerts or games, the deck is almost sadistically stacked against them. But those same fans have been inundated by nonsense from stakeholders in the ticketing business, and at this point, they don't know what to believe".[10]

A local Kansas City television station highlighted the dilemma facing a typical fan when Sporting KC was contending for the MLS Cup in 2013:[11]

> *Tickets on Sporting KC's website sold out in five minutes. Now, ticket brokers are the go-to place to buy a ticket. That's disappointing to Tom Davis, a Lee's Summit man who was hoping to attend the game with his sons. Sporting KC had tickets for sale starting at 10 a.m. Monday. By 10:05, the tickets were sold out.*

> *"I was on the Sporting KC website searching for the tab to buy tickets and it had already been taken down," Davis said. "It's just a shame that we have such wonderful venues like Sporting Park and the Sprint Center and we live here in town; but it's tough to get tickets."*

Davis had hoped to be able to purchase $60 tickets at the team's website, but quickly realized he would be facing prices between $130 and $170 at ticket broker sites. He and his sons opted to watch the game at home on television.

As such, the online ticketing industry seemed to be at a fork in the road. Jake was aware that a number of industry players felt that one response to ticket buyers' many concerns and complaints with the status quo was to make the resale of tickets "impossible in order to protect fans from being priced out by brokers."[12] In some cases, the legal system was moving in the direction of supporting teams, leagues, and venues that wanted to aggressively limit where and when fans could buy tickets.

In stark contrast, SeatGeek represented a very different approach to answering consumers' concerns by creating an **open ticketing network** that not only allowed third-party websites to sell tickets, but also let fans resell their tickets anywhere and on more than one site at once. A 2015 *Forbes* article described it in this way: "SeatGeek Helps You Scalp the Scalpers."[13] Equally important: According to SeatGeek co-founder Russ D'Souza, "Teams can make way more money by being more open with their inventory …. There is a lot of money being left on the table."[14]

"The goal is to use data, design, and technology to get users to go to more events," said SeatGeek CEO Jack Groetzinger. "There's a lack of advocacy baked into the [ticketing] business. Tickets in North

America are sold via exclusive long-term contracts where buyers can only purchase them from a single venue. This is good only for the ticket vendor".[15]

Decision makers at Sporting KC had spent some time comparing a number of competitors in the ticketing industry (See Appendix A). In the end, Jake and his team members were convinced that SeatGeek and its open ticketing network represented the future of the online ticketing industry – not only for Sporting KC and other MLS teams, but also for myriad other sporting and entertainment venues.

The Players

Sporting KC. Sporting Kansas City began life as the Kansas City Wiz (KCW) in 1995 – one of 10 Major League Soccer (MLS) charter members. The team officially extended its name to "Wizards" following the 1996 MLS season. Before of the start of the 2000 season, the team's offices moved to Arrowhead Stadium in Kansas City, MO, and the Wizards ushered in a new era of success, both on and off the field. The team also unveiled a shade of blue as its primary color alongside white as the organization's official colors for its uniforms.[1][6]

The Wizards got off to a 10-0-2 start and went on to win the regular season championship, the Supporters' Shield,[1][7] and the MLS Cup in 2000. The team is currently recognized with a respectable ranking in the league in MLS Cup titles and Supporters' Shield wins in the past 20 years (See Table 1).

Table 1. MLS Cup Titles and Supporters' Shield Wins

Team	MLS Cups	Year(s) won	Supporters' Shields	Year(s) won	MLS Seasons
LA Galaxy	5	2002, 2005, 2011, 2012, 2014	4	1998, 2002, 2010, 2011	21
D.C. United	4	1996, 1997, 1999, 2004	4	1997, 1999, 2006, 2007	21
San Jose Earthquakes	2	2001, 2003	2	2005, 2012	19
Sporting Kansas City		2000, 2013	1	2000	21
Houston Dynamo	2	2006, 2007		–	11
Columbus Crew SC	1	2008	3	2004, 2008, 2009	21
Chicago Fire	1	1998	1	2003	19
Portland Timbers	1	2015		–	6
Colorado Rapids	1	2010		–	21
Real Salt Lake	1	2009		–	12

New York Red Bulls	–	2	2013, 2015	12
FC Dallas	–	1	2016	21
Seattle Sounders FC	–	1	2014	8
Miami Fusion*	–	1	2001	4*
Tampa Bay Mutiny*	–	1	1996	68

Franchise folded after completion of the 2001 season
Source: www.mlssoccer.com

In 2005, the league embarked on a significant expansion plan that included individual club ownership. To attract new ownership and more money into the league, it encouraged the owners of multiple teams to become the owner of a single team.

As a result, Wizards owner Lamar Hunt (Hunt Sports) announced his intention to sell the team. OnGoal, LLC purchased the club from the Hunt Sports Group on August 31, 2006. The Wizards thus began an era that brought changes to the club's management, coaching staff, and players. The team got its world- class training center Swope Park, Kansas City, MO in 2007. The Wizards moved to a new stadium in CommunityAmerica Ballpark in 2008.[1]8

In 2010, The Wizards were officially renamed as Sporting Kansas City (Sporting KC) and registered as an American professional soccer club and a member of Major League Soccer (MLS). 2011 brought the most significant change in the club's history with the completion and inauguration of the team's new stadium, Children's Mercy Park in Kansas City, KS. The new stadium provided Sporting KC's players and fans a permanent home.[1]9

In 2013, Sporting KC won its second MLS Cup championship by defeating Real Salt Lake at Children's Mercy Park. It also represented the Major League Soccer in the 2013-14 CONCACAF[20] Champions League. The team celebrated its 20th season in MLS by winning the Lamar Hunt U.S. Open Cup, its third Open Cup title in 2015. Sporting KC was ranked 5th in the MLS Western Conference in 2016.[2]1

From the start, the players, executives, and staff members of Sporting KC believed that the team's fans ranked among its greatest strengths. Fans were able to engage with the team through a detailed, well- designed website and various social media platforms, and they readily showed up for games. Indeed, in recent years, two-thirds of the 18,500 stadium seats had been sold to season ticket holders. The club capped the number of seats sold to season ticket holders to leave room for a sufficient number of group seats and single-game-buyer seats, as well as public relations/marketing initiatives.

Selling out games had always been one of the highest priorities for Sporting KC, which meant that one-third of the tickets were up for grabs for any game. Like other teams, Sporting KC found that some games were easier to sell than others, so it wanted to better understand this market to drive profitability and yield. Sporting KC also wanted to make it possible for season-ticket and other ticket holders to resell tickets in the best possible environment for consumers: transparent, convenient, safe and certain.

Even with robust attendance and enthusiastic fans, the club also focused on attracting the next generation of sports fans – Millennials. The club hoped to convert this group from its typical single- game purchase behavior to becoming the next generation of season ticket holders.

To meet these ticketing challenges, Sporting KC signed an official ticket distribution agreement with SeatGeek, an online ticket seller, to sell its primary ticket inventory and to establish an open, official secondary marketplace. This change allows Sporting KC's tickets to be sold anywhere on the Internet.[22] For example, companies like Uber and Hilton could offer deals to an upcoming match and offer tickets to be purchased directly from the SeatGeek app. Tickets could also be purchased via social media platforms when consumers post content about a game.

Sporting KC's previous ticketing agreements generally required it to send fans to official team sites or specific ticketing partners, such as Ticketmaster, to purchase single-game tickets. Fans holding tickets would have to go to secondary sites to sell unwanted tickets if their plans changed. SeatGeek would allow these fans to post the tickets on multiple websites, but they would be conveniently aggregated by SeatGeek's technology. Further, SeatGeek allows Sporting KC to sell its tickets on its official site, and any site or app of the club's choice. This open network was a reflection of the fact that primary and secondary ticket markets were destined to become increasingly blurred. SeatGeek gets a small service charge for transactions that take place on its unique ticketing platform.

Jake is psyched! SeatGeek represents a new opportunity for satisfying Sporting KC's customers and maximizing revenue at Sporting KC.

SeatGeek and Its Competitors. SeatGeek is a "meta" search engine and aggregator of sports, concerts, and theater tickets. It uses both mobile app and desktop platforms that allow users to browse events, view color-coded maps for seat location and best value, purchase tickets, and receive electronic or physical tickets. SeatGeek shows the list of events and prices aggregated from ticket exchanges such as TicketsNow, TicketNetwork, and Razorgator, as well as from fans who post their own tickets for sale via SeatGeek's consumer marketplace tools.

SeatGeek was founded in 2009 by Russell D'Souza and Jack Groetzinger from DreamIT Ventures, a start-up accelerator program in Philadelphia. DreamIT was able to attract more than $3 million in financing over the next two years, including a 2011 investment from Aston Kutcher and Guy Oseary, through their A-Grade Investments fund. SeatGeek continued to grow through rapid growth and consumer adoption of its mobile ticketing applications on iOS and Android, and also via acquisitions of competitors such as FanSnap. More investment groups continued to fund SeatGeek's development and expansion.[23]

By the end of 2013, more than $6 million in transactions took place on its platform every month, a 300% growth from the previous year. It was notable that the bulk of this growth came from its mobile app.

Consumers have cited many reasons for purchasing on SeatGeek. Foremost, SeatGeek guarantees all tickets sold on its platform – so fans can purchase tickets from the site with confidence. Second, fans appreciate SeatGeek's DealScore feature, which takes a wide range of factors such as price, seat location, opponent, day of week and more to produce a 0-to-100 score that grades out each and every ticket listing available for a given game based on its relative value. Third, fans receive customized information that tracks their favorite teams and players, and personal recommendations for upcoming events. They get notified when their favorite teams and players announce a new event near their location. Finally, SeatGeek offers more than 2,000 seating maps across venues in 80 countries.

D'Souza sums it up: Customers "can get not only every ticket by going to SeatGeek, but they can get a better user experience."

SeatGeek knows that it is not the only game in town. From the truly basic (e.g., Craig's List, eBay) to very strong competitors (e.g., Ticketmaster, StubHub, TicketNetwork, sports clubs themselves with a loyal fan base), consumers have an increasing number choices when it comes to buying tickets.

SeatGeek's ability to sell in the primary and secondary ticket markets has also opened up another revenue stream: working with clubs and executives on strategy and tactics in primary ticket sales. For example, SeatGeek will provide ticket inventory distribution for a range of clients of Spectra Ticketing & Fan Engagement, a live entertainment company that sells more than 120 million tickets a year on behalf of its clients.

The agreement with MLS is SeatGeek's first major sports partnership. The growth of MLS attendance[xxxvi] and fan interest, along with a presence at major league events such as the AT&T All-Start Game and MLS Cup, make this a win-win for the teams and SeatGeek.

A New World of Ticket Pricing

All things being equal, a profit objective has tended to be the ultimate determinant of ticket pricing.[24] In general, professional sports teams are profit maximizers whose objective rides on the club's season revenue – primarily gate receipts, broadcasting rights, sponsorship, and merchandising. There is a strong positive correlation between ticket sales and stadium attendance and most other revenue streams. Sponsors are more interested in a successful club, and broadcast companies prefer to cover games that are attended by many people. Also, merchandising revenue historically has benefited from the presence of a large number of spectators being physically present at a particular venue.

In the past, teams would make educated guesses about ticket prices, set pricing tiers for the "face value" of a ticket, and then hope for the best. If the team enjoyed a winning season, many tickets would be re- sold (scalped) for much higher prices on secondary markets. If the team had a difficult season, tickets could go unsold at the going rate. The volatility could be reflected from one match to the next, depending on the popularity of the opposing team. The result was that the secondary market (individuals or commercial venues) would resell the "in demand" tickets, and the "real" going rate for the seat would be established. The secondary-market price also identified how much money the team could have earned had it been better able to estimate how much fans would pay for the ticket. In the words of Russ D'Souza, it represented how

much money teams were leaving "on the table." In 2013, fans paid "an average $211 a ticket for the matchup between Sporting Kansas City and Real Salt Lake" on the secondary market, when tickets for the MLS cup event "originally sold for between $30 and
$150."[2][5]

At the same time, teams were still uncertain about the price that could be charged for less popular matches. Even at discounted rates, filling the stadium would increase the team's attractiveness to team sponsors, and potentially build fan loyalty and engagement for the future.

Sports and live events planners have long been cautious about the secondary market for tickets. Plagued by scalpers, counterfeit tickets, and high service fees, secondary sellers and aggregators have often been marked with unsavory reputations in the past. Due to lack of sales information and forecasting abilities, the sports clubs could not manage – never mind control – the secondary market, and seemed to avoid it altogether. Clubs also did not want to alienate fans if ticket prices changed too quickly. "Going for the last buck" seemed to be anti-fan.

Still, the potential to adjust prices to meet demand was attractive to the franchises. The existence of the secondary market reflected the fact that ticket prices and fan demand were often mismatched by the clubs. Some tickets could sell for much more than the official ticket price. For particularly desirable games, the secondary market could earn large profits lost to the franchise. When the San Francisco Giants tried dynamic pricing for 2,000 leftover seats in the furthest corners of the stadium, they sold 25,000 extra tickets and earned an additional $500,000 in one season. Likewise, the NBA's Cleveland Cavaliers tested dynamic ticket pricing on 20,000 seats over the span of 25 games. The average price increased by $9.25 per ticket and the franchise earned more money as a result.[2][6]

Jake and his team had kept track of changes in the ticketing industry, so they were aware that much of the aversion to secondary sales had changed in recent years with the advent of Internet sites like Stubhub. com, which could gather meaningful databases on secondary (reseller) ticket prices.[xxxvi] With more and more fans buying tickets on these sites, the "real" price of the ticket could be seen by both the buyer and the sports franchise. This market information allowed the clubs to model and forecast demand and price tickets dynamically, similar to hotels and airlines. Today, it is possible for ticket prices to vary by specific event, predicted demand, and date purchased. Major League Baseball, which was the first to substantively adopt dynamic pricing, saw large benefits due to the extreme variability of demand game-to-game. Between rotations of popular pitchers, weather, and changes of team performance throughout the season, ticket demand could vary greatly.

Many sports franchises have become more comfortable with the idea of managing both primary and secondary ticket sales through dynamic pricing as fans have become more accustomed with the practice. Most of the tickets are now sold to season ticket holders for a set price or negotiated agreements based on volume, as some customer segments prefer to lock in prices rather than deal with future price volatility. The rest of the tickets are available for primary sale, and offer an important opportunity to manage revenue. Besides the team's ability to control its own pricing, the advantages of a team using dynamic pricing include:[2][7]

- Greater efficiency in setting prices
- Better opportunities in revenue maximization
- Incentives to consumers to purchase season tickets
- The ability of fans to acquire tickets to low-demand games

Some clubs have turned to outside pricing experts, such as Qcue (http://www.qcue.com) and Digonex (http://www.digonex.com) to manage their dynamic pricing programs. These third-party providers provide ticket prices for each game in each section of the stadium and are optimized as often as daily. The pricing is based on (but not limited to) the following data sources:

- Available inventory
- Current sales
- Historical sales patterns
- Television schedules
- Game date/time
- Home team record
- Visiting team record
- Secondary market prices
- Weather

These dynamic pricing experts create separate pricing algorithms for each sports league and customize them to each team. The third-party company sends their experts' pricing recommendations to each team's management, which can approve, modify, or reject the prices prior to the new prices being sent to the team's ticketing venue.

Ticket Purchases Go Mobile

Observers have noted a move toward greater access to ticketing across platforms.[28] Even Ticketmaster moved about 10% of its 100 million tickets sold in North America last year to platforms it does not own. Such moves have been a response to increasing customer demand for convenience -- buying when, where, and how they want, and it better be easy.

Sales on mobile platforms have continued to soar. In early 2015, nearly half of all online retail traffic was through a mobile device, a 26.5% growth. Mobile commerce was 23% of online sales, a growth of 35%.[29,30] Mobile ticket purchases were expected to account for more than 50% of all tickets transacted on digital platforms by 2019, according to a new report from Juniper Research. Digital ticket purchases made from desktop and mobile devices, including tablets and smartphones, were expected to reach $32 billion by 2019, almost twice the amount of $16.2 billion in 2016.[31,32] SeatGeek realized significant growth through its own mobile ticketing sales,[33] and attributed this increase to the convergence of the convenience of buying through a mobile device with target markets that increasingly "live" through their mobile devices.

Following the growth and popularity of mobile payment platforms, SeatGeek identified Apple Pay as its mobile payment platform of choice for a seamless transaction process. Typical conversions to purchase on SeatGeek's mobile site tended to be about 30%, but this percentage rose to 80% when a customer paid with Apple Pay. Groetzinger summed up the strategic importance of convenient payment systems in the mobile environment: "Apple Pay is convenient in a physical store, but you're never going to Wal- Mart because of Apple Pay. It's a triviality. … But you are going to buy tickets on SeatGeek with Apple Pay in a case where you wouldn't have otherwise. That's huge."

Apple Pay makes one-tap shopping easier than multiple taps to enter credit card and other buyer information. Verification is through a fingerprint check. Groetzinger wished that other mobile payment platforms, such as Google's Android app, were as robust and easy to use as Apple Pay.

Attracting Millennials

Like many businesses, Sporting KC had identified Millennials as the next opportunity for growth and long-term customer engagement. Millennials, which the U.S. Census Bureau defined in 2015 as individuals between the ages of 18 and 34, numbered 75.4 million that year, surpassing the 74.5 million Baby Boomers (ages 51-69).[34] The Millennial generation had grown so quickly in part because of young immigrants. Generation X (ages 35-50 in 2015) was also projected to pass the Boomers in population by 2028, as Boomers aged and passed away, and because older immigrants were not making up for this decline.

Sporting KC decision makers were well aware that Millennials are different from previous generations in more ways than mere numbers.[35] Comprising the most racially diverse generation in U.S. history, Millennials also are more likely to be single (26%) compared to when other groups were that age. Many would like to marry, but they are also more likely to have student debt and lower incomes than previous generations. They are putting off marriage until they achieve a more solid financial situation. Instead of belonging to political and religious organizations, their social lives revolve around personal networks of friends, colleagues, and groups through social and digital media.

While many Millennials face economic challenges, more than 8 in 10 say they currently have enough money to lead the lives they want or expect to in the future.[36] In part, this may be explained by their educational attainment, which often leads to better-paying jobs: in 2014, 34% of Millennials have a college degree, and of the 25-32 year-olds, 72% have said that their bachelor's degree has paid off or will pay off in the future.[37] Still, two-thirds of recent bachelor's degree graduates have an average debt of $27,000 compared to an average of $15,000 two decades ago, adjusted for time and inflation.[38]

Millennials have joined the trend of preferring to spend their money on experiences rather than things.[39] By 2020, Mintel's American Lifestyles Report predicts that total spending on so-called "non-essential" categories, including tourism, vacations, and dining out, will grow by approximately 22%. As a result, industries from live entertainment to hotels to restaurants to various lifestyle activities have targeted this group. Businesses in these industries are trying to connect with Millennials where they are naturally engaged, which means following them to the digital environment.

Millennials are heavy users of digital technology and the Internet. However, they are also less trusting than older Americans.[40] This contrast may mean that Millennials are also more savvy consumers in the digital environment, preferring to rely on networks of friends and trusted experts than commercial advertisers and institutions for information and insights.

The Growth of the Digital Environment and Social Media

While Internet traffic keeps growing, mobile traffic exceeded the amount of desktop traffic for the first time in May 2015.[41] The fact that Google's newest algorithms penalized sites that weren't optimized for mobile search should only cause this trend to increase.[42]

"Constantly connected" describes most Americans, and especially the Millennials' relationship with the digital environment.[43] Millennials are further accelerating the growth of the digital environment, often through their participation in social media. For example, where 79% of all adults use Facebook, 88% of the 18-29 year-olds and 84% of the 30-49 year-olds use it.[44] Millennials' median "Friend" count on Facebook is 250 (higher than other age groups), and 55% have posted a on a social media site.[45]

Facebook continues to be the platform on which most users begin their social media lives. Indeed, Facebook's 2 billion users now spend an average of 50 minutes a day on their Facebook and its subsidiary platforms, Instagram and Messenger (does not include its messaging app, WhatsApp.)[46] Other social media platforms also attract a disproportionate share of younger groups (see Table 2). In addition, the percent of Facebook users that interact with another platform is high.

Marketers are particularly intrigued by heavy users of social media through the use of Influencer marketing."[47] These are social media users who have a disproportionate influence over a marketer's target audience. By creating a mutually beneficial situation, or providing useful content, a marketer can make it easy for the influencer by giving them swipe files, and using "click to tweet" or similarly helpful tools.

Table 2. Use of Selected Social Media by Age Groups

	All Ages	18-29	30-49	% that use Facebook
Facebook	79%	88%	84%	-
Instagram	32%	59%	33%	95%
Twitter	24%	36%	23%	93%
LinkedIn	29%	34%	33%	92%
Pinterest	31%	36%	34%	89%

Source: compiled from Greenwood, Shannon, "Social Media Update 2016," PEW Research Center, November 11, 2016. http://www.pewinternet.org/2016/11/11/social-media-update-2016/

The Challenge

Jake continued to ponder the strategic value of Sporting KC's relationship with SeatGeek beyond becoming the online provider of ticketing services for his organization. He understood that a fan's journey, or experience, begins long before he or she steps into the stadium. From the moment fans learned about a Sporting KC soccer match, they had to figure out if they could attend, with whom they wanted to attend, and where they wanted to sit – well before they decided where to obtain the tickets. Those decisions were all part of what could make the experience rewarding and value-driven. Fans' exposure to and experience with SeatGeek could become a prelude to a long-term relationship with Sporting KC and MLS that goes beyond awareness, discovery, and cultivation. It could transcend life- long loyalty and advocacy.

Jake leaned forward and picked up the phone to schedule a meeting with his marketing team. He knew Sporting KC's relationship with SeatGeek would present many new and innovative ways to reach fans in both the primary and secondary ticket markets. With interest in MLS growing, he was convinced that finding the right prices and pricing mechanisms for various market segments, and finding the best ways and venues to engage and communicate that value, could maximize revenue as never before. The key would be to balance this strategy while delivering the best fan purchase experience.

Your assignment is to develop and present a multifaceted distribution plan for Sporting KC to achieve the following goals:
- Ensure maximization of ticket and related revenues
- Identify new revenue streams for Sporting KC, made possible via the MLS partnership with SeatGeek
- Reach and engage new fans, Millennials in particular, by providing outstand ticket-purchasing experience

The plan should prioritize and address each of the goals appropriately, recommend proper strategies to achieve them, and provide guidance to measure their effectiveness. Entertaining the following questions can help further clarify the recommended distribution strategy for Sporting KC:
- Recommend specific ticket distribution partners and marketplaces – opportunities made possible by SeatGeek's unique open ticketing network/platform – which will ensure that Sporting KC provides an outstanding ticket-purchase experience for fans and will allow Sporting KC:
- Reach/engage new fans (in particular, Millennials);
- Identify new, creative revenue streams for Sporting KC, which are made possible via the MLS partnership with SeatGeek, and
- Ensure maximization of ticket and related revenue.

The presentation should prioritize and address each of the goals appropriately, as well as provide guidance for measuring the effectiveness of each strategy recommendation.

The following questions provide guidance for thinking about the possibilities of this relationship.
1. Discuss how partnership with SeatGeek ensures the maximization of ticket and related revenues for Sporting KC.

2. How can Sporting KC take full advantage of SeatGeek's unique ticketing platform by developing relationships with a variety of ticket distribution partners? You may want to focus on one or more of the following factors or the ones you identify:

- Help Jake and his team understand why a sports fan would choose SeatGeek over other online ticketing options when purchasing Sporting KC tickets. You may want to conduct a SWOT analysis for the relationship between Sporting KC and SeatGeek

- SeatGeek's open ticketing system allows Sporting KC to work with a wide range of distribution partners to sell tickets. Identify new opportunities that are made possible to enhance customer value and maximize Sporting KC's revenue stream. What distributors would you recommend SKC partner with to sell tickets beyond pure-play ticketing companies like StubHub or Vivid Seats?

3. How can Sporting KC reach and engage new fans (in particular, Millennials) by taking full advantage of SeatGeek's unique ticketing platform, as well as other opportunities? You may want to focus on one or more of the following factors or the ones you identify:

- What other brands are currently employing effective strategies to market to Millennial sports and entertainment fans? Would any of their strategies or tactics be applicable to Sporting KC's challenge? Does Sporting KC's relationship with SeatGeek offer any particular advantage(s) to target Millennials?

- What should be particular features with key apps or websites that Sporting KC could use to target Millennial fans and direct them to SeatGeek to purchase their tickets?

- Are there specific "premium" periods or games that Sporting KC can use to target and attract Millennial fans? Are there segments within the Millennial group that would be more responsive to Sporting KC's targeting?

4. Identify new opportunities that are made possible, via the MLS partnership with SeatGeek, to enhance customer value and maximize Sporting KC's revenue stream. You may want to focus on one or more of the following factors or the ones you identify:

- SeatGeek posts a "value for the ticket." Is there a way that Sporting KC could add customer value to certain sections or seats to improve their rating score?

- How can Sporting KC use influencer marketing to drive ticket sales?

- What social media strategies can be designed to target and attract Sporting KC fans to online ticket outlets?

- What other types of organizations or events might the managers of Children's Mercy Park seek to use the stadium, and use SeatGeek for their ticketing services? Is there potential for synergy between and among Sporting KC and these other ticketed venues?

5. For each strategy that you recommend regarding the MLS/SportingKC/SeatGeek partnership, identify the specific target market/s of each strategy and indicate how to measure the effectiveness of each strategy. You may want to focus on one or more of the following factors or the ones you identify:

- What are the important metrics that Sporting KC should use to evaluate the success of the SeatGeek relationship?

- What are the important metrics that SeatGeek should use to evaluate the success of the relationship with Sporting KC (and subsequent MLS teams)

Appendix A. Comparison of Online Ticketing Websites

Name of Company	Headquarters	Description	Market/s	Ticket types	Business model	Notes
SeatGeek	New York City	Ticket "meta" search engine, aggregator	Primary, secondary	Sports, concerts, entertainment events	Commission after sale	"DealScore" algorithm for best value, price forecasting feature, makes suggestions based on customer location, goal is 100 e-tickets (no physical tickets), mobile app and desktop, offers Apple Pay for payment
Ticketmaster	West Hollywood, California	Acts as agent for event promoters	Primary	Sports, concerts, entertainment, events	Fees paid by buyers (service charge, building facility charge, processing charge, shipping/e-ticket convenience/ will call charge)	Makes ticket suggestions based on customer location, rated best sports ticketing company 2016 (free shipping of physical tickets, premium parking, gift cards, rewards, return policy), criticized for high customer fees, acquired Getmein.com to serve secondary ticket market
StubHub	San Francisco	Online ticket exchange	Secondary	Any ticket posted by seller	Commission after sale	Owned by eBay, helps customer find best deal, also called "ticket scalper of digital age"
AXS	In the U.S., Los Angeles	Digital marketing platform for AEG venues/ events	Primary, also serves ticket resellers	Sports, concerts, entertainment events	Business model similar to Ticketmaster in that they pay teams/ venues a licensing fee for ticketing which they make back primarily on consumer fees added to base ticket price.	Parent company is AEG (world's largest owner of sports teams/events, second largest presenter of live music/entertainment), recently added "Name a Ticket Price" platform (partnering with ScoreBig), AXS Invite allows customers to reserve seating for friends

The Ticket Experience	Houston	Acts as agent for ticket sellers	Primary	Sports, concerts, theater	Traditional ticket brokerage model where they take on event inventory and sell that for a profit thru distribution channels.	Recently launched B2B secondary market service provider Eventellect
Eventellect	Houston	Provides ticketing solutions for sports and entertainment properties	B2B Secondary	Sports, concerts, theater	Standard consulting business model.	Company is The Ticket Experience, allows ticket sellers access to revenue, data, customers on secondary market
Gametime	San Francisco	Tickets for impulse buyers (mobile ticketing app)	Primary, secondary	Sports, concerts	Distributor for tickets from ticket brokers. They either buy a ticket wholesale and sell it to the consumer at their own markup, or for other listings they may sell a ticket thru from a broker and retain a commission against that sale from the broker's take.	Most sales occur in final two hours before event start, mobile-based
Spectra	Irvine, California	Services provider (venue management, food services/ hospitality, ticketing/fan engagement, fundraising)	Primary	College athletics, performing arts, professional sports	Same model as AXS -- primary ticketer that primarily drives revenues thru consumer fees. Major client focus is on the college market	Goal is to "transform events into experiences" for the customers of their clients; partners with StubHub
TicketIQ	New York City	Ticket search engine, aggregator	Primary, secondary	Sports, music, theater	Ticket aggregator akin to Gametime but web focused. Collects commission on top of a sale of broker tickets.	Low price guarantee, CEO is active disseminating ticket-market information via news media
Tickets.com	Costa Mesa, California	Provides ticketing and other services to teams, entertainment venues, non-profit organizations	Primary	Sports, performing arts	Same model as AXS -- primary ticketer that primarily drives revenues thru consumer fees. Owned by MLB Advanced Media with a bulk of their business in MLB, though they do have an assortment	Parent company is Major League Baseball, partners with Boston Red Sox secondary market Red Sox Replay

						of longer tail clients as well.	
TickPick	New York City	Provides online ticket marketplace for sellers and buyers	Secondary	Sports, concerts, theater	Ticket aggregator akin to Gametime but web focused. Collects commission on top of a sale of broker tickets.	Allows bidding, "Best Deal Ranking System" feature	
Score Big	Los Angeles	Ticket liquidator (allows venues and properties to discreetly move excess primary inventory to a secondary market without cannibalizing existing strategies)	Secondary ("stealth" primary)	Sports, concerts, entertainment events	Now defunct, but business model was primarily centered around cutting deals with teams for distressed inventory, selling it opaquely through their own channel or opaquely thru other distribution channels.	Partners with Ticketmaster, consumers can bid on tickets, self-described "outlet mall for tickets"	
ShooWin	New York City	Connects "real" fans with tickets at face value	Primary	Sports, music	Make money by operating a marketplace where fans can buy team-specific options that entitle them to purchase a face value ticket in the event that their team qualifies for a playoff-caliber game (i.e., college bowl games).	Fans pick a championship team, pick a seating zone, pay the reservation price – if team qualifies, customer has locked in seats at face value; "created by fans"	

Endnotes

[1] Sporting Kansas City website. http://www.sportingkc.com/

[2] http://www.sportingkc.com/post/2016/07/28/sporting-kansas-city-and-seatgeek-announce-landmark-ticketing-partnership

[3] https://www.fastcompany.com/3065478/the-fast-company-innovation-festival/four-lessons-from-seatgeeks-fan-friendly-assault-on-tic

[4] Ibid.

[5] http://searchcio.techtarget.com/definition/digital-disruption

[6] https://blog.tickpick.com/ticket-industry-ticket-resale-ticketmaster/

[7] https://hbr.org/2016/03/the-industries-that-are-being-disrupted-the-most-by-digital

[8] http://www.techradar.com/news/world-of-tech/who-are-the-digital-disruptors-redefining-entire-industries-1298171

[9] https://theringer.com/ticket-industry-problem-solution-e4b3b71fdff6#.7y106qu96
[10] http://www.kshb.com/sports/soccer/sporting-kc-tickets-sold-out-in-five-minutes-on-the-teams-website

[11] http://www.bloomberg.com/news/articles/2016-07-27/mls-moves-to-open-its-ticket-markets-unlike-the-rest-of-sports

[12] http://www.forbes.com/sites/briansolomon/2015/01/21/the-hottest-ticket-in-mobile-seatgeek-helps- you-scalp-the-scalpers/#15c9407a3c03

[13] http://www.bloomberg.com/news/articles/2016-07-27/mls-moves-to-open-its-ticket-markets-unlike-the-rest-of-sports

[xxxvi] https://www.fastcompany.com/3065420/secrets-of-the-most-productive-people/at-sundar- pichais-google-ai-is-everything-and-everywhe
[14] http://www.sportingkc.com/club/history

[15] https://en.wikipedia.org/wiki/Supporters%27_Shield

[16] Ibid.

[17] Ibid.

[18]CONCACAF is an annual continental soccer club competition that represents soccer teams in North America, Central America, and the Caribbean.

[19] www.mlssoccer.com

[20]Perez, A.J. "SeatGeek Enters Into Partnerships with MLS, Sporting Kansas City," USA Today, July 27, 2016. http://www.usatoday.com/story/sports/mls/2016/07/27/mls-seatgeek-tickets/87616062/
[21] Strauss, Karsten, "SeatGeek Snuffs Out Competition, *Forbes,* December 19, 2013. http://www.forbes.com/sites/karstenstrauss/2013/12/19/seatgeek-snuffs-out-competition/#14bb0840277f [22] Average Per Game Attendance of the Five Major Sports Leagues in North America 2015/2016." The Statistics Portal. https://www.statista.com/statistics/207458/per-game-attendance-of-major-us-sports-leagues/

[23] Fort, R. and Quirk, J. Owner Objectives and Competitive Balance. Journal of Sports Economics. February 2004, 20-32.

[24] http://www.bizjournals.com/kansascity/news/2013/12/04/fans-paying-record-prices-for-mls-cup.html

25 Parket, T. Why The Prices Of Sports Tickets Vary So Much. Investopedia http://www.investopedia.com/financial-edge/1012/why-the-prices-of-sports-tickets-vary-so-much-.aspx#ixzz4QUJbwZwt

[26] *Economist*, "Sports Ticketing: The Price Is Right." January 9, 2012. http://www.economist.com/node/21542621/
[27]Rishe, Patrick, "Dynamic Pricing: The Future of Ticket Pricing in Sports," Forbes, January 6, 2012. http://forbes.com/sites/prishe/2012/01/06/dynamic-pricing-the-future-of-ticket-pricing-in-sports/
[28]Groetzinger, Jack, "New TIcketing Technologies Will Open More Doors to Live Entertainment, July 20, 2016, techcrunch.com. http://techcrunch.com/2016/07/20/new-ticketing-technologies-will-open- more-doors-to-live-entertainment

[29]Fisher, Eric, "Ticketing on the Go," *Sports Business Journal,* April28-May4, 2014, http://www.sportsbusinessdaily.com/Journal/Issues/2014/04/28/In-Depth/Ticket-apps.aspx

[30] Sterling, Greg, "Mobile Drives Nearly Half of E-Commerce Traffic, but PC Still Rules - Sales Report. MarketingLand, February 17, 2015. http://marketingland.com/mobile-drives-nearly-half-e-commerce-traffic-pc-still-rules-sales-report-118629

[31] Solomon, Brian, "Forget Stores: ApplePay Is Already Taking Over Mobile Shopping," Forbes, January 22, 2015. http://www.forbes.com/sites/briansolomon/2015/01/22/forget-stores-apple-pay-is- already-taking-over-mobile-shopping/#d3abe6b5b56f

[32] Samuely, Alex. "Mobile Ticketing Transaction Volume to Double by 2019: Report." *Mobile Commerce Daily*. 14 Apr. 2015. Web. 16 Sept. 2015. Data retrieved by Juniper Research.

[33] Strauss, Karsten, "SeatGeek Snuffs Out Competition, *Forbes*, December 19, 2013. http://forbes.com/sites/karstenstrauss/2013/12/19/seatgeek-snuffs-out-competition/#1bb0840277f

[34] Fry, Richard, "Millennials Overtake Baby Boomers as America's Largest Generation," April 25, 2016. Pew Research Center. http://www.pewresearch.org/fact-tank/2016/04/25/millennials-overtake- baby-boomers/

[35] Drake, Bruce, "6 New Findings About Millennials."PEW Research Center, March 7, 2014. http://www.pewresearch.org/fact-tank/2014/03/07/6-new-findings-about-millennials/

[36] Drake, ibid.

[37]"The Rising Cost of not Going to College," PEW Research Center, February 11, 2014. http://www.pewsocialtrends.org/2014/02/11/the-rising-cost-of-not-going-to-college/

[38] Millennials in Adulthood: Detached from Institutions, Networked with Friends," Pew Research Center, March 7, 2014. http://www.pewsocialtrends.org/2014/03/07/millennials-in-adulthood/

[39] Schultz, Brian, "Not just Millennials: Consumers Want Experiences, Not Things," Advertising Age, August 18, 2015. http://adage.com/article/digitalnext/consumers-experiences-things/299994/

[40] Millennials in Adulthood, op cit.

[41] Rand, SEth, "A Look Inside: What WIll Be the Big Online Marketing Trends for 2016?" business.com, December 9, 2015. http://www.business.com/online-marketing/a-look-inside-what-will- be-the-big-online-marketing-trends-for-2016/

[42] Ibid.

[43] American Lifestyles 2015: The Connected Consumer - Seeking Validation from the Online Collective US - April 2015. Mintel Resaerch. http://store.mintel.com/american-lifestyles-2015-the-connected-consumer-seeking-validation-from-the-online-collective-us-april-2015.

[44] Greenwood, Shannon, "Social Media Update 2016." PEW Research Center, November 11, 2016. http://www.pewinternet.org/2016/11/11/social-media-update-2016/

45 Millennials in Adulthood, op cit.

[46] Stewart, James, "Facebook Has 50 Minutes of Your Time Each Day. It Wants More," New York Times, May 5, 2016. http://www.nytimes.com/2016/05/06/business/facebook-bends-the-rules-of- audience-engagement-to-its-advantage.html?_r=0

[47] http://www.business.com/online-marketing/under-the-radar-digital-trends-you-need-to-know-about/

Team Survivor New York – Getting Back on Track

By

Deborah Fain, Pace University

Wendy sipped her chai latte as she described her situation as the program leader for Team Survivor New York City (TSNYC). The New York chapter was part of the national organization dedicated to promoting health and fitness for women who are cancer survivors. When Wendy started with the organization, five years ago, she imagined that the New York group would grow and be self-sustaining through grassroots efforts and word-of- mouth. But participation in activities had started to dwindle at the same time as Wendy's own career as a financial consultant was consuming more of her time. TSNYC was something she did on a volunteer basis.

Wendy noted that TS chapters were well attended in other parts of the country. There was certainly a need for such a program in NYC, as a significant number of cancer cases occurred there. The cost to participants was not an issue as all activities were free or very low cost. There was a market and the price was right, so why could she not get more women cancer survivors interested? Wendy mused that perhaps since she had never had cancer she was missing out on some unknown factor for running such an organization. Surely she could figure this out, after all she had an MBA! But this problem had been gnawing at Wendy for a couple of years now. She had talked to a lot of people, including those running successful chapters in other parts of the country. She even asked her business professor friends to allow her to present her materials in an undergraduate and graduate Customer Relationship Management (CRM) class and get suggestions from their students, but Wendy still did not have a clear path to making TSNYC successful.

Mission of Team Survivor (Source: Team Survivor Startup Information)

The mission of Team Survivor is to enable women with a past or present diagnosis of cancer to take an active role in their health and well-being.

The National Association of Team Survivor provides training and support for local Team Survivor organizations and promotes the concept of cancer wellness thorough exercise and physical activity across the country.

Local Team Survivor programs provide exercise and health education programs to women in their communities who have been affected by cancer. These programs, which combine fun fitness activities with emotional support, are an important part of the ongoing healing process for women living with cancer.

(See materials from National Association of Team Survivor in Appendix C.)

Background Information about Team Survivor

(Source: Team Survivor website (http://www.teamsurvivor.org/doc.aspx?3))

<u>What</u>: Team Survivor is a nonprofit 501(c)3 organization. Affiliates provide group exercise and support programs for women with a present or past diagnosis of cancer.

The National Association of Team Survivor (NATS) provides resources and guidance for Affiliates to develop programs and communicate their missions within their local markets.

<u>Who</u>: Women of all ages and fitness levels and in all stages of cancer treatment and recovery are welcome. Team Survivor is open to women who have been diagnosed with any type of cancer.

<u>History</u>: Team Survivor was founded in 1995, as a grassroots program offshoot of the Danskin® Women's Triathlon Series to provide a fitness opportunity for female cancer survivors to train for and participate in their first triathlon. Austin, TX, and Seattle, WA were the first to run year—long programs.

<u>Programs</u>: Team Survivor programs vary from city to city. All Affiliates focus on providing fun group exercise opportunities, fitness education and peer support. Some program offerings at present include:

- Walk/Run Groups ("Walk & Talk")
- Dragon Boat Racing
- Swimming
- Tennis
- Yoga
- Cycling (Road and Mountain)
- Golf Clinics
- Pilates
- Triathlon Training

Team Survivor New York

Team Survivor NYC (TSNYC) formed in August 2006 with Wendy as Executive Director and Founder and four board members. As stated on the TSNYC website:

Our mission is to create a network for women affected by cancer, providing a variety of fitness activities, education and support while taking an active role in their well-being.

To that end, TSNYC listed a variety of programs in their online monthly calendar. Some of these are led by TSNYC, such as the weekly walks in Central Park. The TSNYC calendar also serves as a clearing house for other organizations' programs for cancer survivors, for example, OM Yoga's class-- Yoga for Women Cancer Survivors ($5 per class) and the Jewish Community Center (JCC) Renewal Water Exercise Program for women with cancer.

Other events are coordinated with other organizations and events. For example, Spin4Survival is an indoor cycling event created to raise money for essential cancer research and important cancer survivorship programs. TSNYC sponsored a team of four to participate in the cycling event. All proceeds benefited Memorial Sloan Kettering Cancer Center. In the past, TSNYC members participated in other established cancer fund raising events as a group – such as the Susan G. Komen Race for the Cure and the NYC Revlon 5K.

Wendy admitted that the TSNYC website was out of date. The board member who had been in charge of updating the site had married and moved out of the area and Wendy had not found someone to replace her technical skills. TSNYC members could log into the website and access a Buddy Board to find workout partners, post interesting events, share ideas or meet for coffee. However, there were no recent posts. Photos on the website highlighted TSNYC members participating in events, but these were dated from 2007. Photos showed TSNYC participants in the Susan G. Komen Race for the Cure, NYC Revlon 5K Walk, and the Danskin Triatholon.

Market Competition

Wendy described some of the challenges in the NYC market:

A lot of the hospitals at the corporate level think that we're competitors. And so for example Sloan

Kettering … when we reached out to them they pretty much shut us down. And they say that explicitly that we're competitors…they have their own health and fitness programs that people pay for that they provide to the city.

We have a big problem there because it's true there are a lot of New York hospitals that already have these [programmatic] activities going on. And I'm sure that they're afraid if their patient can go somewhere for free, why on earth would they pay for their services.

Wendy described another stumbling block:

And then the other part is that we've tried to partner with gyms, but their philosophy is 'if we do it with one nonprofit then we have to do it for all,' so they just make a blanket policy of no partnership. I have been trying to think of creative ways to reach out to the community besides leaving brochures or letters with each oncologist that we know of which by no means covers the spectrum.

Next Steps

Wendy asked Professor Mary, her friend at a local university, if she had any ideas. They decided that some additional market research was in order. Professor Mary agreed to conduct in-depth interviews of TSNY former members. She also suggested to talk to people more at the organization level to see what they are doing in other parts of the country that is different and could be applied to Wendy's situation here in New York. A summary of the in-depth interviews with five former TSNYC members can be found in Appendix

A. The next section provides highlights of the conference call with Wendy and leaders of two successful TS chapters in other parts of the country.

Conference Call

The conference call took place with the leaders of Team Survivor-Madison (Diane), Team Survivor-Tri-State (Ronnie) and TSNYC (Wendy). There was a lot to think about from the over one hour long phone conversation (see Appendix B for a partial transcript).

Wendy was particularly struck by Diane's thoughts on what works in Madison:

> What worked for us, and what I can continue to see is working for us, is that it's the constant. And what's the constant in what you're trying to do right now? I mean, it sounds like you had the Central Park thing and it wasn't working. And again I'm just speaking for what was successful for us is that we found a location.

And it was a constant that for most Sundays in the winter, we had a program there every Sunday and we had volunteer instructors. We have always said also that what constitutes a program is two members, which not everybody will do. And let me tell you I've been to many programs and sat through a yoga or a Tai Chi, Chi-gong, a step program, boot camp, where it's been myself and one member. But we've held the program. It's tough when there's only two of you, but the return on the investment can be high.

Diane also spoke about their flagship events:

But this meeting happens usually the third week of January because it's the anniversary of our first meeting when literally it was at the Panera Bread and 21 women showed up and it was 25 below zero and 45 below windchill that night. And 23 women showed up because they have gotten an email about something about fitness, and exercise, and survivorship. And so every January we have that event. Again, this last couple of weeks ago in January, a couple of months ago, we have the event again but we've done is turn it into a social night. Again because we want to try and streamline and get some business done at the same time, we unveil our calendar for the year. We allow people to sign up to do volunteer things through our organization and the other community events we volunteer for.

But our other big flagship event over the summer we have our dragon boat program that basically runs May to the end of September.

And then our other big fundraiser is the Labor Day weekend we do the Chocolate Chase bike ride which is this would be our fifth annual. It's a family friendly, again like I said we try to have that ripple effect in the household. So it's family friendly. There's a 4, 10 or 20 mile ride. Trek Bicycle Store here is our partner. And last year we had over 300 riders.

So would I say I think finding some kind of an event that you can get people to engage in as a starting point and launch pad is a really good idea.

Appendix A

Summary of In-Depth Interviews of TSNYC Participants

Five TSNYC participants were interviewed via telephone in March 2011. These were members who had participated in past events, but were not currently active.

The participants found out about TSNYC through a combination of word-of-mouth and online search. Other than posting materials at medical facilities – one person suggested chemo nurses could make referrals -- no one had any suggestion as to how to make it easier to find the group.

Motives for Joining TSNYCs:

TSNYC participant motives for joining were short-term, to get them through a "rough period." Participants could be segmented into two groups:

Those who already exercised and wanted to continue to stay in shape during or post-treatment.
Those who had not exercised much in the past but who viewed cancer as a wake-up call to get a healthier lifestyle, through exercise and nutrition.

Activities:

The participants interviewed ran the gamut from those who just did the walks to one who had completed two triathlons with the organization. Organized cancer walks (e.g., Revlon), yoga classes, aromatherapy, and cooking classes were other activities that these women mentioned.

Reflections:

Those participants in the second group (new to exercise) could stay with the organization long-term if TSNY had more/better activities. As to what those activities might be, it varied. For those who were already exercisers, walking was too low-key. The one participant interviewed who had completed the tri was used to working out pre-cancer. Those new to exercise were intimidated by the thought of training for the triathlon or actually found it too difficult. Another person said the time commitment for training was too great. They want regularly scheduled activities but there was no consensus on what those activities should be. On a positive note, all of the interviewees mentioned the sense of camaraderie and doing things in a group as a good motivator for exercising.

The participant who did the tri expressed that she would never cancel on the trainer, he made her get out of bed.

The key theme reiterated by all of the participants was the need for regularly scheduled activities. They lose touch over the winter and then it becomes hard to restart with TS. As one participant put it:

"If you don't hear [from TS] for a few months, you go on to other things -- it's New York!"

Someone else noted that at times they forget about the organization. Perhaps a general meeting or coffee hour could be used for defining the group:

"I don't have a sense of who is in the group…what is our mission, who are we?"

One person stated that she felt guilty being called a survivor and taking things people give for survivors. She claimed her cancer situation was easier, she did not have full chemo or radiation or lose her hair. She noted:

"I don't think I deserve the pass that everyone else is given…I try to get people who are sicker than me in…I don't want to define my life for the time I had cancer."

Moving Away from TSNY:

While on the one hand, participants stated that more regularly scheduled activities would be a good way to decrease attrition, others have moved beyond TSNY. In addition to segmenting by high/low exercisers, one can also segment by level of association with cancer and survivorship. Several participants noted that the further out from cancer treatment, the less important it was to be associated with anything cancer related:

" It's not my life…I don't want to be reminded. It brings me back and down."

"It's always there [cancer] but you'd like to forget about it. The further out you go, you feel back to yourself, it's not so important to connect on a cancer level."

Appendix B

Conference Call with National TS

Diane – TS Madison Wisconsin founder 2002

"I mean I'm lucky enough to have a day job that pays my bills but I'll tell you it takes every twenty-three and a half hours of every day for me to keep the organization going. "

"…we're all volunteer, non-profit, grass-roots and people fall in and out of this organization as it fits their lives. No strings attached."

(Ronnie: About 300 virtual members in Tri-State and 25-50 participate on a regular basis in events.)

"Right now we have an active membership base of about 130… and some of them do all of the summer events, and none of the winter events and some members who do everything.

What we defined as virtual members because we adhere to the guidelines of the national organization. You are a member as long as you complete that annual membership form, the medical release.

And we have a little member application. We compiled it into one document.

Our monthly newsletter goes out to about 130. And then as you can see on our website and I haven't been out to the website for a while. But then in the peak seasons, we will list a calendar of event of some of the things that are upcoming and then usually have the disclaimer that you have to be a member to participate. One of the things that we worked hard at the last I would say couple of years maybe 2 to 3 years but certainly in the last couple of years is again feedback from our membership is this notion of and I think it's again that broader, we can get into that broader marketing appeal of the fact the impact that we have only to that survivor but to their household whatever that means.

If it's kids, if it's a spouse, if it's a partner, if it's just friends in their community or network at wok so that we purposely plan programs. And if you again looked at some of the language that we have used on our websites, it's we'll note a program is open to a TSM member, Team Survivor Madison, a TSM member and their family and friends kind of thing. And that have certain programs that, for instance we do snowshoe events. So that snow shoe event is open to not only the member but if they want to bring their spouse or their neighbor, they can do that.

We don't want to lose the brand and the brand is that we're open to woman surviving any diagnosis. And so I think the other piece of that in terms of the conversation not only on the national level but other chapters that I've tried to help get going here in our local region is, it will go without saying that our chapter has been dogged about recruitment across all cancers. And I think that's another reason why we are as successful as we are.

(Mary) How do you guys go about recruiting?

So we started with the healthcare. We went to the hospitals. We had a world renowned cancer center here. So we went to the cancer centers and had conversations. And at that time I mean I had to tell you, I was sitting there across the table from the external relations person and the only thing that I had going for me is that I could speak external relations and that I was a survivor. But it was that wing and a prayer thing. It was like this is what we want to do. This is what we want to bring to Madison.

In those days we were asking for, you know, we're going to have an informational meeting, will you put something in your newsletter. Can we put something out on your bulletin board that we made at home on our computer?... This has morphed into something that now we're asking for space and staff.

And I always say you know thank god that Lance Armstrong put fitness and survivorship on the map because we've taken it to the next step... Again when we were asking that question back in 2001-2002, people were like not so hot about saying that we were supposed to be standing there with our poles next to our beds because we were on chemo and not supposed to be going out and try to do a triathlon. So I think society has come along and I think that conversation is easier. But I would say that the healthcare and the fitness and community, and again because I think Madison is what it is. It's very recreationally minded. So we targeted healthcare entities, fitness, health clubs. Then you know and again these are the things that are continuing to be what we called our community partners. The other big ones is all of the outdoor, I don't know if you guys have REI. Do you have REI out there?

Our paddling program is with the local paddle shop -- Rutabaga. We wouldn't have a dragon boat program had it not been for the conversation with those folks back in 2002 where they gave us two old canoes and said we're just going to toss these in the backyard unless you want them. And that's how our paddling program started. And again it sounds cliché but I will say that if you build it they will come and I think you have to have the patience to build it.

Mary: There's REI I think in New Jersey. I saw that on your website. I thought it was interesting that you were targeting the sports stores too.

Diane: It's huge.

[Ronnie]:   Yeah, we did that as well.

Because early on I mean we couldn't get anything in the Madison newspaper. We couldn't get on the local TV stations… One of the local TV personalities did the triathlon with our group because she's a survivor and actually joined the organization that year and participated.

Our biggest recruitment tool right now the oncologist. Know the oncologist they know of. And again depending on where and what like I said we served all cancers but probably the majority of our members are still breast cancer.

It still comes back to there is a different in the camaraderie and the theme that resonates when it's a survivor only program.

Wendy: I think both of you, Ronnie and Diane, mentioned that you both have flagship events. Do you mind sharing with us what those events are?

And now it's our annual informational meeting…. we've done is turn it into social night. Again because we want to try and streamline and get some business down at the same time, we unveil our calendar for the year. We allow for people to sign up to do volunteer things through our organization and the other community events we volunteer for.

We also let them bring in there annual renewal and medical release form that they get from their doctors cause people don't want to mail them, whatever. They can drop them off in person.

Mary: Do you see like different segments of participants in the organization or is there a typical participant?

This is Diane. I mean I would say that our age range is 30 to 85. Personally in seeing the ebb and flow of the organization I frankly see the people that are the most active on a regular basis are the people that prior to a diagnosis were probably not active. And I think again you know we can talk about the fact that I think our median age for participants easily is probably close to 45 or 50. And I would say these are women that were pre- title IX so they never participated in any organized fitness activity or high school sport.

Now members are getting younger because we are getting members that are being diagnosed younger unfortunately.

We don't have a lot of members that you would say are fit iron man. We have women that say the beauty of it is that they're accepted because it's all ages, shapes, sizes and abilities.

Yeah sure it's about the fitness but you know it's about the friendship and the camaraderie of the special connection.

Mary: … an interesting point that if people who stay long term and they're getting all this stuff for free, do you hear anything like that from anybody?

Diane: I think we hear it with a little bit different spin. And I think part of the way we package our message out of really know the school of hard knocks and also just necessity is, and again if you heard some of the words that I'm using today that I served these women and we served each other. And there's ways that we can serve and give back to the community. And so again one of the things, for instance there are a number of thing that happen throughout the year where we will serve as the volunteer core for a particular event or something. I think the other thing that we have learned in terms of our programming depending on the program and you know and again it's from that whether it's a business sense or whatever it is. That we have asked for a nominal registration fees or deposits to basically get the commitment and accountability.

You know, dovetailing into existing program and then you go as a group. And even if it's a community program the fact that you all show up as a group.

And I think the other thing we've really tried to do with our members is again we deputized. We call them program ambassadors. So I always say that the organization is where member driven and member lead.

Ronnie

"And I think Diane hit on a really important point and I could say the same for Tri-State which is if you look at our virtual members we probably have about 300. But there's probably only about anywhere from 25 to 50 depending on the events, that actually participates in the events on the regular basis."

We try to email everybody on a regular basis. We do monthly newsletters.

[Wendy]: Hey Ronnie, how did you guys go about recruiting when you first started?
So one thing that we did that I would say probably at least 70% of our membership came from was from local newspapers. My background is in PR so obviously I took that and I pitch the story to all the local papers and we got so much coverage. Every single local paper in the area did a story on us and it was fabulous.

So that's where'd I say most of our recruitment came from. We could do that in the New Jersey area because we have all these local papers. You guys have it a lot tougher cause your competition in that media market is seriously harsh.

Flagship event?
We do about I would say four really key events a year. One is the triathlon, the Danskin or Trek whichever happens to be is more convenient. That's usually here, usually in September. Then we do usually two races, running races a year usually one half marathon and one 5K, the same ones every year. And then we do one fund raising brunch. We don't do a dinner we do a brunch. And at that brunch we used it as a fund raiser but we also used it as a time to get a motivational speaker come in and talk to people. And for that like Dianne said it's the member and then they bring their husbands or their friends or whatever or they can have a nice brunch and then hear a really fabulous speaker. So those are the four things that we usually do.

I find that the triathlon is obviously the most popular. And I think the reason for that is because most women whether they're survivors or not never think that they can actually do a triathlon. But we have a pretty serious training program. So we have a triathlon coach who volunteers his time and trains all our ladies to complete one. So it's more formalized than just go out there and train on your own. So we found that to be really helpful. In conjunction with that, we also do a triathlon training camp which is usually a day or a weekend where we borrow some space from the local gym and they usually just donate the space to us. And then our coach comes in. We used the pool. We go outside and do some biking. We do some running. And we basically just tell them what they're going to expect especially if they're first timers.

And then like I said a 5K which is easy to get a lot of people in. We encourage a lot of walkers so you don't have to be a runner. And then for those who want a more challenging experience we offer them the half marathon and we get all our race registrations for free. Most of the time the race will donate the registrations for us especially if we volunteer for the weekend of the race, help with registration and pre-registration in exchange for some free [registrations].

Segments?
Nobody ever talks about cancer in our classes. And I found that there's pretty much two groups of people. One are really really active members, those who participate in the triathlon and the marathons. I would put them in the younger crowd. I would say they are between mid-20s to mid-40s. And these are the people who they really got the exercise bug. I mean they're competitive. These people are the ones who when we first started the group in 2005 never did a triathlon. Always thought it would be neat to do one. Never actually did one. They did their first sprint and they got hooked. And now they do Olympic and you know they do marathons and they're competitive. And they tack their time. So there's definitely two groups. And then there's the other group of women who's probably range from mid 20 all the way up to 60s.

And they're the ones, they just like to come to class once a week. So our most popular classes are spinning class and our yoga class. And they just come once a week. And they just want to take the class and they want to chow with their friends and they don't want to work too hard but they want to feel like they're moving their bodies and doing something. So I would say that those are the two groups of people.

We also have an online message board. We do it through yahoo group. And basically anybody who is involved with the affiliate can go ahead and log in and talk to each other. And that is a lot of fun. That's used a lot. Like I said the more active participants will talk about hardcore training and then there are some who just want to know do you have a good recipe for green veggies. So that's another good way to engage people without too much time and effort.

Conclusion

Wendy kept looking at all the materials she had acquired as she tried to make TSNYC a success. Maybe she needed to pass the leadership on to someone with more time to devote. Maybe she should take the advice of both classes and hire a paid intern to get everything into good order first. Maybe she should seek help from the national Team Survivor people. She was an Ivy League MBA with excellent health care experience. Where had she gone wrong and how could she turn this around?

Appendix C

Materials from National Office Team Survivor

Welcome to Team Survivor NYC!

We ask that you please complete this short survey so that we are better able to design and tailor activities for members

Personal Information

Name: _____

Mailing Address: _____

E-mail: _____

Phone: _____

What is the preferred method of communicating activities and events with you?

_____

_____

Interests and Goals for Participation

What kinds of activities would you be most likely to participate in with Team Survivor NYC (walking, running, cycling, yoga, triathlon training, swimming, etc.)?

_____

_____

What are your fitness or other goals for participation in Team Survivor NYC?

_____

Are there any other particular events or activities that you would like Team Survivor NYC to organize

_____

(guest speakers, clinics, etc.)?

Are you interested in fundraising or otherwise volunteering your time to organizing and expanding Team Survivor NYC activities?

_____

If so, approximately how many hours per week are you available?

_____

What other information do you want to provide?

_____

_____

_____

Introduction

Welcome to Team Survivor! We are so pleased that you will be launching Team Survivor activities in your area and are confident that you will find it a fun and rewarding venture.

These materials are designed to be used by individuals who are starting local Team Survivor programs in their area. They include detailed information on program development and management and organizational issues.

If you have not reviewed the introductory startup materials provided by Team Survivor, please do so before using this guidebook.

Background/History of Team Survivor

Team Survivor was founded in 1995, in conjunction with the Danskin Women's Triathlon Series. Sally Edwards, National Spokeswoman for that Series, believed that women dealing with cancer would benefit both physically and emotionally from tackling a significant fitness challenge. She conceived of the idea of creating "teams" of breast cancer survivors to participate in the Danskin Women's Triathlon Series. Her goal was to honor cancer survivors, build cancer awareness and put a face on the Official Series Charity, The Susan G. Komen Breast Cancer Foundation. Sally brought her idea to Maggie Sullivan, VP of Sports Marketing at Danskin and Director of the Danskin Women's Triathlon Series, who agreed to support those teams. Cancer survivors together with their coaches, doctors and other volunteers spread the word of this innovative exercise program called Team Survivor. Sixty women across the country participated in the first Danskin Team Survivor program in 1995, with the first team beginning in Austin, Texas.

During the training for the 1995 event, National Coach Lisa Talbott and Seattle Team Physician Julie Gralow, M.D. met numerous women who wanted to exercise but needed more support than a 3-4 month triathlon training program could provide. Lisa and Julie decided to create year-round exercise programs that would give women with any type of cancer a safe place to recover physically from their treatments and surgeries. Together with the help of the University of Washington Cancer Center they founded the nonprofit organization Team Survivor Northwest. This project was created with the enthusiasm and help of numerous volunteers from the cancer, medical and fitness communities. It was designed to promote regular exercise, new and challenging physical goals, emotional and social support, and an emphasis on wellness. Over the next five years, Team Survivor Northwest helped other Team Survivor groups form around the U.S.

In 2001, the National Association of Team Survivor (NATS) was formed to assist Team Survivor groups to begin, grow and maintain. The intention informing the National Association was to ensure protection of the Team Survivor name and program quality and to formalize the process of assisting Team Survivor groups to form and help one another. It is our hope that some day every woman who seeks participation in a Team Survivor program will have that opportunity.

Mission of Team Survivor

The mission of Team Survivor is to enable women with a past or present diagnosis of cancer to take an active role in their health and well-being.

The **National Association of Team Survivor** provides training and support for local Team Survivor organizations and promotes the concept of cancer wellness through exercise and physical activity across the country.

Top Drawer Soccer: Can a Startup Score Points with User Information?

By:

Seth Burleigh, California State University, Northridge
Kristen Walker, California State University, Northridge
Mary Curren, California State University, Northridge
Sean Keyani, California State University, Northridge

> *I have faith in my management team at Top Drawer Soccer; it's just that we cannot continue like this anymore. When we bought this website, it was not in as great a shape as it is now, but we should still have improvement plans. Continuing to pour capital into TDS will not be an option very soon. I expect us to come up with a plan and improve the way we collect user data and generate revenue for this company. We should make this website profitable. – Joseph, CEO Top Drawer Soccer*

Seth, Vice President of Operations at Top Drawer Soccer (TDS), was frustrated. His attempts to improve TDS's website and data collection strategies were hitting a wall. TDS needed to collect more details from users/subscribers to be able to segment effectively. The next day he would only have 30 minutes to convince Joe to adopt his plan to improve user data collection. He had to take into account that when a site requires users to provide many personal data points, it may cause them to abandon personal data sharing altogether. Seth's improvement plan had to be achievable and effective or his plan wouldn't be adopted and he would lose credibility. Will improving TDS's website actually encourage users to provide data? Seth needed to answer that question based on his experience with the company, the constantly changing technology, and ultimately the guidelines and restrictions on the collection and use of consumer data.

Company Background

As of 2011, Top Drawer Soccer (TDS) was the only online destination for club and college soccer news, scores, schedules, rankings, and analysis. The website also had recruiting features and tools for youth players (ages 14-aspiring to play soccer in college (after age 18). Joseph Konowiecki bought the website from its original owner in 2008. Like most start-up websites, TDS began simply. The original TDS was like a starter home, or as Seth described it, "The site architecture, like the home's design, the backend, like the structure of the walls and electrical wiring, and the frontend, everything visible to the homeowner, was basic, nothing was too complicated." The goal for TDS had been to become a profitable website within three years. After three years TDS was not yet profitable.

Typical of many start-up companies, the staff was youthful, and originally consisted of only three people, two of whom were under 25. Funds were tight, and everyone fulfilled multiple roles. The CEO of TDS was Joseph Konowiecki, a successful lawyer and healthcare executive turned entrepreneur.

Similar to other start-ups, the first iteration of the website was short-lived. Less than five months after the new site launched, a redesign was already in the works with a more user-friendly layout. Another redesign followed less than a year later with improved navigation menus and new features including college standings and more robust rankings. After yet another redesign (the third since launch) TDS has stretched its current platform to its limits with complicated hacks and unconventional modifications. Because TDS had evolved so quickly and changed so often in such a short period of time, its programmers never had time to properly "clean-up" the system before moving to the next project. Thus, the site had become bloated, the code was messy, and TDS programmers said if any further changes were to be made, a major overhaul would be required. Marketing strategies were focused on acquiring users.

Initial growth: 2008 to 2011

TDS experienced modest website traffic and revenue growth from 2008–2011, but struggled to build a big enough audience in its niche market to generate any significant revenue (See Appendix A). The website had established a foothold in the space, with few viable competitors, but still struggled to attain a sufficient audience base.

Partnering with NSCAA: Late 2010, Early 2011 NSCAA Partnership Drives Site Change

Toward the end of its initial growth (late 2010/early 2011), TDS had strengthened its relationship with the National Soccer Coaches Association of America (NSCAA)–the largest coaching organization in America. Unhappy with its technology partner for its national college soccer scoreboard, NSCAA approached TDS about collaborating to create a new one.

The opportunity was undeniable: partnering exclusively with the NSCAA on the college scoreboard provided a competitive advantage that no other website would be able to duplicate. This partnership would expose TDS to an audience they had struggled to capture and could be the catalyst for the growth it desperately needed. TDS would have direct access to thousands of college coaches and their programs, and tons of data to create new features. Additionally, because the NSCAA would be financially invested, they would be equally focused on its success. Lastly, TDS would benefit tremendously from the SEO (Search Engine Optimization) opportunities that having a vast amount of college team and player data would provide by allowing programmers to create highly shareable content (an important element in SEO) and college athletics relevant content. However, creating the scoreboard would be challenging.

Scalability and Maintenance, Not User Experience

Ideally, a healthy website should be built in such a way that it can be expanded easily as business needs require. TDS was originally built using PHP (a type of programming language) and Joomla, a free content management system (CMS). A CMS allows the site administrator to input all information, such as articles, pictures, and other data that appear on the site. The administrator does not actually program, rather he uses pre-designed interfaces that allow non-programmers to manage the site content. Additional programming "underneath" the CMS translates the administrator's actions into the final product on the public website. PHP is great for content-only sites (i.e., those with articles, pictures, galleries), but is not ideal for database-driven sites like TDS's with its myriad rankings, player and team profiles, and scores. TDS needed to make the new scoreboard successful for its end users and allow colleges to input the necessary information to make the scoreboard useful for the college soccer community. Hacking Joomla, as it had for the last three years, was no longer an option. The programmers recommended a rebuild from scratch using Java, a programming language capable of more advanced features. While it would take six to nine months to create a proprietary system, the resulting platform would better support current features, enable the scoreboard to function correctly, and allow further enhancements (e.g., improving page loading time and fixing bugs faster).

Becoming Data-Rich: More Data, Better Data

After inking a major partnership with the largest soccer coaching association in the nation in early 2011, TopDrawerSoccer.com (TDS) was poised to become the official college soccer scoreboard—a service it would provide for over 2500 college soccer teams. However, the current website was not very well equipped to handle the influx of data that would be entered by college admins and coaches and accessed by tens of thousands of college soccer fans per day. VP of Operations, Seth Burleigh, knew that recoding the entire site might take too long for this college soccer season; however, it was possible to have the user registration system completed by July 1. Seth had to decide which fields to include on the new user registration page to collect sufficient data for TDS to generate revenue and provide Director of Sales, Ron Dvorkin, with a compelling sales tool without creating a negative user experience.

Marketing

Aside from the internal staff who focused on direct marketing to industry contacts and community forums, and email newsletters to TDS users, TDS did not spend much money on marketing or advertising activities (See Appendix A for budget details). Because TDS was a website without a tangible product to sell, staff did not purchase Google or Facebook ads online. While purchasing ads could have increased brand exposure, Seth and Marketing Director, Max, determined that the return on investment (ROI) for more visits/traffic to the website was not justified by the cost of those advertising methods. TDS sent staff or freelance writers and occasionally a videographer to the most popular soccer events nationwide to provide editorial and video coverage of major youth soccer events.

User Experience and Generating Revenue

Monetizing a content-based website (versus an e-commerce site) was difficult without significant traffic (see Appendix B). Traditionally, websites only implemented banner ads that generated minimal revenue without significant scale. Some websites found creative ways to generate revenue through content or feature sponsorships, while others placed content behind a paywall, only accessible to those who paid for access (e.g., *Wall Street Journal* or *Harvard Business Review*). Some even sold products alongside their regular content through affiliate relationships with larger ecommerce platforms such as Amazon or small ecommerce stores built into their sites. Other sites sold their data (directly or indirectly) for third-party marketing purposes.

TDS had two sources of revenue—digital advertising (traditional banner ads, site sponsorships, email blasts, and social media integrations) and subscriptions. The two subscription options were a monthly plan for $4.95 and an annual plan for $49.95. Both plans automatically renewed each month or year unless the customer notified TDS that he or she wanted the subscription cancelled.

The TDS sales process started with Ron closing the sale and then passing the management on to Jennifer (Account Manager) and Seth. While Jen managed most of the campaign, Seth was involved in certain elements that required more technical expertise and campaigns that had an email component requiring the use of the TDS email database. Seth and Jen did not have any influence over the prices charged to clients, regardless of current industry trends and market prices.

Banner Ads

Banner ads are a common form of website advertising. These ads are typically placed at the top of each page and along the left or right side (sometimes both) of a website and come in several different sizes depending on the location on the web page (See Exhibit 1). Websites earn revenue based on a CPM (cost per one-thousand impressions), CPC (cost per click), or CPA (cost per action) model. A $1 CPM rate means that a website earned $1 for every 1000 banner impressions served to users. CPM rates typically fall into the $5-8 range, but vary significantly based on the advertiser, website, and industry. CPM rates could be as low as $0.50 or as high as $12. Its niche audience (i.e., mostly parents of high school, club, or college soccer players) enables TDS to earn CPMs in the $10-15 range. TDS earns $20 CPM for site takeovers, which occurs when one advertiser purchases all the available banner inventory for a given time period.

Site Sponsorships

Advertisers who want more exposure or who want to be associated with certain higher profile or unique features pay more to have special graphics or naming rights surrounding specific elements of the site. These sponsorships are typically based on a flat fee and often include other digital advertising assets (banner ads and email blasts) to enhance the overall sponsorship (See Exhibit 2).

EXHIBIT 1: *Banner advertisement sample*

Source: TDS internal company records

EXHIBIT 2: *Sponsorship*

Source: TDS internal company records

Email Blasts

Email was one of the earliest forms of electronic communication and remains in high demand by advertisers for its potentially more personalized and targeted format. Email lists cost more to rent from list brokers than do traditional mail order (i.e., direct mail addresses) lists, typically as much as $85/CPM. For example, an email list of 60,000 emails at $85/CPM could cost $5,100 to rent for a one-time use. Of course, companies with their own internal email database of users can charge any price they want and send to those users who have explicitly opted- in to promotional messages; many charge significantly less than the going market rate.

EXHIBIT 3: *eblast sample (Inclusive)*

Source: TDS internal company records

EXHIBIT 3: *eblast sample (exclusive)*

Source: TDS internal company records

TDS was one such company that did not charge the market rate for use of its email database. In fact, it often charged 80%-90% less than the market rate or gave clients free e-blasts (either inclusive or exclusive) as a way to close the sale.

Inclusive means an advertiser could include its graphics in one of TDS' email newsletters that went several times a week to its email database. Exclusive means that the advertiser received its own email blast with a unique message and graphics sent on a day that TDS did not send a regular email newsletter; thus, justifiably warranting a higher charge to the advertiser (See Exhibit 3).

Social Media Integration

Advertisers often purchased Facebook posts or Twitter mentions as part of their entire package with the goal of reaching TDS' highly engaged audience.

Subscriptions

Some TDS users paid an annual subscription fee for access to exclusive features on the site; mainly part of the site that was used as recruiting tools. Paying users also received access to content such as rankings, analysis, and content otherwise unique to TDS (i.e., content not readily available elsewhere).

Resources

Office Space

TDS leased a 1500 sq. ft. office in a downtown Long Beach office building and provided free parking to all employees.

Human Resources

(See Appendix C for organizational chart of TDS)

Seth Burleigh – Vice President of Operations

Seth managed all aspects of the website and internal operations pertaining to the website. He interfaced with the development team in Romania, worked with the graphic designer on site features, handled all customer support inquires, updated the site with new content daily, configured and managed all email marketing, and maintained the subscription element of TDS. Seth also managed all internal IT needs (procuring new computers, troubleshooting basic computer problems, managing all employee email accounts, etc.)

Seth handled almost everything internal to the company, including project management, subscription program support, website maintenance, content editor and customer support. He constantly focused on the user experience, which included, but was not limited to, ensuring information was easy to find and interpret, creating a clear and logical flow when users entered information, finding and fixing errors, and maintaining website performance and speed. He also made sure that the content staff had the necessary tools to perform optimally and supported them to maintain editorial consistency and efficiency.

Seth believed in making fact-based decisions. He referenced site data, industry trends, and used customer feedback to make decisions on projects and improvements to the website. Recoding the site was his biggest management project to date, and he worked diligently with programmers to ensure each element would be recoded and designed to the specifications outlined.

> *I have faith that TDS will become profitable; we have a wonderful team and loyal users. I am confident we will eventually succeed. I believe we need a little more capital investment and a comprehensive plan. We are on the right track to build a trustworthy, competitive, and profitable website, and eventually, the big boys will beg us to sell them this site. That is when we have reached our goal and we can come up with a plan for a new startup, take on the next challenge, and ace it.*

Ron Dvorkin – Director of Sales

Ron single-handedly generated the majority of revenue for TDS through advertising packages sold to endemic advertisers (i.e., clients in the soccer industry–camps, tournaments, products, etc.). He did not handle major clients such as Nike, Gatorade, or Under Armour who are participants in the soccer industry. Ron was older than most of the staff and much less tech-savvy (for example, he did not know what Google was when he started at TDS). He hailed from the east coast and had a hustler attitude. Ron was willing to do almost anything to get a sale closed—including slashing prices or adding more impressions for free. He could be very emotional with his requests or opinions. In an internal meeting Ron said:

> *I get things done fast, and I get them done right the first time. If you ask anyone in this office, they pretend to know sales and customer acquisition and retention, but I am not sure if any of them really do. I have been doing this for years; these kids were not even on this planet when I became a professional in this field. What I say is very simple but very effective. I say it does not matter what you are selling, if you are a good salesperson, you find the leads; you do your homework well, approach them with confidence, and close the deal in a sec. These kids sometimes tell me I delete my emails by mistake and I tell them, what's the big deal? I can bring money in that pays our salaries; can you really do what I do?*

Ron respected Seth as a peer and Joseph as the CEO/Owner of the business, but had no fear voicing his concerns about the business:

> *Seth is a good and smart kid, but sometimes I feel Seth and Joe are choking this business; I have shared this with them too. The startup companies do not make a ton of profits in the first few years. I have been around long enough to know that. This business needs more money in so it can generate more revenue, and the solution is not to pay those guys overseas to clean the website or to set up a system that gets more email addresses from the users. We need to physically be more present in the market, hire more professional sellers and relationship builders and increase revenue, that's where the additional money should go. What else do we need? The right commodity*

to sell: quality user data that could be segmented properly and easily, our customers don't want to waste their resources on people who are not their target market. These are the ABCs of marketing.

Max – Marketing Director

Max was responsible for all non-endemic sales (i.e., sales with non-soccer-specific companies). He also managed most of the marketing.

Joseph – CEO

Despite being the CEO, Joseph had become much less involved after moving to the new office in 2011. He owned other companies and started to devote more time to those than to TDS. Max, Seth, and Ron reported directly to Joseph, but managed the company's day-to-day operations. Joseph has said:

> *I believe we need to think and act more strategically, and this business needs to, for lack of a better expression, grow up! I have shared my vision with my team here numerous times: our goal is for TDS to become the leading source of information for soccer fans in the United States. Being a leader in this environment is not something that comes easy. We have worked long and hard to get here and we need to work smarter and more strategically to get to where we should be. We will make this website profitable without being too greedy about collecting user data; it's a fine line.*

Outsourcing: TDS did not keep all functions in-house: it outsourced web development, accounting, and legal functions. Web development was handled by a firm in Romania that was paid a retainer for one full-time programmer. Payroll, accounts receivables, and accounts payable were handled by a third-party accounting firm paid annually for its services. When legal counsel was needed, usually pertaining to intellectual property, TDS used an outside firm specializing in intellectual property.

Competition for Digital Soccer Audiences

While TDS had direct competitors, no soccer website could match the size of TDS' audience. Here, we briefly discuss two websites that share some features with TDS:

Soccer America (www.socceramerica.com)

Soccer America had both a print magazine and a website. It provides some college news, Top 25 college team rankings, and scores for a very limited number of games each week for men's and women's college soccer. Historically, it was the most referenced source of college and youth soccer, but had lost popularity. Soccer

America also covered the men's and women's National Teams and parts of American professional soccer.

College Soccer News (www.collegesoccernews.com)

College Soccer News provided news, weekly Top 30 team rankings, and some scores for men's college soccer only. It also provided youth player rankings for high school juniors and seniors. Although it had been around since 2001, it did not have TDS' presence or clout within the college soccer community.

Online User Data Collection Guidelines

In 2015, the Federal Trade Commission provided guidelines for businesses in how to collect, handle, store and process consumer information. In its "Start with Security" guide for business based on lessons learned from FTC cases, the FTC recommended only collecting necessary personal information so that you limit what's at risk of being stolen. FTC's guidance to reduce a company's risk was organized around these 10 lessons:

1. *Start with security.*
2. *Control access to data sensibly.*
3. *Require secure passwords and authentication.*
4. *Store sensitive personal information securely and protect it during transmission.*
5. *Segment your network and monitor who's trying to get in and out.*
6. *Secure remote access to your network.*
7. *Apply sound security practices when developing new products.*
8. *Make sure your service providers implement reasonable security measures.*
9. *Put procedures in place to keep your security current and address vulnerabilities that may arise.*
10. *Secure paper, physical media, and devices.*

Source: https://www.ftc.gov/system/files/documents/plain-language/pdf0205-startwithsecurity.pdf (p.3)

Regulatory Environment: What is CAN-SPAM Law?

TDS operations are subject to many regulations. One important regulation is CAN-SPAM—Controlling the Assault of Non-Solicited Pornography and Marketing Act. The CAN-SPAM law requires all emails to provide an explicit choice for consumers to unsubscribe. U.S. Congress passed this law in 2003 to mitigate the risk of receiving unsolicited emails. According to the FTC website, the law bans false or misleading header information, prohibits deceptive subject lines, and requires emails to explicitly provide an opt-out method. Senders who receive an opt-out request have 10 business days to stop sending emails to requestor's email address. The CAN-SPAM law also requires that commercial email be identified as an advertisement and show the sender's physical postal address (The United States Federal Trade Comission, 2006).

How Much User Information? Culling Data without Creepiness

Director of Sales, Ron Dvorkin, frustrated with the lack of user demographic data to better segment email marketing campaigns for advertising clients, frequently argued with Seth about data usage best practices, the potential consequences of violating CAN-SPAM laws, and the ethical implications of using the user database for sales-related email blasts. However, both knew the significance that the user database played in securing potential advertisers for the website and the value of such a database.

When designing the new website, specifically the user registration page, Seth researched best practices and learned that the more friction users experienced from start to finish (e.g., the more fields they had to complete), the less likely they would be to voluntarily complete the form. In fact, according to research conducted in 2013 by Forrester, 11% of adults have abandoned a purchase form because it asked for too much information. While the TDS form was not a purchase form, industry research still recommended only requesting necessary user information (Sheldon, 2012).

Marketers have increasingly turned to email to communicate specific messages with unique audiences that were previously unavailable due to the high costs (specifically printing and postage) of direct mail marketing.

Companies can sell user email information to list brokers or directly to clients for as much as $150 per thousand email addresses. They can also charge fees for additional targeting within the complete list, such as age, sex, or zip code (DM Carney Direct Marketing, n.d.).

In management discussions about redesigning the entire TDS site, everyone recognized it as an opportunity to collect more user information for marketing purposes. Ron's position was that TDS should collect extensive user information so that he could segment the list better for potential clients. Seth worried that asking for more information might hurt the user experience and had recently familiarized himself with the FTC guidelines regarding the collection, handling, storing and processing of consumer information.

Seth's Presentation Tomorrow: To Collect or Not to Collect?

Seth has to develop and present a plan to improve user data collection, determining what 'necessary' information TDS should collect. Technically, the only information TDS needs from its users to create an account is an email address and a password. Seth wonders whether TDS should request that users provide additional personal statistics such as age, gender, education level, location (zip code), ethnicity, race and family size. He's not sure how much personal information is too much to request. How much personal information can be gathered without losing potential users? Seth also knows that he must consider whether TDS could become profitable without changing. Seth is considering:

- If TDS creates a new form, how much and what type of user information should TDS request?
- Will a richer user profile enable TDS to package, rent and/or sell the information for more revenue?
- Are there ethical concerns that are being ignored about gathering, storing, and selling user information?

APPENDIX A

Balance sheet of TDS in 2011 (in USD)

TDS Profit and Loss Sheet	
AQCxRByb2Z	Jan - Dec 11
AQAAAAkFAS	
Income	
Advertising Income	$ 297,193.31
Fees	$ 56,944.43
Other Income	$ 1,000.00
Subscription Income	$ 62,624.87
Total Income	$ 417,762.61
Gross Profit	$ 417,762.61
Expense	
GENERAL & ADMINISTRATIVE	
Bank and ADP Payroll Charges	$ 9,752.04
Computer & Internet Expense	$ 9,891.08
Insurance Expense	$ 41,514.60
Legal Fees	$ 6,388.05
Office Expense	$ 50,464.86
Professional Fees	$ 30,000.00
Rent Expense	$ 65,283.73
Tax Expense	$ 1,898.02
Telephone	$ 17,029.90
Total GENERAL & ADMINISTRATIVE	$ 232,222.28

LABOR COSTS

Outside Services	$	322,385.52
Payroll Tax Expense	$	44,938.49
Salary Expense ADP	$	496,665.36
Total LABOR COSTS	$	863,989.37

PROGRAM EXPENSES

Baltimore Tradeshow 01/2011	$	14,260.69
Europe Tour	$	(27,540.64)
PDL Expenses	$	30,295.96
Philadelphia Tradeshow 1/2010	$	1,223.02
Production Expense	$	13,291.00
Scouting Expense	$	9,382.16
Soccer Broadcast Expense	$	2,595.00
Soccer Showcase	$	1,110.00
Total PROGRAM EXPENSES	$	44,617.19

SELLING EXPENSE

Advertising & Promotion	$	36,826.24
Meals & Entertainment	$	114.93
Trade Show	$	9,603.33
Travel Expense	$	19,420.58
Total SELLING EXPENSE	$	65,965.08
Total Expense	$	1,206,793.92
Net Income	$	(789,031.31)

Source: TDS internal company records

APPENDIX B: Traffic, revenue and page visit information

Traffic historical information of TDS

Year	Visits	Unique Visits	Page views	Revenue
2008	442,453	174,938	2,687,451	$ 75,006
2009	1,030,120	399,733	6,301,806	$ 201,475
2010	1,315,819	487,685	7,290,842	$ 376,874
2011	3,264,065	1,888,514	14,321,093	$ 417,763

Source: TDS internal company records

Revenue historical information of TDS

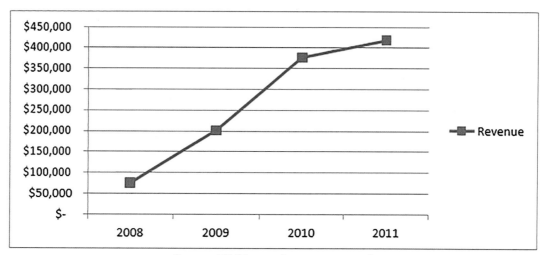

Source: TDS internal company records

Page visit historical information of TDS

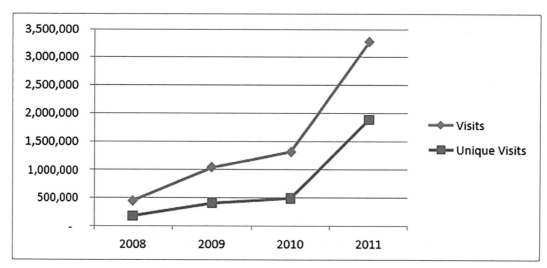

Source: TDS internal company records Page views historical information of TDS

Page views historical information of TDS

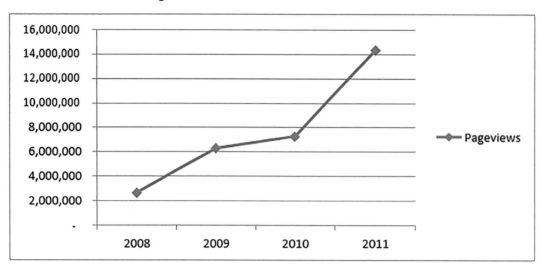

Source: TDS internal company records

APPENDIX C: Organizational Chart

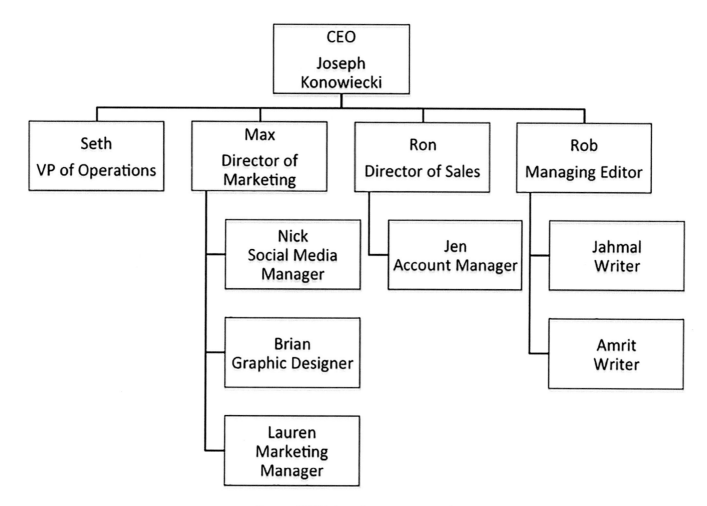

Source: TDS internal company records

Bibliography

DM Carney Direct Marketing. (n.d.). *DataCards*. Retrieved April 21, 2016, from carneydirect.com: http://lists.carneydirect.com/market;jsessionid=AE109DED35F114CF2C1D8B7B3C7C5679?page=rese   arch/datacard&id=385120

Sheldon, P. (2012, February 20). *Have You "Signed In" With Facebook Recently?* . Retrieved April 20, 2016, from Forrester: http://blogs.forrester.com/peter_sheldon/12-02-20- have_you_signed_in_with_facebook_ recently?cm_mmc=RSS-_-MS-_-1711-_-blog_2684

Federal Trade Commission. (2006, September). *CAN-SPAM Act: A Compliance Guide for Business*. Retrieved April 25, 2016, from Federal Trade Commission: https://www.ftc.gov/tips-advice/business- center/guidance/can-spam-act-compliance-guide-business

Federal Trade Commission. (2015, June). *Start With Security*. Retrieved May 27, 2016 from Federal Trade Commission: https://www.ftc.gov/system/files/documents/plain-language/pdf0205-startwithsecurity.pdf

72939807R00173

Made in the
USA
Middletown, DE